Oxford AQA History

A LEVEL AND AS

Revolution and Dictatorship: Russia 1917–1953

REVISION GUIDE

 RECAP   APPLY   REVIEW   SUCCEED

Rob Bircher

OXFORD

OXFORD
UNIVERSITY PRESS

Great Clarendon Street, Oxford, OX2 6DP, United Kingdom

Oxford University Press is a department of the University of Oxford.
It furthers the University's objective of excellence in research,
scholarship, and education by publishing worldwide. Oxford is a
registered trade mark of Oxford University Press in the UK and in
certain other countries

British Library Cataloguing in Publication Data
Data available

978-0-19-843252-4

1 3 5 7 9 10 8 6 4 2

Digital edition: 978-0-19-843293-7

Paper used in the production of this book is a natural, recyclable
product made from wood grown in sustainable forests.
The manufacturing process conforms to the environmental
regulations of the country of origin.

Printed in India by Manipal Technologies Limited

Acknowledgements

The publisher would like to thank Sally Waller for her work on the
Student Book on which this Revision Guide is based and Chris Rowe
for reviewing this Revision Guide.

We are grateful to the authors and publishers for use of extracts
from their titles and in particular for the following:

E. Acton and T. Stableford: *The Soviet Union: A Documentary History*,
Volume 1, (University of Liverpool Press, 2005). Reproduced with
permission from University of Liverpool Press.

R. V. Daniels: *A Documentary History of Communism in Russia:
From Lenin to Gorbachev*, (University Press of New England, 1993).
Reproduced with permission from University Press of New England.

Gorky, Radek, Bukharin, Zhdanov and others: *Soviet Writers'
Congress 1934*, (Lawrence & Wishart, 1977). Reproduced with
permission from Lawrence & Wishart.

V. Serge: *Memoirs of a Revolutionary*, translated by Peter Sedgwick,
(NYRB Classics, 2012). Copyright © 1951 by Editions de Seuil.
Translation copyright © 2012 by the Victor Serge Foundation.
Published in English by New York Review Books.

M. Zoshchenko: Nervous People, (Indiana University Press, 1963).
Copyright © 1951 by Editions de Seuil. Translation copyright © 2012
by the Victor Serge Foundation. Reproduced with permission from
Penguin Random House, LLC.

We have made every effort to trace and contact all copyright holders
before publication, but if notified of any errors or omissions, the
publisher will be happy to rectify these at the earliest opportunity.

Cover: Fine Art Images/Heritage Images/Getty Images

Artwork: QBS Learning

Links to third party websites are provided by Oxford in good faith
and for information only. Oxford disclaims any responsibility for
the materials contained in any third party website referenced in this
work.

Contents

PART ONE   AS AND A LEVEL

The Russian Revolution and the Rise of Stalin, 1917–1929

| | RECAP | APPLY | REVIEW |

SECTION 1   Dissent and revolution, 1917

SECTION 2   Bolshevik consolidation, 1918–1924

SECTION 3   Stalin's rise to power, 1924–1929

Contents *continued*

Introduction

The *Oxford AQA History for A Level* textbook series has been developed by a team of expert teachers and examiners led by Sally Waller. This matching revision guide offers well-researched, targeted revision and exam practice advice on the new AQA exams.

This guide offers you step-by-step strategies to master your AQA History exam skills, and the structured revision approach of **Recap, Apply** and **Review** to prepare you for exam success. Use the progress checklists on pages 3–4 as you work through the guide to keep track of your progress. Other exam practice and revision features include the **'How to...' guides** for each AQA question type on pages 6–7 and a **Timeline** of key events to help you see the themes.

RECAP

Each chapter recaps key events and developments through a variety of concise points and visual diagrams. **Key terms** appear in bold and red; they are defined in the glossary.

 indicates the relevant Oxford AQA History Student Book pages so you can easily cross-reference for further revision.

SUMMARY highlights the most important points at the end of each chapter.

 Key Chronology provides a short list of dates to help you remember key events.

APPLY

Carefully designed revision activities help drill your grasp of knowledge and understanding, and help you apply your knowledge towards exam-style questions.

 Apply Your Knowledge activity tests your basic comprehension, then helps apply your knowledge to exam questions.

 Plan Your Essay activity prepares you for essay exam questions with practical essay plans and techniques.

 Improve an Answer activity shows you one or more sample student answers, and helps you to evaluate how the answers could be improved.

 A Level essay activities (for example, **To What Extent** or **Assess the Validity of This View**) are extension activities that help you practise the A Level essay question.

 Revision Skills provides different revision techniques. Research shows that using a variety of revision styles can help cement your revision.

 Examiner Tip highlights key parts of an exam question, and gives you hints on how to avoid common mistakes in exams.

 Source Analysis activity helps you practise evaluating sources and prepares you for the sources exam question.

 Key Concept covers the concepts, which are strongly linked to the essay question you might find in your exams. This activity helps to drill your understanding of the key Revolution and Dictatorship: Russia concepts:

- Marxism
- communism
- Leninism
- Stalinism
- ideological control and dictatorship
- issues of political authority
- the interrelationship between governmental, economic and social change.

REVIEW

Throughout each chapter, there will be opportunities to reflect on the work you have done, and support on where to go for further revision to refresh your knowledge. You can tick off the Review column from the progress checklist once you've completed this. **Activity Answers Guidance** and the **Exam Practice** sections with full sample student answers also help you review your own work. Also don't forget to refer to the **Top Revision Tips for A Level History** on page 142 to help you organise your revision successfully.

The topic Revolution and Dictatorship: Russia is a **Component 2: Depth Study**, which means you should be familiar with the key concepts relating to the topic and the skill of evaluating primary sources.

The **AS LEVEL** exam lasts 1.5 hours (90 minutes), and you have to answer two questions.

The **A LEVEL** exam lasts 2.5 hours (150 minutes), and you have to answer three questions.

On these pages, you will find guidance on how to tackle each type of question in your exam.

How to master the AQA sources question

In **Section A** of your Revolution and Dictatorship: Russia exam, you will encounter one sources question that you must answer. Here are the steps to consider when tackling the sources question:

1 Look at the question posed
Note (underline) the focus of the question.

EXAMINER TIP

AS LEVEL You have to answer one sources question on **two** primary sources (worth 25 marks). Try to spend about 50 minutes on this question.

A LEVEL You have to answer one sources question on **three** primary sources (worth 30 marks). Try to spend about 60 minutes on this question.

2 Read the first source (including the provenance) carefully
Keep the focus in mind. Underline or highlight the parts of the source that offer a view relevant to the focus of the question. This will give you the author's 'overall' view.

EXAMINER TIP

If you're aiming for top grades, look again at the source: see if there are any sub-arguments or views. Underline or highlight these in a different colour.

3 Begin your evaluation
Analyse the provenance, as well as the content and argument of the source. Use your own knowledge where appropriate to support your evaluation. You should consider the following (where relevant) in relation to the focus of the question:

❏ Author (as an individual and as a representative figure; position and intent)

❏ Date and context

❏ Target and actual audience

❏ Tone and emphasis (tone can add to or detract from value; emphasis shows the author's key concerns, which may affect value).

EXAMINER TIP

You should begin your answer with the overall view of the source, and cite material which both supports and challenges this. Remember to comment clearly on the source's value for the focus of the question. To achieve top grades, repeat step 3 for any sub-arguments.

4 Make a judgement
Consider how valuable the source is in relation to the focus of the question.

5 Repeat steps 2–4 for the next source or sources
At you will need a further paragraph in which you **compare** the two sources directly and give a judgement on the more valuable.

At you **don't** need to make any comparative judgements and there is no need for an overall conclusion.

REVIEW

Take a look at the Exam Practice sections on pages 66 and 105 of this guide to reflect on sample answers to the sources question.

How to master the AQA essay question

In **Section B** of your exam, you will encounter a choice of essay questions. Here are the steps to consider when tackling an essay question:

1 Read the question carefully
Note (underline) key words and dates.

EXAMINER TIP

 You have to answer one essay question (worth 25 marks) from a choice two questions. Try to spend about 40 minutes on this question.

 You have to answer two essay questions (each worth 25 marks) from a choice of three questions. Try to spend about 45 minutes on each answer.

2 Plan your essay and form a judgement
Use whichever approach will best enable you to answer the question – this may be chronological or thematic.

EXAMINER TIP

Plans can be in the form of columns, spider diagrams, mind-maps, flow charts and other styles, but should both help you to form a judgement and to devise a coherent structure for your answer.

3 Introduce your argument
Having made a judgement, advance this in your introduction. The introduction should also be used to show your understanding of the question, particularly key terms and dates, and to acknowledge alternative views and factors.

4 Develop your argument
The essay should proceed logically, supporting your balanced argument through the opening statements of the paragraphs. Remember: comment first, followed by specific and precise supporting information.

EXAMINER TIP

Don't forget to write analytically. Your job is to argue a case and evaluate events, developments and ideas, rather than simply describing what happened in a story-telling (narrative) fashion.

EXAMINER TIP

To achieve top grades, remember that a good argument will have balance. You should examine alternative ideas and factors, and explain why they are less convincing than those you are supporting.

5 Conclude your argument
Your conclusion should repeat the judgement given in the introduction and summarise your argument. A good conclusion will not include any new information and will flow naturally from what has gone before.

REVIEW

In the Exam Practice sections on pages 26 and 125, you will find sample answers and helpful examiner tips to the essay exam question.

AQA AS and A Level History mark schemes

Below are simplified versions of the AQA mark schemes, to help you understand the marking criteria for your **Component 2: Depth Study** History exam paper.

AS LEVEL	Section A: Sources	Section B: Essay
5	Good understanding of provenance and tone of the sources. Very good knowledge, with argument linked to the question. Comparison contains a substantiated judgment. [21–25 marks]	Good understanding of the question. Range of knowledge, with specific supporting information. Analytical, well-argued answer. Structured effectively. Substantiated judgement. [21–25 marks]
4	Good understanding of provenance and tone of the sources. Good knowledge, with argument linked to the question. Comparison partly substantiated. [16–20 marks]	Good understanding of the question. Range of knowledge. Analytical, balanced answer. Structured effectively. Limited judgement. [16–20 marks]
3	Reasonable understanding of provenance and tone of the sources. Shows awareness of knowledge, with argument linked to the question. Partial comparison. [11–15 marks]	Reasonable understanding of the question. Some knowledge, with limited scope. Answer contains some balance or is one-sided. Structured adequately. Partial judgement. [11–15 marks]
2	Partial understanding of provenance and tone of the sources. Some knowledge, with limited link to the question. Undeveloped comparison. [6–10 marks]	Partial understanding of the question. Some knowledge, with very limited scope. Answer contains limited balance, or is descriptive. There is some structure. Undeveloped judgement. [6–10 marks]
1	Little understanding of provenance and tone of the sources. Limited knowledge, not all linked to the question. Comparison is vague or too general. [1–5 marks]	Limited understanding of the question. Limited knowledge. Answer is vague or too general. Structure is limited. Unsupported judgement. [1–5 marks]

A LEVEL	Section A: Sources	Section B: Essays
5	Very good understanding of provenance and content of the sources. Balanced argument, substantiated judgement. Very good knowledge, linked to question. [25–30 marks]	Very good understanding of the question and of the issues/concepts. Range of knowledge, with specific and precise supporting information. Full analytical, balanced answer. Good organisation, structured effectively. Well-substantiated judgement. [21–25 marks]
4	Good understanding of provenance and content of the sources. Partial or limited judgement. Good knowledge, linked to question. [19–24 marks]	Good understanding of the question and of the issues/concepts. Range of knowledge, with specific and precise supporting information. Analytical, balanced answer. Good organisation, structured effectively. Some judgement. [16–20 marks]
3	Some understanding of provenance and content of the sources, may contain imbalance. Judgement is not fully convincing. Awareness of knowledge, linked to question. [13–18 marks]	Reasonable understanding of the question, with some awareness of the issues/concepts. Range of knowledge, may contain imprecise supporting information. Answer links to the question and contains some balance. Structured effectively. Partial judgement. [11–15 marks]
2	Partial understanding of provenance and/or content of the sources (accurate for 1-2 sources or provenance or content only). Unconvincing judgement. Some knowledge is present, may contain limited link to question. [7–12 marks]	Partial understanding of the question, with some awareness of the issues/concepts (may contain generalisations). Some knowledge, with limited scope. Answer contains limited balance, or is descriptive. There is some structure. Undeveloped judgement. [6–10 marks]
1	Partial understanding of provenance and/or content of the sources (accurate for at least one source, may be inaccurate). Judgement is lacking. Limited knowledge is present, not all linked to question. [1–6 marks]	Limited understanding of the question, with inaccurate or irrelevant understanding of issues/concepts. Limited knowledge. Answer is vague or too general. Structure is limited. Unsupported judgement. [1–5 marks]

Timeline

The colours represent different types of events and developments as follows:

● Blue: economic events   ● Red: political events
● Black: international events (including foreign policy)   ● Yellow: social events

1917	**Feb–March** – February/March Revolution
1917	**April** – Return of Lenin
1917	**July** – July Days
1917	**Aug** – Kornilov coup
1917	**Oct–Nov** – October/November Revolution
1917	**Oct** – Establishment of Sovnarkom
1918	**March** – Treaty of Brest-Litovsk
1918	**April–May** – Civil War starts
1919	**March** – Comintern established
1920	**May** – Start of the Russo-Polish War
1921	**March** – Kronstadt rising
1921	**March** – Launch of the NEP
1921	**March** – Treaty of Riga signed, formally ending the Russo-Polish War
1922	**April** – Rapallo Treaty
1924	**Jan** – Lenin's death
1926	**April** – Treaty of Berlin
1927	**Nov** – Trotsky, Zinoviev and Kamenev expelled from the Party
1927–29	Stalin's 'Great Turn'
1928	First Five Year Plan
1929	War on kulaks and mass collectivisation announced
1932–33	Famine in Ukraine and elsewhere
1933	Second Five Year Plan
1934	**Dec** – Kirov's murder
1934	**Sept** – USSR enters the League of Nations
1935	Stakhanovite movement begins
1936	**June** – Family code restricts abortion and divorce
1936	**Aug** – Show trial of Zinoviev, Kamenev and others
1936	Stalin constitution
1936	**Sept** – Soviet intervention in the Spanish Civil War
1937	Start of the Yezhovshchina
1937	**May–June** – The military purge
1938	Third Five Year Plan
1938	**March** – Show trial of Bukharin, Rykov and others
1939	**Aug** – The Nazi-Soviet Pact
1940	**Aug** – Death of Trotsky
1941	**June** – Germany invades the USSR
1941	**Sept** – Siege of Leningrad begins
1941	**Oct–Dec** – Battle for Moscow
1942	**Aug** – Battle of Stalingrad begins
1943	**Feb** – German surrender at Stalingrad
1945	**Feb** – Yalta Conference
1945	**May** – Soviet victory in the Great Patriotic War
1945	**July–Aug** – Potsdam Conference
1946	Zhdanovshchina begins
1947	**Oct** – Cominform established
1948–49	Berlin blockade
1949	Leningrad Affair
1949	**Aug** – Soviet atomic bomb successfully tested
1952	Doctors' Plot
1953	**March** – Death of Stalin

1 Dissent and revolution, 1917

REVISION PROGRESS

1 The condition of Russia before the revolution of February/March 1917

 RECAP

- Russia in 1917 was a developing country, with the majority of its population living as peasants.
- Industrialisatio n had been rapid before the First World War, but the workers endured harsh working and living conditions.
- Liberals were frustrated by the autocratic system that shut down any opportunities to share power, while the tsarist secret police forces battled with radical groups who plotted to overthrow the Tsar.

The Tsar and political authority

Russia before the February/March Revolution was an **autocracy**: a rule by one person with no limits to their power. That person was Tsar Nicholas II, whose personal failings as a leader had seriously weakened his political authority by 1917.

Nicholas' personality
- Nicholas believed completely in his divine right to rule.
- He was stubborn and saw advice as criticism.
- He undermined his ministers to stop anyone challenging his authority.

Alexandra and Rasputin
- Rasputin was a self-styled 'holy man', trusted by the royal couple after he was able to help their son Aleksei, who suffered from haemophilia.
- Alexandra encouraged Nicholas to listen to Rasputin's advice. Rasputin became more powerful than many ministers, which undermined support for the Tsar at court.
- Rasputin had a reputation for sexual promiscuity. Rumours about Rasputin and Alexandra were especially damaging to Nicholas' authority.

Reasons for Nicholas' weakened authority

Nicholas and the State Duma
- Nicholas was forced to allow a State Duma (an elected representative assembly) to form in 1906.
- The Duma held meetings to debate politics and legislation.
- Nicholas refused to share any real power with the Duma, frustrating those who were hoping for a more democratic approach to Russia's government.
- This meant that Nicholas remained responsible for Russia's problems.

Nicholas and Russia's problems
- Nicholas and Alexandra believed there was a religious bond between the Tsar and the people.
- They believed Russia should put its faith in God and tradition.
- This meant that Nicholas did not actively try to solve Russia's problems, believing instead that they were in God's hands.

Opposition to tsarism

In Russia in 1917, there were three main groups of political opposition to the Tsar's rule:

Liberals	The Social Revolutionaries (SRs)	The Social Democrats (SDs)
• A loose collection of groups that favoured reform and a constitutional monarchy. • Included the Constitutional Democrats (known as the Kadets), the Octobrists and the Progressives.	• The Socialist Revolutionary Party was founded in 1901. • It chiefly represented peasant interests, including land reform. • It suffered from internal divisions. Some extreme SRs believed in political assassination, but the moderate wing gained influence after 1905.	• The All-Russian Social Democrat Labour Party was founded in 1898. • It represented the proletariat (the industrial working class). • It split in 1903 into Mensheviks and Bolsheviks, following arguments about how to apply **Marxism** to the Russian situation.

The Russian war effort

In July 1914, Nicholas mobilised Russia's armies to support Serbia in its war against Austria-Hungary. When Germany joined the war as Austria's ally, Russia experienced several very serious defeats. By early 1917, Russia's involvement in the First World War was a major cause of discontent.

- A lack of weapons, ammunition, equipment and clothing for the Russian troops contributed to numerous defeats.
- For example, at the Battle of Tannenberg in August 1914, around 300,000 Russians were killed or wounded and thousands were taken prisoner.

- The liberal **zemstva** and others saw the government failures as a call to action.
- A 'Union of Zemstva' was set up to provide the medical facilities which the state seemed to neglect.
- Factory owners and businessmen set up a Congress of Representatives of Industry and Business to help coordinate their production for the war effort.

- In June 1915, the All Russian Union of Zemstva and Cities was formed. This was chaired by Prince Lvov (later to lead the Provisional Government).
- Nicholas refused to let this civilian organisation take any part in his government's management of the war.

- In August 1915, a 'Progressive bloc' in the State Duma (made up of more than half of all the Duma deputies) demanded that responsibility for the war effort be handed over to a civilian government.
- Unable to accept this challenge to his autocratic rule, Nicholas refused. This increased liberal discontent with the tsarist government even further.

- In September 1915, Nicholas took on the role of Commander in Chief of Russia's armed forces, despite lacking enough military experience.
- This made him directly responsible for everything that went wrong in the war.

- Nicholas effectively left Alexandra to govern in Petrograd.
- Alexandra's reliance on Rasputin, a peasant, appalled the aristocracy.
- One of the Tsar's relations, Prince Yusupov, assassinated Rasputin in December 1916.

The economic and social state of Russia

The costs of the war caused major economic problems and had a significant social impact. Two of the most important impacts were food shortages in the towns and cities, and a soaring cost of living because of runaway inflation.

Reasons for food shortages	Reasons for the soaring cost of living
- The millions of men conscripted into the army caused labour shortages on farms and in factories, reducing food supplies. - Peasants hoarded their grain rather than sell it. - Food supplies were prioritised for the army, leaving towns undersupplied. - The railway system was turned over to transporting military supplies. Supplying towns was a lower priority.	- To pay for the war, the government raised taxes and took on huge loans. - Shortages of food and manufactured products raised prices higher and higher, leading to inflation. - Unemployment increased as non-military factories were forced to close because of a lack of supplies.

- The food shortages and insanitary conditions led to an increase in the death rate of workers in the towns and cities.
- This, combined with the increased cost of living and rising unemployment, led to unrest and strikes.
- In January 1917, 30,000 workers went on strike in Moscow and 145,000 went on strike in Petrograd.

Discontent in Russia

- Most of the discontent was expressed towards those in positions of power: employers, landlords, and officers in the army. It was expressed in strikes, unrest in the countryside and desertions from the armed forces.
- The Tsar's refusal to cooperate with the Progressive bloc increased political discontent. Progressives discussed the Tsar's possible abdication.
- Although workers and soldiers were increasingly open to radical political influences, most radical opponents of tsarism were in exile or in prison.

SUMMARY

- By early 1917, the strain of war had intensified the underlying economic and social problems of Russia.
- Tsar Nicholas II's political authority had weakened by 1917, partly due to his inability to take a firm lead in increasingly difficult circumstances.
- The First World War was a disaster for Russia, with military defeats and serious food shortages blamed on government failures.

APPLY

APPLY YOUR KNOWLEDGE

Complete the table below by explaining for whom each of the following situations increased discontent, and why.

	For which groups of people did this increase discontent?	Why did this increase discontent?
Rasputin's position at court		
Nicholas' relationship with the State Duma		
Nicholas' refusal to share responsibility for the war effort		
Russia's involvement in the First World War		

EXAMINER TIP

Being able to use a range of clear and specific information to support your answer is an important way of demonstrating your knowledge and understanding of the topic.

APPLY YOUR KNOWLEDGE

a Complete this spider diagram of the challenges facing Russia in January 1917.

b Which of these challenges do you think might have contributed the most to the discontent among the Russian population in 1917? Explain your reasoning.

EXAMINER TIP

This exercise will help you to answer questions about the significance of the challenges facing Russia before the 1917 revolutions, and whether some factors can be considered more significant than others.

PLAN YOUR ESSAY

AS LEVEL **'Tsar Nicholas II was the main cause of discontent in Russia in 1917.' Explain why you agree or disagree with this view.**

a Look at the spider diagram on page 10. Write a sentence explaining how each of the four main factors in the spider diagram supports the statement in the question above.

b Now use the information on pages 10–11 to write counter-arguments, explaining the importance of the war and social and economic problems in causing discontent.

c Use your answers to **a** and **b** to write an essay plan to answer the question above. Include an indication of whether you agree or disagree with the statement, and the reasons why.

EXAMINER TIP

Planning your exam answers is essential so it's important to practise writing essay plans. There are lots of different ways to write essay plans – you could use bullet lists, spider diagrams, tables or short paragraphs. Try to find a way that works for you.

KEY CONCEPT

Economic and social change is a key concept in the study of revolution and dictatorship in Russia 1917–53, especially the role and influence of individuals and groups in these changes.

This exercise will help you to understand the role of individuals in economic and social change between 1914 and February/March 1917. Can individual actions explain the changes, or are other factors more important in influencing the changes?

a   Complete the following table. The first row has been done for you.

Social or economic change	Role of individuals?	Other factors?
Russia's disastrous and costly First World War	The Russian leadership decided to mobilise to support Serbia. Poor leadership explains some of Russia's military defeats.	Russia's outcome in the First World War also depended on the actions of other nations and powers. The war would have been costly and probably caused economic problems regardless of its leadership.
Industrialisation and terrible living and working conditions		
Inflation and food shortages		
Rising opposition to autocracy		

b   What conclusions can you draw from this table about the importance of individuals and their actions in the social and economic changes sweeping Russia before 1917?

REVIEW

For a reminder about economic and social change in Russia before 1917 you may want to re-read the textbook for further revision. The icon in the top right-hand corner of each double page indicates the relevant Oxford AQA History Student Book pages for this Section of the revision guide.

ASSESS THE VALIDITY OF THIS VIEW

 'The loss of royal authority by early 1917 was mostly due to Tsar Nicholas II's decision to make himself Commander in Chief in 1915.' Assess the validity of this view.

a   Write a sentence explaining what is meant by 'royal authority' in the context of the Russian Empire at the start of the twentieth century.

b   Compare the impact of Nicholas' decision with other factors that might explain the decline in royal authority. For example:

- other decisions made by Nicholas
- the influence of Rasputin
- the impact on tsarist government of the First World War
- political challenges, such as from the Progressive bloc in the State Duma.

c   Decide what you think was the main factor (or factors) in the loss of royal authority by early 1917. What are your reasons?

d   Now use your answers to **a**, **b** and **c** to write a complete answer to the question.

EXAMINER TIP

You must provide balance in an A-level answer. Even if you have a strong view on a topic, you should consider alternative viewpoints and the reasons for them.

2 The February/March Revolution of 1917

The causes and course of the revolution

The February/March Revolution began as a spontaneous uprising triggered by bread shortages, but it was rooted in long years of suffering and frustration under an autocracy that was unable to adapt to change but absolutely unwilling to give up power.

Key events during February 1917	
Tuesday 14 February	• There were strikes in Petrograd. • News that bread would be rationed from 1 March brought long queues and riots. The police struggled to keep order.
Wednesday 22 February	• 20,000 workers were locked out of the Putilov Steel Works after pay talks collapsed. • Workers in other factories went on strike in support.
Thursday 23 February	• Striking workers joined the traditional march for International Women's Day. • Students and women from the bread queues also joined the march. • The city fell into chaos and order was not restored until the evening.
Friday 24 February	• 200,000 workers were on strike and there were spontaneous demonstrations. There was no obvious organisation of the crowds from any of the radical political parties.
Saturday 25 February	• 250,000 people (over half the capital's workforce) were on strike. • Shalfeev, in charge of the mounted police, was dragged from his horse and shot. • Civilians were shot by soldiers on the Nevskii Prospekt, but some Cossacks refused to attack the strikers.
Sunday 26 February	• Rodzianko, the Duma President, sent the Tsar a telegram warning him of the serious situation in Petrograd. • Nicholas ignored the warning and ordered the Duma to dissolve the next day.
Monday 27 February	• Nicholas ordered Khabalov, Commander of the Petrograd Military District, to restore order by military force. Around 40 demonstrators were killed. • A mutiny began in the Volynskii regiment. Soldiers joined the protestors, arming them with rifles. • The Duma held a meeting, despite the Tsar's orders, and set up a Provisional Committee to take over the government. They were supported by the army's High Command. • The same evening, revolutionaries set up the Petrograd Soviet, which also intended to take over the government. It began to organise food supplies for the city.
Tuesday 28 February	• Nicholas started to make his way back to Petrograd. • He sent a telegram offering to share power with the Duma.

Issues of leadership

Almost all the major Bolshevik leaders were absent at the time of the revolution. For example, Lenin was in exile in Switzerland and Stalin was in Siberia. The revolution appeared spontaneous and leaderless; it is not clear to what extent any of the small groups of local Bolshevik activists played a part in instigating or influencing the course of it.

During and following the revolution, local socialist groups helped to set up soviets (councils). The most important was the Petrograd Soviet, which represented workers and soldiers. It had 3000 members by 10 March.

On 1 March the Petrograd Soviet produced a charter of soldier's rights called 'Order No. 1'. The order stated that:

- All military units were to elect a deputy to the Petrograd Soviet and agree to be under the control of the Petrograd Soviet.
- The Military Commission of the Duma was only to be obeyed if its orders agreed with the Petrograd Soviet's orders.

Order No. 1 also aimed to improve the rights and respect given to soldiers, for example by giving them full citizens' rights when off duty.

The abdication of the Tsar

- At the end of February, Nicholas tried to get back to Petrograd from his military headquarters but was forced to stop at Pskov, 200 miles south of his destination, after his train was diverted.
- On 1 March, Nicholas' Chief of General Staff tried to convince him to abdicate.
- Nicholas agreed to abdicate on 2 March. Nicholas and his family were placed under house arrest, along with most of his Council of Ministers.

The establishment of the Dual authority: the Provisional Government and the Petrograd Soviet

Nicholas named his brother Mikhail as the new tsar because his son's haemophilia made him unsuitable, but Mikhail refused the position. As a result, political authority passed to two bodies: the Provisional Government and the Petrograd Soviet. The Provisional Government met in the right wing of the Tauride Palace and the Petrograd Soviet in the left wing.

The Petrograd Soviet

- Its executive committee was made up of **socialist** intellectuals (mainly Mensheviks and SRs).
- Members of the executive committee were elected, unlike the Provisional Government.
- Generally considered by workers, soldiers and peasants to be a more democratic, less elitist organisation than the Provisional Government.

The Provisional Government

- Headed by Prince Lvov, an aristocrat and zemstvo leader.
- Made up of former supporters of a constitutional monarchy.
- Planned as a temporary ('provisional') government until a Constitutional Assembly could be elected.
- Supported by the old tsarist civil service, army officers and the police.

The workings of the Dual authority

Alexandr Kerensky, a member of the Socialist Revolutionary Party and the State Duma, was the only member of both the Provisional Government and the Petrograd Soviet. He helped negotiate 'Dual authority', through which Russia was governed by an uneasy alliance of the Provisional Government and the Petrograd Soviet.

While the Soviet did not block Provisional Government reforms, there were many areas of conflict:

> The Soviet's Order No. 1 said that soldiers and workers should obey the Provisional Government, but only where the Soviet agreed with the Provisional Government's decisions.

> Although the Provisional Government was committed to holding elections for a Constituent Assembly, any elections in 1917 would clearly be won by the SRs, which the liberals of the Provisional Government were desperate to avoid.

> The Provisional Government wanted to improve discipline in the army to stop more desertions, and also wanted to restore order in the countryside. But the Soviet encouraged soldiers, workers and peasants to defy authority and assert their rights.

> The Provisional Government wanted an all-out effort to win the war, while the Soviet wanted to end Russia's involvement in the war as quickly as possible as long as this did not mean giving up territory to the Germans.

> The Soviet was essentially reactive – it saw its role as being to protect workers', soldiers' and peasants' rights. This was an obstacle to the Provisional Government being able to get things done, and the Soviet did not offer any alternative leadership of its own.

SUMMARY

- The February/March Revolution of 1917 was a largely spontaneous uprising against tsarist authority, fuelled by food shortages and poor living and working conditions.
- Nicholas was forced to abdicate and power passed to two bodies: the Provisional Government and the Petrograd Soviet.
- Although the Provisional Government dominated, the control the Soviet had over soldiers and workers made it virtually impossible for the Provisional Government to get anything done.

APPLY

APPLY YOUR KNOWLEDGE

Complete the spider diagram below with the causes of the February/March Revolution.

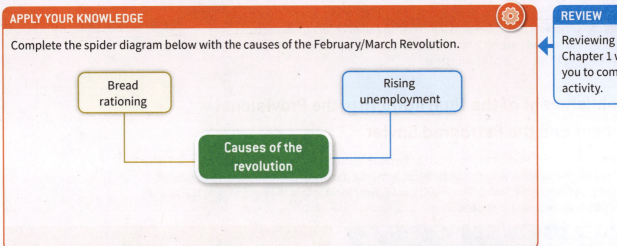

Bread rationing

Rising unemployment

Causes of the revolution

REVIEW

Reviewing Chapter 1 will help you to complete this activity.

SOURCE ANALYSIS

SOURCE A

Events of 3 March 1917, from the diary of the writer Mikhail Prishvin, who kept his private diary from 1905 to 1954; it was published in 1991, long after his death.

A beautiful March day – sunny and frosty – filled by the people's increasing joy. There was enormous traffic on Nevsky Prospekt. Imperial coats-of-arms were being taken down, piled in a heap and burned. In shop windows there were signs announcing the abdication of the Tsar. There were processions of soldiers and workers with banners calling for a socialist republic. They were singing the Russian version of the *Marseillaise*; it's as if 'God Save the Tsar' no longer exists. A really great victory is being celebrated. 'Comrade,' says my cab-driver to the crowd, 'Mind your backs, please!' 'Comrade,' says an officer to another cabby, 'Take me to Liteyny'. Huge paper flowers are all the rage, with soldiers sticking them on their chests and stomachs. But a huge angry crowd followed one soldier, and you could hear them shouting, 'Arrest him!' This was just because he had been heard saying: 'Just you wait. Socialism is going to cause you all a lot of trouble'.

SOURCE B

From 'Order No. 1' of the Petrograd Soviet, issued 1 March 1917 in response to the Provisional Government's command that all soldiers should return to barracks and obey their officers.

The Soviet of Workers' and Soldiers' Deputies has resolved:

- All orders issued by the Provisional Government shall be carried out, except those which run counter to the orders and decrees issued by the Soviet of Workers' and Soldiers' Deputies.
- All weapons shall be placed at the disposal and under the control of the company and battalion committees of soldiers and sailors and shall by no means be issued to the officers, not even at their insistence.
- In formation and on duty, soldiers shall strictly observe military discipline; however, off duty soldiers shall fully enjoy the rights granted to all citizens.
- In particular, standing to attention and obligatory saluting of officers off duty shall be cancelled.
- Likewise, officers shall be addressed as Mr. General, Mr. Colonel, etc., instead of Your Excellency, Your Honour, etc.

SOURCE C

From the Provisional Government's manifesto of 3 March 1917. The Provisional Government was formed from Duma deputies on 2 March, following Nicholas II's abdication. It was led by Prince Lvov.

A great event has taken place. By the mighty assault of the Russian people, the old order of tsarism has been overthrown. A new, free Russia is born. The great revolution crowns long years of struggle.

All our attempts to bring the Tsar's Government to its senses failed, and the titanic world war, into which the country was dragged by the enemy, found the Government in a state of moral decay, cut off from the people, not caring about Russia's fate, and full of corruption. And when Russia, because of the illegal and fatal actions of her rulers, was facing the most terrible disasters, the nation had to take the power into its own hands.

The revolutionary enthusiasm of all the people and the determination of the State Duma have created the Provisional Government, which considers it to be its sacred duty to fulfil the hopes of the nation, and lead the country out onto the bright path of free civic organisation.

 With reference to these sources and your understanding of the historical context, assess the value of these sources to an historian studying the February/March Revolution of 1917.

a   Copy and complete the following table to consider the provenance of each source.

	Who produced the source?	What type of source is it?	When was it produced?	What was the purpose of the source?	Who was the intended audience of the source?	How does the provenance affect the value of the source?
Source A						
Source B						
Source C						

b   Briefly summarise each source. What is it saying? Pick out one or two phrases in each source that help to support your explanation.

c   Use your answers to **a** and **b** to write a complete answer to the exam question above.

EXAMINER TIP

Remember that to answer source analysis questions effectively, you need to consider the provenance and content of each source and apply your own knowledge to your evaluation of both.

3 Developments between the revolutions of 1917

The return of Lenin

- At the time of the February/March Revolution of 1917 the Bolshevik Party was still small, with only 23,000 members.
- The soviets were dominated by SRs and Mensheviks, and there were only 40 Bolsheviks in the Petrograd Soviet.
- The Bolsheviks in Petrograd agreed with the policy of the Petrograd Soviet: to give support to the Provisional Government while protecting workers' rights.

The Bolshevik leadership played no part in the February/March Revolution of 1917. It was a surprise to them and they scrambled to respond to it.

- Kamenev and Stalin were the first leaders to return to Petrograd, from exile in Siberia.
- Lenin was in exile in Switzerland. He was permitted to travel back to Russia via Germany on a sealed train. The Germans allowed this as they could see how Lenin and the Bolsheviks might be able to further destabilise Russia, possibly even pulling Russia out of the war. The sealed train meant that Lenin could not cause trouble among Germany's Marxists on his way through the country.
- Lenin returned to Russia on 3 April 1917. His return would change Bolshevik policy.

Lenin's ideology and the April theses

Lenin's political programme challenged the traditional Marxist ideology about revolution that the Petrograd Soviet was following.

Marxist theory and the Petrograd Soviet	Lenin's ideology
A socialist revolution could only happen after a bourgeois revolution.	The Russian middle classes were too weak to carry through a revolution; the workers, backed by the peasants, needed to do it.
The Russian proletariat was still developing. There was still a long wait, maybe decades, before a socialist revolution could happen.	Russia was different: the soviets were a ready-made socialist government, and Russia was primed for a socialist revolution.
There was no quick way to socialism; Marx had identified natural laws that had to be followed.	The rest of Europe seemed close to socialist revolution; Russia would surely be supported by socialist neighbours.

The April Theses

The April Theses, which were published on 7 April 1917, explained Lenin's political programme. They set out his ideology and made demands that were summarised in two slogans: 'peace, bread and land' and 'all power to the soviets'.

All power to the soviets!

Peace — The war should be brought to an immediate end

Bread — Food shortages should end

Land — All land should be taken over by the state and allocated to peasants

Russia should be handed over to the soviets to run

Lenin's role as leader

Lenin did not immediately receive full support for his proposals. Some argued that the Bolsheviks were not yet powerful enough oppose the Provisional Government, while others feared that his radical proposals would do more harm than good.

- Lenin gained support through a mixture of persuasion, compromise, threats of resignation and appeals to the rank and file.
- He abandoned his call for an immediate overthrow of the Provisional Government, helping him to convince those who were worried about civil war.
- He sought out supporters at Party and factory meetings.
- He claimed credit for the social changes already happening in Russia, such as the peasant land seizures, which helped him to appear in control of events.

By the end of April, Lenin had won over most of the Party's Central Committee but was still struggling to gain wider support. For example, on 3 June the Petrograd Soviet passed a vote of confidence in the Provisional Government by 543 votes to 126 votes.

The July Days

- In July 1917, sailors from the Kronstadt naval base organised an armed demonstration that spread to the centre of Petrograd, with workers and soldiers joining them. Rising prices and unemployment contributed to the unrest.
- When the demonstrations turned violent, the Bolsheviks were blamed.
- The Provisional Government brought in troops to crush the demonstrations, and the Mensheviks and SRs of the Petrograd Soviet supported the Provisional Government in this.
- Bolshevik newspapers were shut down and Lenin and Stalin fled, while other Bolshevik leaders (such as Trotsky) were arrested and put in prison.

The Kornilov coup and the role of the Provisional Government and Trotsky

Despite the setback of the July Days, the Bolsheviks grew more powerful during the summer and autumn of 1917. They were the main beneficiaries of the Kornilov coup, which unfolded as follows:

> In June 1917, there is an increase in desertions from the army following heavy losses in the war.

> Kerensky appoints General Lavr Kornilov as Commander in Chief to bring back discipline.

> The Petrograd Soviet criticises Kornilov's army discipline and right-wing views. However, landowners and businessmen see Kornilov as saving them from socialism.

> In August 1917, Kornilov orders troops to march on Petrograd, presumably in an attempt to establish a military **dictatorship**.

> Kerensky panics and allows the Bolsheviks to arm workers to halt Kornilov's advance.

> Kornilov's march is stopped and the coup leaders are arrested.

By September, the Bolsheviks had majorities in both the Petrograd and Moscow soviets. Trotsky became Chairman of the executive committee of the Petrograd Soviet on 26 September. Membership of the Bolshevik Party had increased from 23,000 in February to 200,000 by the beginning of October. Reasons for this included the following:

> The Provisional Government had failed to improve food supplies to the cities and prices were far higher than wages. The Bolsheviks promised to end the food shortages.

> The war was still continuing, and Russia's offensive in June 1917 had failed. The Bolsheviks' promised an immediate end to the war.

> The Provisional Government had pushed back land redistribution until a Constituent Assembly could be elected. The Bolsheviks promised land for the peasants.

> Kornilov's coup showed the revolution was under threat from the Right, just as the Bolsheviks had warned.

> The Bolsheviks could portray themselves as the saviours of the revolution, and as a result of the Kornilov coup they had an armed wing of 10,000 Red Guards.

> The Bolsheviks were able to play on fears of further right-wing attacks. This led the Petrograd Soviet to adopt a resolution written by Trotsky, to create a Military Revolutionary Committee (MRC) to protect Petrograd.

> Kerensky was weakened by Kornilov's coup. He had appointed Kornilov in the first place and then had to rely on the Bolsheviks to deal with him.

Lenin and the Central Committee of the Bolshevik Party

- From mid-September onwards, Lenin (who was still hiding in Finland) demanded the Bolsheviks get ready to seize power.
- Kamenev and Zinoviev, two leading members of the Bolshevik Central Committee, disagreed with Lenin. They feared Russia was not yet economically ready for a revolution, and did not want to act until after the Constituent Assembly had been called.
- Trotsky also thought an armed uprising could be avoided if the Bolsheviks became the leading socialist party at the Congress of Soviets, which was planned for 26 October.
- Frustrated by this resistance, Lenin returned in disguise to Russia in October, and eventually convinced the Central Committee that 'an armed uprising is the order of the day'. At a meeting on 10 October it took him all night to convince the Central Committee to vote in his favour. Even then, Kamenev and Zinoviev refused to support his plan.
- Trotsky's strong organisational skills led Lenin to put him in charge of organising the seizure of power. Trotsky gathered **Red Guard** militias at Bolshevik headquarters and sent Commissars to get the loyalty of Petrograd's garrisons.
- On 16 October, Trotsky and Dzerzhinsky established the Military Revolutionary Committee. In total, this came to control 200,000 Red Guards, 60,000 Baltic sailors and 150,000 soldiers of the remaining Petrograd garrison units.

> **SUMMARY**
> - Lenin's return was a turning point for the Bolshevik Party; his April Theses gave the Party a new focus that made it more popular.
> - However, the July Days were a disaster for the Party, which looked to be in trouble until Kerensky's handling of the Kornilov coup gave the Bolsheviks a major propaganda victory.
> - Lenin had to fight hard to convince his Party's Central Committee to commit to an uprising. Once the decision was made, Trotsky's role in organising troops to back the revolution was significant.

APPLY

APPLY YOUR KNOWLEDGE

a   Select ten events or developments between the abdication of the Tsar in March 1917 and the Bolshevik seizure of power in October/November 1917, and use them to construct a key chronology.

b   Choose the three most important events or developments that help to explain why the Bolsheviks were able to come to power in October 1917. Explain your choice.

EXAMINER TIP

Having a secure knowledge of when these events happened, in what sequence, and their significance will help you with questions asking you to assess the reasons for the increase in popularity of the Bolshevik Party between the revolutions, and the reasons for the success of the Bolshevik seizure of power in October/ November 1917.

IMPROVE AN ANSWER

AS LEVEL 'Between March and the end of September 1917, Lenin was personally responsible for the growing appeal of the Bolshevik Party in Russia.' Explain why you agree or disagree with this view.

Read the paragraph below which is an introduction to this question.

Answer

The February/March Revolution meant that Lenin and the other leaders of the Bolshevik Party could return to Petrograd from exile and prison. From his arrival on 3 April, Lenin set about focusing the Bolshevik Party in a new direction – leading an armed uprising against the government to seize power in the name of the workers and peasants. Although his ideas were rejected by the Mensheviks, he succeeded in convincing most of the Bolshevik Central Committee to back his radical political programme. At the end of August, the role of the Bolsheviks in seeing off Kornilov's coup attempt had made the Bolsheviks more popular, as had the slogans inspired by Lenin's April Theses: 'peace, bread, land' and 'all power to the soviets'. This would have convinced more senior Bolsheviks that Lenin was right, but with Lenin still in hiding in Finland, this reduced his control over the Party. Kamenev and Zinoviev argued against his orders and on 10 October Lenin spent the whole night arguing with the Central Committee to get them to back an armed uprising.

a   Which two of the following statements do you think best summarises the strengths and weaknesses of this introduction?

- The introduction shows accurate and relevant knowledge of this topic area.
- The introduction clearly indicates the student's judgement on whether they agree or disagree with the view in the question.
- Most of what the student has written is not relevant to the question.
- It is not easy to tell what the student's judgement is – whether they agree with the view in the question or disagree with it.

b   Using your answers to **a** to help you, as well as the examiner tip opposite, rewrite this introduction so it is better focused on the question's requirements.

EXAMINER TIP

This question is asking you to consider arguments for and against Lenin being personally responsible for the growing appeal of the Bolshevik Party during a specific period of time: between March and September 1917. Make sure that when you rewrite this introduction, you include a clear judgement that makes it obvious what your argument will be.

ASSESS THE VALIDITY OF THIS VIEW

A LEVEL 'The increased strength of the Bolsheviks by September 1917 owed more to the weaknesses of rivals than to Lenin's political skill.' Assess the validity of this view.

a Write a sentence explaining what you think 'increased strength' means. For example, in the context of the Bolshevik Party, does it refer to military strength, political influence, number of supporters, or something else?

_____

_____

_____

REVIEW

If you are not sure about the reasons for the growth in Bolshevik support, look back at page 19.

b Make a list of reasons for the increase in the Bolsheviks' strength by September 1917. Which reasons do you think are the most significant?

_____

_____

_____

_____

_____

_____

c How many of the reasons are related to the weaknesses of the Bolsheviks' rivals? Highlight these or underline them.

d Use your answers to **a**, **b** and **c** to write a complete answer to the essay question.

EXAMINER TIP

To write an effective answer you need to provide balance. Here you could compare Lenin's strengths as a leader with the significance of Kornilov's coup, along with other reasons for the Bolsheviks' increased support, such as disillusionment with the Provisional Government.

PLAN YOUR ESSAY

AS LEVEL 'The failure of the Provisional Government in 1917 was due to its own mistakes.' Explain why you agree or disagree with this view.

REVIEW

Page 15 in Chapter 2, which examines the workings of the dual authority, may help you to answer this question.

a Copy and add to the following spider diagram to identify reasons for the Provisional Government's failure in 1917. Some reasons have been identified already.

Lack of decisive leadership

Reasons for the Provisional Government's failure in 1917

Failure to improve the economy

Not elected by the people

b Highlight reasons on the diagram that were due to mistakes made by the Provisional Government.

c Use the highlighted diagram to write a plan for your answer.

4 The October/November 1917 Revolution

 **RECAP**

The causes of the October/November Revolution

On 10 October 1917, Lenin returned to Russia in secret and spent the night convincing the Bolshevik Central Committee to agree to an armed uprising. The following factors contributed to his decision that the time was right for the Bolsheviks to lead a revolution:

- The Bolsheviks dominated both the Petrograd and Moscow soviets, as well as other soviets across Russia.
- The Provisional Government was very weak; Kerensky's credibility was greatly reduced after the Kornilov coup.
- The Bolsheviks had the Red Guards, armed by Kerensky during the Kornilov coup.

After the Military Revolutionary Committee (MRC) was established on 16 October, 15 out of the 18 Petrograd garrisons declared allegiance to the MRC, not the Provisional Government. On 23 October, Kerensky attempted to reduce the power of the MRC. He sent troops to cut off a Bolshevik area of the city from the centre, and ordered two Bolshevik newspapers to close down. The Bolsheviks used this as their excuse to act.

The course of the October/November Revolution

KEY CHRONOLOGY	
October 1917	
24 October	The Red Guards, supported by soldiers and sailors from Kronstadt, capture key positions in Petrograd
25 October	After a shot from the battleship Aurora to signal the attack, the Red Guards enter the Winter Palace
	The Second Congress of Soviets meets; some Mensheviks and right-wing SRs protest against the Bolsheviks' seizure of power
26 October	All remaining members of the Provisional Government are arrested
	The Congress votes to take power into its own hands
	The Congress agrees unanimously to Lenin's Decree on Peace
27 October	The Congress agrees to Lenin's Decree on Land
	A Central Executive Committee is set up, with the majority of members being Bolsheviks or left-wing SRs
	Sovnarkom is set up to run the government

The extent of the October/November Revolution

- The revolution involved 25,000–35,000 people at the most (approximately five per cent of the workers and soldiers in Petrograd).
- 10,000–15,000 people may have been present during the 'storming' of the Winter Palace, but many may have been spectators only.
- The revolution involved very little fighting; there were probably no more than five deaths.
- The revolution focused on the takeover of a few strategic targets; much of Petrograd (and the rest of Russia) carried on with life as usual during the revolution.

Lenin's role in the revolution

Historians have taken differing views on Lenin's importance in the revolution.

> Soviet historians idealised Lenin's role and portrayed him as the heroic leader of the Bolshevik uprising.
>
> After Lenin's death and Trotsky's fall from power, Soviet historians downplayed Trotsky's role in organising the Red Guard and directing the actual seizure of power.

> Critics of the 'heroic Lenin' approach argue that Lenin was not the driver of the revolution and was absent for most of 1917.
>
> These critics often prioritise the failures of the Provisional Government over Lenin's leadership in bringing the Bolsheviks to power.

> During the Cold War, Western historians tended to claim that the revolution was a coup d'état (an overthrow of the government carried out by a small group of people), not a popular revolution.
>
> However, more recently historians have identified that there was at least some radicalism and spontaneous rebellion that the Bolsheviks were able to exploit.

The establishment of Bolshevik authority

- The October/November Revolution transferred power to the All-Russian Congress of Soviets.
- When the Bolsheviks won a majority of seats on its executive committee, the Mensheviks and right-wing SRs walked out, leaving the Bolsheviks and left-wing SRs in control.
- The Soviet of People's Commissars, also known as **Sovnarkom**, was set up to take charge of running the government, with Lenin as its Chairman.

- Sovnarkom initially consisted of just Bolsheviks, although Lenin begrudgingly allowed seven left-wing SRs to join in November.
- Sovnarkom was reluctant to share power and sidelined the Petrograd Soviet.

It took the Bolsheviks a while to establish their control:

- At first, civil servants refused to work for the Bolshevik government and bankers refused to allow the Bolsheviks access to the state's funds. It took ten days and the threat of armed intervention to persuade the State Bank to hand over its reserves.
- The Bolsheviks had to establish their authority outside of Petrograd, and combat the opposition forces organised by Kerensky (mainly made up of Cossacks).
- The Bolsheviks' military force was also weakened as many Petrograd garrison soldiers went back to their homes in the countryside after the revolution.

KEY CHRONOLOGY

October–November 1917

29 October	The Red Guard puts down an army cadet rising up against the Bolsheviks
31 October	Bolsheviks take control of Baku and 17 provincial capitals
2 November	Kerensky's opposition forces are defeated
3 November	The Bolsheviks gain control of Moscow after a ten-day battle
	Kamenev, Zinoviev and Rykov leave the Bolshevik Party after Lenin's ultimatum to end division within it
5 November	Lenin announces that the revolution has succeeded

By the end of 1917 the Bolsheviks dominated the larger towns and cities and controlled the railways. However, huge areas of countryside were still not under their control.

Lenin's decrees and actions to December

Lenin's decrees

Between the Bolsheviks' seizure of power and December 1917, Lenin issued a large number of decrees.

Decree on Peace
- Promised an end to war
- An armistice followed in November

Decrees on workers' rights
- Workers' decree: limited the working day to eight hours
- Social insurance decree: gave old-age, health and unemployment benefits
- Decree on Workers' Control of Factories: allowed workers to 'supervise' managers

Decree to establish the Cheka
- Created a secret police force known as the Cheka to root out opposition

Lenin's early decrees

Social decrees
- Press decree: banned the opposition press
- Judicial decree: established people's courts
- Decree to outlaw sex discrimination: gave equal rights for women
- Decrees on the Church: removed marriage and divorce from Church control

Decree on Land
- Abolished private ownership of land
- Legitimised peasant seizures of land from landlords
- Reduced peasant support for the SRs

Lenin's actions

Lenin was cautious about how quickly Russia should become fully socialist. For example:

- On the one hand, Vesenkha (the Supreme Soviet of the National Economy) was set up in December 1917. It answered to Sovnarkom and was responsible for gaining state control over the economy, starting with the State Bank.
- On the other hand, Lenin resisted calls to completely nationalise all industry.

Lenin took steps to combat opposition to Bolshevik control of Russia:

- The Cheka, led by Felix Dzerzhinsky, could arrest anyone it suspected.
- Members of opposition parties were arrested and imprisoned.
- Anti-Bolshevik newspapers were shut down.

SUMMARY

- The Bolsheviks were easily able to remove the weak Provisional Government in their revolution of 25 October. However, establishing wider control over Russia proved more difficult.
- Lenin's government was resolutely Bolshevik. Only the left-wing SRs were allowed to have any role in a government that was otherwise dominated by Bolsheviks.
- The establishment of the Cheka showed Lenin's conviction that active repression of 'counter-revolutionary' enemies was needed to safeguard the 'dictatorship of the proletariat'.

APPLY

APPLY YOUR KNOWLEDGE

Sort the events below into chronological order, then group them according to whether they happened during the February/March Revolution of 1917, or the October/November Revolution of 1917.

Group the events into a table like this one:

Events of the February/March Revolution	Events of the October/November Revolution

- The Provisional Committee is set up by the Duma
- Kamenev and others leave the Bolshevik Party
- The government announces bread rationing
- Sovnarkom is set up to run the government
- Members of the Provisional Government are arrested
- There is a lock-out at the Putilov factory
- Kerensky's opposition forces are defeated
- The Duma president sends a telegram to Nicholas II warning him of the riots
- Red Guards 'storm' the Winter Palace
- The International Women's Day March
- The Second Congress of Soviets agrees to Lenin's Decree on Land
- The Petrograd Soviet is set up

EXAMINER TIP

This exercise will help you to revise the key events of both the 1917 revolutions, and to keep these events separate in your mind – they can be easy to muddle up!

REVIEW

To review the events of the February/March Revolution, go back to Chapter 2.

ASSESS THE VALIDITY OF THIS VIEW

> **A LEVEL** 'Lenin played a more important part than any other individual or group in the success of the October/November 1917 Revolution.' Assess the validity of this view.

a Copy and complete the following table by including evidence of the contribution of each individual or group to the success of the revolution.

Individual or group	Contribution to the success of the revolution
Lenin	
Trotsky and the MRC	
The Bolshevik Central Committee	
Red Guard soldiers and sailors	
The Second Congress of Soviets	

b Use the table to write a complete answer to the exam question.

PLAN YOUR ESSAY

 'The October/November Revolution was the result of the failures of the Provisional Government.' Explain why you agree or disagree with this view.

a Make a list of the main failures of the Provisional Government. One has been added to get you started:

Failure to solve Russia's economic problems

_____

_____

_____

_____

b Use your list as a starting point to fill in the table below. Remember that you need to link the failures of the Provisional Government to the reasons for the October/November Revolution.

How the weaknesses of the Provisional Government contributed to the revolution	Other factors that contributed to the revolution

c Use your table to write an essay plan for the exam question above.

EXAMINER TIP

The causes of the October/November 1917 Revolution are debatable. From your point of view, there isn't a single right or wrong answer to this question – what is important is how well you can argue your case.

KEY CONCEPT

Political authority is a key concept in the study of revolution and dictatorship in Russia 1917–53.

'Political authority' refers to political power and the basis on which that power rests. It suggests the ability to influence and control, and to make decisions affecting the people who are subject to those holding this power.

a On what basis did the political authority of the Bolsheviks rest immediately after the October/November Revolution?

b What was the extent of the Bolsheviks' political authority by the end of 1917? As part of your answer, give specific examples of where the Bolsheviks had or had not yet gained political authority.

c Write a paragraph to summarise how the Bolsheviks' political authority changed between the October/November Revolution and the end of 1917.

AS Level essay sample answer

 REVIEW

On these Exam Practice pages you will find a sample student answer for an AS Level essay question. What are the strengths and weaknesses of the answer? Read the answer and the corresponding Examiner Tips carefully. Think about how you could apply this advice in order to improve your own answers to questions like this one.

 AS LEVEL 'The Bolsheviks played a decisive role in undermining the Provisional Government in 1917.' Explain why you agree or disagree with this view.

25 marks

Sample student answer

The Bolsheviks had an important role in undermining the Provisional Government in 1917, criticising the failures of the government and constantly promoting government by the soviets as the alternative to the Provisional Government. But other factors were important in undermining the Provisional Government, including the actions of the government itself, and these other factors were more decisive than the Bolsheviks' actions.

There was a lot of frustration in Russia in 1917 that food was still so hard to get in the cities, and that land had not been taken away from the big landlords and given to the peasants in the countryside. Soldiers were demoralised by the war and workers were tired of long hours of difficult factory work for low pay and in dangerous conditions. Through 1917, the Bolsheviks benefited from this frustration because they were talking about the things that workers, soldiers and peasants wanted.

The Provisional Government's own actions were more decisive in undermining its own authority than anything the Bolsheviks did. For example, the Brusilov offensive in June 1917 was a huge gamble by the government that lost 400,000 Russian soldiers (with as many again deserting from the army) and millions of square miles of Russian land. This disaster was very important in convincing soldiers to support the Bolsheviks, who were the only political party that promised to end the war. It was a colossal mistake. If Kerensky (as Minister of War) had worked on a peace deal with Germany instead of launching the disastrous Brusilov offensive, then the Provisional Government would have had a lot more support, and the Bolsheviks would have gained a lot less support.

REVISION SKILLS

AS questions will contain a quotation advancing a judgement followed by 'explain why you agree or disagree with this view'. Read page 7 for details on how to master the essay question.

EXAMINER TIP

This introduction mentions two ways in which the Bolsheviks undermined the Provisional Government and one other balancing factor: the actions of the Provisional Government itself. It thus shows some balance and the final sentence expresses a view. However, there is no attempt to show a more nuanced judgement or to present the full range of ideas that will be considered in the essay.

EXAMINER TIP

There are some useful points being made in this paragraph, but the student has not developed them to show how they are relevant to the question. There is no comment that is explicitly directed to assessing the Bolsheviks' role in undermining the Provisional Government. This could have been done by saying the Bolsheviks were offering positive solutions, while the Provisional Government quickly became a symbol of oppression – like tsarism – because it was not responding to people's needs.

EXAMINER TIP

The student includes some good detail here and links the paragraph to the question focus. However, the paragraph takes a very one-sided view of the Brusilov offensive (which was not necessarily a 'colossal mistake'). It is also too speculative, as it is only possible to guess at what might have happened if the Brusilov offensive had not gone ahead.

The army was also important in undermining the Provisional Government. This was because most of the officers wanted to keep the army the same as under tsarism, while many of the ordinary soldiers were attracted to the socialism of the Petrograd Soviet. The most the Petrograd Soviet would support was a defensive war, in which Russia tried to hold on to the territory in the West that it still had. But the Provisional Government was under pressure from its Western allies to lead new offensives against Germany and Austria, which the Soviet was against. From the start, Dual Authority with the Petrograd Soviet undermined the Provisional Government, especially in relation to the army, and tensions over the war increased this.

The July Days brought a series of uprisings which may have been planned by Bolshevik activists, but no one really knows. The Provisional Government and Petrograd Soviet worked together to put down these uprisings, and many Bolsheviks were imprisoned as a result, although Lenin fled to Finland. This was not a case of the Bolsheviks undermining the Provisional Government, but more the other way round.

I believe that the Kornilov coup was the decisive factor in undermining the Provisional Government in 1917. Kornilov believed in the restoration of the monarchy in Russia and he saw the Provisional Government as being under the control of the Petrograd Soviet. Even before his coup, Kornilov tried to bring back traditional discipline to the army, and his coup was an attempt to crush the Soviet and bring military control to Russia – which would have completely undermined the government's commitment to democracy.

Before Kornilov's coup, the Bolsheviks were in no position to undermine the Provisional Government. Lenin was in hiding and the rest of the Bolshevik leaders were under arrest. When Kornilov did not call off his advance on Petrograd, things changed very quickly. Trotsky and other senior Bolsheviks were freed. 40,000 Red Guards were given weapons to defend Petrograd – and did not return them. Kerensky's own authority was completely undermined; he lost support on the right because of 'betraying' Kornilov and on the left because he had appointed Kornilov and it was suspected that Kerensky had agreed to Kornilov's plan before he got cold feet about it. The Bolsheviks were able to portray themselves as defending Russia from counter-revolution, and their support increased rapidly: they won their first majority in the Petrograd Soviet at the end of August and by the end of September there were possibly 350,000 Bolshevik Party members. But by this point the Provisional Government was not in a position to stop the Bolsheviks.

EXAMINER TIP

The points being made in this paragraph are potentially good, but are not very clearly expressed, perhaps because two different points seem to be combined together here: tensions in the army as a factor undermining the Provisional Government, and relations with the Petrograd Soviet as another factor undermining the government. Keeping these as two separate points, in two separate paragraphs, would help to make the student's argument clearer and easier to follow. The addition of more substantive evidence would also improve the paragraph.

EXAMINER TIP

This paragraph is rather descriptive, although it does make a comment in relation to the question at the end. It would have been better had the argument come first and the supporting information followed – perhaps with a little more development.

EXAMINER TIP

Although this paragraph begins with a clear statement that is explicitly linked to the question, what follows loses its focus. The points about Kornilov show good knowledge of the period, but need to be tied more directly to the theme of the answer: how was the Provisional Government undermined? Also, there is no mention of Kerensky's possible complicity in the Kornilov affair.

EXAMINER TIP

This paragraph makes a lot of points without fully developing them, but the overall effect is quite convincing. A sentence at the beginning that links to the essay question would improve the paragraph. In fact, the previous paragraph could have been cut and this paragraph could then have begun: 'The Kornilov coup was the decisive factor in undermining the Provisional Government in 1917.'

The Bolsheviks took advantage of a Provisional Government that was already so undermined that it was unable to do anything to stop the Bolsheviks from taking over. It was the Kornilov coup that played the decisive role in undermining the Provisional Government, because after this the government was left with no supporters either on the right or on the left, while the Bolsheviks – almost wiped out as a political force in July – were able to rapidly gain support as the defenders against more Kornilov-style counter-revolutionaries.

EXAMINER TIP

The conclusion reinforces the argument that the Kornilov coup was decisive in creating an opportunity for the Bolsheviks. However, this is not quite what the question asks about. It is not entirely clear whether the Bolsheviks 'played a decisive role' here or whether it was the Provisional Government's own mistakes that undermined its power.

OVERALL COMMENT

The answer shows a good knowledge of key events of the period between the revolutions in 1917, and a good understanding of the implications of these events for the Provisional Government. The answer provides a good deal of comment on the question, but coverage of the Bolsheviks' role in undermining the Provisional Government is not given much space, and while there is a view (that the Bolsheviks' role was not decisive), this is never fully developed. The essay would also have benefited from more substantive examples to back up relevant comments. The information and analysis would enable the answer to reach a low Level 4, but more direct consideration of the Bolsheviks would have been expected for higher marks.

OVER TO YOU

Give yourself 40 minutes to answer this question on your own. Then review the Examiner Tips on these pages to check whether you have avoided making the same mistakes as the sample student answer.

❏ Did you explicitly link each of your paragraphs to the question?

❏ Did you fully develop your arguments to explain how your evidence shows what the decisive roles or factors were in the undermining of the Provisional Government in 1917?

❏ Did you make a judgement and sustain it from the introduction through to the conclusion?

Go back and look at pages 14–21 to help you refresh your knowledge of the Provisional Government and its troubles.

5 The consolidation of the Communist dictatorship

 RECAP

By the end of 1917, the Bolsheviks had seized control of Petrograd and Moscow, and had made great strides in establishing their power. However, they were only one of the various groups competing for power amidst the chaos of war and revolution. Vast areas of Russia were completely beyond their control and they still faced a huge task in consolidating their power.

The Bolsheviks had to enforce authority on the central government; if successful, they then had to extend their control outwards across a vast and diverse nation. Furthermore, they had to do this while Russia was still involved in fighting a world war.

The establishment of one-party control

The Bolsheviks had seized power in the name of the proletariat – the industrial working class of Russia. Their most powerful slogan was 'all power to the soviets', which implied that councils of working people would help to run all aspects of Russia, from its factories to its national government. However, the reality was quite different.

On 25 October 1917, the delegates of the second All-Russian Congress of Soviets voted 500 to 170 for a socialist government to replace the overthrown Provisional Government. They were expecting this to be a socialist coalition government, along the lines of the Petrograd Soviet.

But Lenin did not want to share power. He believed the Bolsheviks were acting in the interests of the working class and that this gave him complete authority.

The removal of the Constituent Assembly

The Provisional Government had organised elections for the long-awaited Constituent Assembly to be held in November 1918, and Lenin allowed these to go ahead.

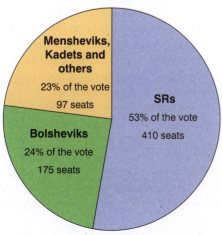

The SRs won the majority of seats. Lenin immediately declared that 'elections prove nothing'. The Constituent Assembly met for one day, attempted to redraft the Bolshevik decrees, then was closed by troops and never opened again.

Lenin justified this by saying that Russia was now governed by a 'dictatorship of the proletariat'. This meant that Lenin's government had taken control of the state on behalf of the proletariat, and would use state power to turn everything to benefit workers and peasants instead of the bourgeois.

The ending of involvement in the First World War

Lenin had a number of reasons for ending Russia's involvement in the First World War:

> The Bolsheviks had promised peace, and much of their support came from soldiers who were tiring of the war.

> Lenin was convinced that Germany was about to have its own revolution. Soon both Russia and Germany would be part of a new international communist system, which meant that any peace-deal terms which negatively impacted Russia would only be temporary.

> Lenin knew the Russian army could not stop a German invasion of Russia, which would end Bolshevik control.

> Lenin believed that national boundaries were less important than the proletariat's shared common values. He believed the end of the war would allow workers everywhere to rise up against the oppressive capitalist classes.

An armistice with Germany was agreed in December 1917. However, agreeing an acceptable peace treaty to end Russia's involvement in the war proved to be extremely challenging.

- Germany was already occupying large swathes of Russian territory and demanded major concessions as the price of a ceasefire.
- Lenin and Trotsky did not agree on their negotiating stance. Trotsky opposed agreeing to a peace deal that would involve harsh terms for Russia. Lenin was less concerned about the peace terms for the reasons given above.

- Once negotiations began, there were further splits in the Central Committee. Bukharin led the 'revolutionary war group' which argued against peace with the Germans at all. Others saw this as betraying the Bolsheviks' promise to end the war.
- Trotsky was put in charge of the Bolshevik negotiating team. He dragged proceedings out, probably hoping that the German revolution would have started before any peace terms had been agreed.
- Trotsky's delaying tactics annoyed the Germans. They ended the armistice and began to advance again into Russia.
- Lenin demanded that Trotsky negotiate peace at any price, but the harsh terms of the Treaty of Brest-Litovsk (signed on 3 March 1918) were deeply unpopular.
- The left-wing SRs walked out of Sovnarkom in protest. Only by threatening to resign could Lenin force the Bolshevik Central Committee to agree to the treaty – by a majority of one.

Terms of the Treaty of Brest-Litovsk

In exchange for peace, the Bolsheviks had to give up a huge area in the west of Russia, meaning the loss of:

- 62 million people (one sixth of Russia's population)
- 2 million square kilometres of land, responsible for one third of Russia's agricultural production
- a quarter of Russia's railway lines
- three quarters of Russia's iron and coal supplies.

The Bolsheviks also had to pay 3 billion roubles in war reparations.

The consolidation of the one-party state

New decrees from Sovnarkom helped to define the one-party state.

- Workers were put in the charge of the railways.
- Government support for the Church ended, and Russia became a secular state.
- Industries were nationalised and land ownership was abolished. Now only the state owned land and made it available to those who would farm it for the good of the community.

In March 1918, Trotsky became head of the new Red Army (after the Red Guards were disbanded). The capital was moved to Moscow, to be more central to the country. In July 1918, the first Soviet Constitution was proclaimed.

These events took place against a background of crisis. Left-wing SRs attempted to seize power in Moscow but were crushed; this was followed by the imposition of the Red Terror by the newly formed secret police, the Cheka (see page 40). For the Constitution to become political reality, the Bolsheviks would have to win a civil war (see pages 33–36).

The 1918 Constitution

The Soviet Constitution of July 1918 set out the power structure of the new regime. On the surface it looked like a fully democratic system:

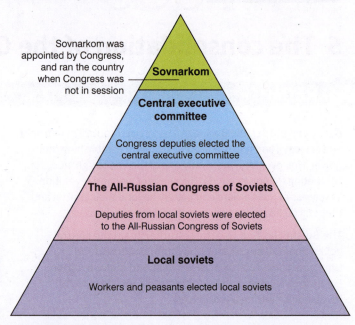

Sovnarkom was appointed by Congress, and ran the country when Congress was not in session

Sovnarkom

Central executive committee

Congress deputies elected the central executive committee

The All-Russian Congress of Soviets

Deputies from local soviets were elected to the All-Russian Congress of Soviets

Local soviets

Workers and peasants elected local soviets

However, in practice Lenin and Sovnarkom held most of the power:

- The Congress of Soviets only met at intervals throughout the year. Between those times, Sovnarkom ruled Russia.
- Although Sovnarkom was officially appointed by the Congress of Soviets, it was actually chosen by the Central Committee of the Bolshevik Party.
- Sovnarkom consisted solely of Bolsheviks after the left-wing SRs walked out in protest over the Treaty of Brest-Litovsk.
- In July 1918, members of the former 'exploiting classes' were banned from voting or holding office.
- Worker's votes were worth five peasant votes.
- In the elections to the Congress of Soviets, the electorate were invited to choose between Bolshevik nominees. There was no free choice of candidates.

SUMMARY

- The Bolsheviks' lack of a majority in the Constituent Assembly undermined any democratic right to rule Russia. Lenin closed the Constituent Assembly, justifying this by saying government was now a 'dictatorship of the proletariat'.
- The Treaty of Brest-Litovsk was very costly for Russia, and was strongly opposed even within the Bolshevik Party. Lenin however could see no alternative and was confident that Germany would soon join Russia in having its own socialist revolution.
- The Bolsheviks made the direction of their new one-party state clear in the early months.
- By the end of 1918, the Bolshevik regime was still in power, but was threatened by a range of hostile forces in a developing civil war. The process of consolidating power was far from complete.

APPLY

SOURCE ANALYSIS

SOURCE A

From an article by Peter Kropotkin, published in April 1919 in the British socialist newspaper *The Labour Leader*. Kropotkin was a Russian anarchist, committed to socialism without central state control.

The idea of soviets – that is to say, of councils of workers and peasants – controlling the economic and political life of the country is a great idea.

But as long as the country is governed by a party dictatorship, the workers' and peasants' councils stop having any real significance. A council of workers stops being free and being of any use when freedom of the press no longer exists, and we have been in that condition for two years – under a pretext that we are in a state of war. But more still. The workers' and peasants' councils lose their significance when the elections are not free, when the elections are carried out under pressure by a party dictatorship.

a What is the attitude in Source A to:

- the soviets
- the election process
- the Bolsheviks' 'dictatorship of the proletariat'?

b How might the author, date, audience and purpose of this extract affect its value to an historian studying the consolidation of the Bolshevik government?

c How valuable is this source to an historian studying the consolidation of the Bolshevik government? Use your answers to **a** and **b** to help you.

REVIEW

The diagram and text about the 1918 Constitution on page 30 will help you put your analysis of this source into context.

EXAMINER TIP

Try to avoid writing generic statements such as 'the writer would be biased'. Make sure you explain why you think the writer adopts their opinion and link this explanation to the content of the source.

APPLY YOUR KNOWLEDGE

a This map illustrates the territorial losses caused by the Treaty of Brest-Litovsk. Add annotations to the map to show relevant details of the losses. One has been done for you.

Key

Territorial losses as a result of the Treaty of Brest Litovsk.

Boundary of Soviet territory, March 1921

NORWAY

FINLAND

BOLSHEVIK RUSSIA

SWEDEN

ESTONIA

Baltic Sea LATVIA

LITHUANIA

GERMANY

Ural Mountains

In total, Russia lost Finland, Estonia, Latvia, Lithuania, Poland, Bessarabia, Georgia, Belarus and the Ukraine.

POLAND

CZECHOSLOVAKIA   Ukraine

HUNGARY

ROMANIA

Caspian Sea

MONTE-NEGRO

Black Sea

YUGOSLAVIA

BULGARIA

ALBANIA

ITALY   GREECE   TURKEY

0   400 km

b Which of the losses caused by the Treaty of Brest-Litovsk do you think would have been most significant to the Russians? Explain your answer.

EXAMINER TIP

This activity will help you answer questions about the impact of the Brest-Litovsk treaty on Russia. It is important to understand not just what the terms of the treaty were, but also their significance.

REVIEW

If you can't think of ways in which of these losses would have had an impact on the Russians, it may help to look ahead to the next chapter on the civil war.

PLAN YOUR ESSAY

AS LEVEL 'The Constitution of July 1918 granted power to the Party, not the people.' Explain why you agree or disagree with this view.

a Use the information on page 30 to help you complete the table below. A few details have been added to get you started.

How the Constitution granted power to the people	How the Constitution granted power to the Party
The Constitution recognised the working class as the ruling class of Russia.	Local soviets had to carry out all orders given by the Congress of Soviets.
All men and women over 18 had the right to vote and be elected to soviets, as long as they earned their living through work that was useful to society.	

b Do you agree with the statement in the question? Write a paragraph that explains your reasoning.

TO WHAT EXTENT?

A LEVEL To what extent does Bolshevik ideology explain why the Treaty of Brest-Litovsk was signed?

a Use the information on pages 29–30 to list the main reasons for why the Bolsheviks agreed to the Treaty of Brest-Litovsk.

b Highlight the reasons that were connected to Bolshevik ideology, rather than other factors.

c Use your list to write a complete answer to the essay question.

EXAMINER TIP

To assess effectively whether the 1918 Constitution did grant power to Bolshevik Party rather than to the people, you will need to compare the rights it gave to the people with what the Party allowed to happen in reality.

6 The Civil War

 RECAP

Lenin's insistence that peace with Germany be achieved at any price was hugely resented throughout Russia. Civil war broke out as different opposition groups tried to overthrow the Bolsheviks by force. From early 1918 until the end of 1920, the regime had to fight for survival in a complex and wide-ranging civil war. Even after they won the war, their consolidation of power was not yet complete.

The causes of the Civil War

By the early months of 1918, a substantial section of the Russian population had turned against the Bolsheviks. Their reasons varied:

On the left

> Lenin had forced the Kadets and right-wing SRs out of his government.

> Lenin had closed the Constituent Assembly after the SRs won the most seats (see page 29).

> The Bolsheviks were sidelining the soviets and imposing a one-party dictatorship (see page 30).

On the right

> Aristocrats and the bourgeoisie were alienated by Bolshevik ideology. Russians with land, money or businesses stood to lose everything from Bolshevik economic and social policies.

> Some still yearned for the old tsarist regime, although they did not necessarily want Nicholas II himself back on the throne. This group included army officers, some of whom objected to the peace treaty with Germany.

> Food shortages hit the bourgeoisie the hardest as the rationing system meant that they were given the smallest share.

Other causes

> The Bolsheviks had seized power by force in Moscow and Petrograd in October/November 1917. Their opponents claimed they had no right to rule Russia; they had not submitted to popular elections; and they had largely ignored the Petrograd Soviet which had helped to place them in power.

> Many were angered by the concessions of the Treaty of Brest-Litovsk (see page 30).

> Much discontent was caused by the Bolsheviks' inability to solve Russia's economic problems.
> Ongoing food shortages and severe rationing of essentials were exacerbated by distribution problems, as well as the loss of agricultural land from the Treaty of Brest-Litovsk.

> National minorities who had been part of the old Russian Empire, such as the Georgians, were uncertain that Bolshevik promises to grant self-determination were to be believed. These groups saw an opportunity in the prevailing chaos and uncertainty to fight for their independence.

> Those of limited allegiance to any political group simply viewed the fluid political situation, brought by the Bolshevik revolution and the economic chaos of war, as an opportunity to win old battles and play out local rivalries.

The course of the Civil War

The Civil War was fought between the Bolshevik Red Army and a range of different opposition groups, motivated by different aims.

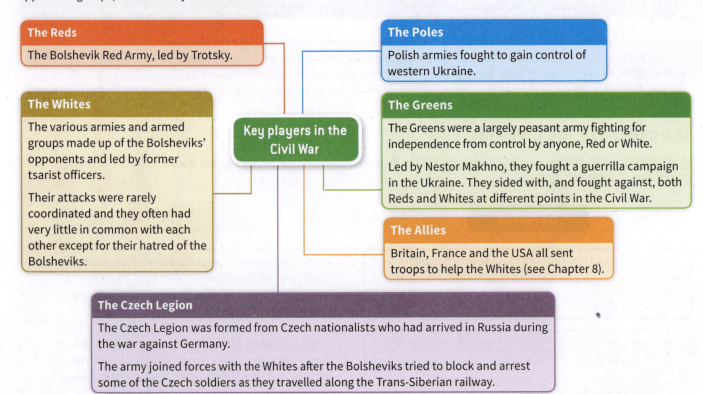

The Reds

The Bolshevik Red Army, led by Trotsky.

The Poles

Polish armies fought to gain control of western Ukraine.

The Whites

The various armies and armed groups made up of the Bolsheviks' opponents and led by former tsarist officers.

Their attacks were rarely coordinated and they often had very little in common with each other except for their hatred of the Bolsheviks.

Key players in the Civil War

The Greens

The Greens were a largely peasant army fighting for independence from control by anyone, Red or White.

Led by Nestor Makhno, they fought a guerrilla campaign in the Ukraine. They sided with, and fought against, both Reds and Whites at different points in the Civil War.

The Allies

Britain, France and the USA all sent troops to help the Whites (see Chapter 8).

The Czech Legion

The Czech Legion was formed from Czech nationalists who had arrived in Russia during the war against Germany.

The army joined forces with the Whites after the Bolsheviks tried to block and arrest some of the Czech soldiers as they travelled along the Trans-Siberian railway.

There were two main stages to the Civil War:

- The first (1918–20) was mainly fought in the east and south of Russia. The Bolsheviks held the area around Moscow and were attacked on different sides by the Whites.
- The second (1920–21) was more of a nationalist conflict against the Polish armies that had invaded western Ukraine. Russian forces, led by General Tukhachevsky, were able to drive the Poles back. This led to the Treaty of Riga in March 1921.

The timeline below gives an overview of the course of the Civil War, but to learn more about Allied involvement in it, see Chapter 8.

1918		
April–May	The Czech Legion seizes parts of the Trans-Siberian railway. War begins.	When Bolsheviks tried to arrest Czech soldiers travelling across Russia on the railway, the Czechs joined the Whites and began advancing towards Moscow.
August	Denikin and Kolchak's White armies make rapid advances.	General Denikin's army attacked from the south-west of Moscow, and Admiral Kolchak's army attacked from the east.
November	Kolchak declares himself 'Supreme Ruler' of Russia.	The Whites appeared poised for success but Red counter-attacks prevented Denikin and Kolchak from linking up.
1919		
October	Denikin's army advances to within 200 miles of Moscow. Yudenich's army advances to the outskirts of Petrograd.	This was the closest Denikin got to victory. Trotsky counter-attacked to force Denikin south towards the Crimea. Red troops were able to repel General Yudenich's small army of 15,000 men.

2 BOLSHEVIK CONSOLIDATION, 1918–1924

1920		
February	Kolchak is captured and shot.	Kolchak had been in retreat since 1919. He was captured and handed over to the Bolsheviks.
March	Denikin's army is evacuated to the Crimea.	White armies continued to retreat.
May	Beginning of the Russo-Polish War.	The new campaign distracted Bolshevik forces.
October	Wrangel's army is evacuated from the Crimea. The Bolsheviks establish control.	Baron Wrangel took over from Denikin in the Crimea. His army was defeated by Nestor Makhno's Green peasant army, and evacuated by British and French ships. The Bolsheviks gained victory over the Whites, but fighting against the Poles continued into 1921.
1921		
March	The Treaty of Riga is signed.	This treaty granted independence to Poland and a number of other states, including Estonia and Latvia.

The role of Trotsky

Although Trotsky had no military training, he was excellent at military organisation and successfully directed the Red Army in the Civil War. The Whites had no leader as effective as Trotsky.

He travelled around the different fronts of the war in a special train, meeting commanders and troops. The train carried food, equipment and cigarettes for the troops and also had a propaganda unit, all of which were important for Red Army morale.

He insisted on strict discipline. If a unit retreated without being ordered to, Trotsky said the first to be shot would be the political commissar, and then the unit commander. Deserters were also shot (the Cheka was used to round them up).

His ruthless approach ensured the Red Army had food (by requisitioning grain from the peasants) and weapons.

Trotsky's role in the Civil War

He did not let ideology get in the way of winning. For example, he recruited 50,000 former tsarist officers to train new troops, even though they were ideological enemies of the working class. Political commissars watched the tsarist officers for any sign of disloyalty.

He turned the Red Army into a professional military force, reintroducing traditional ranks and practices. Soldier soviets no longer elected their officers, for example.

The murder of the Tsar

- At the start of the Civil War, the Bolsheviks worried that the Tsar and his family might be important to the Whites as a figurehead of resistance against the Bolsheviks.
- In July 1918, the royal family was being held in Yekaterinburg, in the Ural mountains. The Cheka police guarding the royal family murdered them when they heard that White troops were nearby.
- Although the murder was carried out by local Bolsheviks, it is almost certain that Lenin authorised the killing. If so, this was evidence of the way that Lenin's government was moving towards greater radicalisation and terror.

Reasons for the Red victory

Some of the main reasons for the Red victory are summarised here:

Geography	Unity and organisation	Leadership	Support	Other
The Reds commanded the hub of communications, the armaments factories and the most densely populated regions of central Russia (including Petrograd and Moscow). The Whites were widely dispersed in less-developed parts.	The Reds were united in their aim to survive and ideologically committed in a way the Whites were not. White generals operated independently and fought for different objectives, whereas the Reds had a unified command structure.	The Red Army became a well-disciplined fighting force under Trotsky's leadership. Whites had few competent commanders, and ill-discipline and corruption were rife.	Although peasant support varied, generally the Reds' land policies were more popular than the Whites' association with traditional tsarist policies.	Foreign involvement did not greatly aid the Whites. However, hostility to foreign involvement gave the Reds a useful propaganda platform. The national minorities were suspicious of the Whites, whose slogan was 'Russia One and Indivisible'.

Government and control in wartime

The Civil War led to greater governmental centralisation and increased Party control. It had a lasting influence on how the USSR was governed.

- Half a million Party members fought for the Red Army. They became used to obeying orders and acting with whatever force was necessary.
- To organise the war, the Soviet bureaucracy grew much larger until there were more bureaucrats than workers. Soviet government remained highly bureaucratic.
- In wartime it was essential that orders from the centre were communicated quickly and carried out without delay. This continued after the war. Instead of policies and decisions being created at local soviet level, they were created in the centre and carried out without question at the local level.
- In 1919, the Politburo was formed from the Party's Central Committee. Because the Politburo's members were also key government officials, the Politburo quickly took over the running of both the Party and the government. Sovnarkom gradually met less frequently during the 1920s, as the Politburo increasingly bypassed it to give orders directly to the government ministries represented in the Central Committee.
- 'Central controls' were brought in to deal with food shortages (see pages 39–40). Central control of the economy increased after the war.
- The Bolsheviks adopted a 'siege mentality' while surrounded by enemies in the Civil War. Defending their revolution from enemies demanded extreme ruthlessness and brutality. This mentality continued after the war; Stalin was heavily influenced by it.
- The Bolsheviks used terror to ensure that people obeyed orders from the centre, and to eliminate anyone suspected of opposition.

After the civil war, areas conquered by the Red Army either became a part of the Russian Soviet Federal Socialist Republic (the name given to the Bolshevik State in January 1918), or were allowed to remain as separate soviet republics (such as the Ukraine and Georgia).

At the end of 1922, the Union of Soviet Socialist Republics was officially established, known as the USSR or Soviet Union.

SUMMARY

- The Civil War broke out because the Bolsheviks had seized power in a coup and faced opposition both within Russia and from foreign powers.
- The Civil War was fought on several fronts. The White forces comprised various separate groups, whereas the Bolsheviks were more united and held the central ground. The Bolsheviks also had Trotsky, a ruthless and inspiring commander.
- The Civil War was a brutal affair, symbolised by the murder of the royal family.
- The Civil War led to greater governmental centralisation and increased Party control. These changes lasted beyond the war, and the experience of this time influenced communist attitudes for years to come.

 **APPLY**

 How significant was the role of Trotsky in bringing about victory for the Reds in the Civil War?

a   Complete the spider diagram below by adding reasons for the Reds' victory in the Civil War.

b   Highlight the reasons where Trotsky made a significant contribution.

> There was no single White leader to coordinate the White armies

> The Reds controlled central Russia, making it easier to supply and coordinate troops

> **Reasons for the Reds' victory in the Civil War**

> Trotsky insisted on strict discipline, making sure that deserters were shot

---

IMPROVE AN ANSWER

 To what extent did the Civil War change how the USSR was governed?

Below is the introduction from a student's answer to the exam question above.

You will notice that the introduction is very one-sided. Rewrite the introduction so it is more balanced.

Answer

The Civil War did not have a very big influence on how the USSR was governed because Lenin and the Bolshevik leadership had already decided the main government structures before the Civil War began. For example, Sovnarkom was set up on 25 October 1917, during the October Revolution. Sovnarkom made the decisions that ran Russia, with the Congress of Soviets rubber-stamping what Sovnarkom said it should. This was the model that the Bolshevik Party followed after the end of the Civil War.

REVIEW

It will be useful to read Chapter 7 before you rewrite this introduction, as war communism had a significant influence on how the USSR was governed.

EXAMINER TIP

The introduction given here is not balanced because it focuses only on supporting the argument that the Civil War did *not* change how the USSR was governed. While it is important to give a clear view, it is better to show you also understand the alternative argument, even if you intend to challenge it.

PLAN YOUR ESSAY

AS LEVEL '**The Treaty of Brest-Litovsk was the most significant cause of discontent with Bolshevik rule in 1918.' Explain why you agree or disagree with this view.**

a   Write a sentence or two to explain how you could assess what the most 'significant' cause is. What makes one cause more 'significant' than another?

b   List the main reasons for the discontent with Bolshevik rule in 1918.

c   Decide whether you think any of these reasons are more significant than the Treaty of Brest-Litovsk.

d   Write a paragraph that could serve as a conclusion to the essay question. You should explain whether you agree or disagree with the statement in the essay question, and give the main reasons why.

ASSESS THE VALIDITY OF THIS VIEW

A LEVEL '**By March 1921, the Bolsheviks still had only a fragile grip on power.' Assess the validity of this view for the years 1918 to 1921.**

a   Explain what you understand by the phrase 'fragile grip on power'. Include an example or examples of what might indicate that a government has a fragile grip on power, rather than a strong grip on power or no grip at all.

b   Copy and complete the following table by identifying what the challenges were for each of the different themes. A start has been made to help you.

Theme (e.g. social/economic/political)	Challenges to the Bolsheviks' grip on power in 1918	Challenges to the Bolsheviks' grip on power in 1921
Political opposition	The Bolsheviks' seizure of power was widely disputed. Wide-ranging opposition to the closure of the Constituent Assembly. Strong condemnation across the political spectrum for the terms of the Treaty of Brest-Litovsk.	
International opposition		
Social challenges		
Economic challenges		
Internal divisions (within the Bolshevik Party)		

c   Using the table to help you, write a complete answer to the essay question above.

EXAMINER TIP

Your conclusion is where you restate your judgement on whether you agree or disagree with the view given in the essay question. It is very important that you substantiate this judgement, although at this point you should not introduce new arguments or evidence. Instead you should recap the reasons why you reached that judgement.

REVIEW

Use Chapters 5 and 6 to complete the sections in this table. It will also help to look ahead to Chapter 7 to consider the economic and social challenges posed by the Civil War.

EXAMINER TIP

There are two main ways you could structure your answer: by considering arguments for and against the view, or by focusing each section on a different theme (such as political, economic and social issues). Although the arguments for/against approach is effective, thematic essays are usually more successful because they produce a more balanced consideration of the wide range of factors influencing a historical issue or situation.

7 Economic and social developments

 **RECAP**

The Bolsheviks were motivated by their commitment to an ideology of economic and social transformation. Implementing communism was the core objective, but it was not easy or straightforward to achieve this.

- It was essential for the Bolsheviks to gain political control and secure the regime against their enemies.
- It was necessary to resolve the internal debates within the Party and to hammer out the precise policies to be implemented.
- The Bolsheviks also needed to adapt their ideology and policies to the terrible conditions of a country faced by revolution, civil war and economic hardship.

KEY CHRONOLOGY		
1917–18		**State capitalism**
1917	February	Decree on Land (abolished private ownership of land)
	November	Decree on Workers' Control of Factories (gave workers greater control over the running of factories)
	December	Nationalisation of the banks
1918–21		**War communism**
1918	June	War communism introduced
	September	Intensification of the Red Terror Nationalisation of factories and railways
1919	January	Start of compulsory grain requisitioning
1920	August	Outbreak of the Tambov Revolt
	December	Industrial production at 20 per cent of 1913 levels
1921 onwards		**New Economic Policy**
1921	March	The Kronstadt rising; NEP introduced
	June	Final defeat of the Tambov Revolt

State capitalism

After the Bolsheviks came to power, an approach to the economy evolved known as **state capitalism**: a 'halfway house' between capitalism and socialism. Until the USSR was ready to fully embrace socialism, the state would manage key parts of the economy while private markets continued in other parts of the economy.

Examples of state control included:

- The nationalisation of Russia's banks (1917) and railways (1918).
- The establishment of Vesenkha (see page 23), which was set up in 1917 to start managing Russia's economy.
- The establishment of GOELRO, which was formed in 1920 to organise the production and distribution of electricity across Russia.

Three of the main problems with state capitalism were:

> Many Bolsheviks did not want a 'halfway house': they demanded state control of every part of the economy. Lenin's measures were a disappointment.

> Allowing factories to be taken over by their workers caused sharp drops in production because the workers lacked the necessary management skills.

> Letting peasants have control over the selling of grain meant higher prices. But state-controlled industries needed cheap grain so that workers did not have to be paid higher wages.

Conditions in cities and the countryside during the Civil War

Many Russians faced severe hardships during the Civil War. Some of the main reasons for this included the following:

Problem	Further detail
Falling industrial production	• Factory supplies were disrupted by the fighting. • Workers left to join the Red Army or to return to the countryside. Between January 1917 and January 1919, Russia's urban proletariat declined from 3.6 million to 1.4 million. • The drop in production led to rising prices, producing inflation. • As there were no products for peasants to buy, they stopped selling grain and hoarded it instead.
Fighting in the countryside	• Peasants could grow the food they needed to live on, so they were often better off than urban workers. • However, villages were attacked and sometimes destroyed by both Whites and Reds.
Food shortages in the cities	• Important agricultural regions were lost because of the Treaty of Brest-Litovsk. • Trade blockades meant hostile foreign powers refused to supply Russia with grain. • Peasant hoarding was a major reason for the food shortages. • By early 1918, the bread ration in Petrograd was only 50 grammes per person per day. • Many resorted to buying food or trading for it through the black market.
Disease and starvation	• Unsanitary living conditions, food shortages, and a lack of medical supplies and doctors led to millions of deaths. • Approximately 5 million people died during the Civil War from starvation and disease.

War communism

The Bolsheviks introduced **war communism** in June 1918, primarily to ensure that the Red Army was supplied with munitions and food.

War communism's centralised planning ensured that the Red Army had the supplies it needed to win the war. It was much more socialist than state capitalism, because the state now controlled production and private trade was banned, but whether such a radical move towards socialism was planned or not is disputed by historians.

Key features of war communism

Nationalisation

- By November 1920, nearly all factories and businesses had been nationalised.
- Private trade and manufacture were banned.
- The railways were placed under military-style control.

Grain requisitioning

- The Food Supplies Dictatorship was set up in May 1918 to organise the requisitioning of peasants' grain to feed the Red Army and workers in the cities.
- Peasants were supposed to be paid a fixed price for their grain, but low-value vouchers were often offered instead (to be exchanged for money at a later date).
- Peasant opposition to requisitioning meant a key feature of war communism was violent repression. The Cheka had to be used extensively to make the policy work at all.

Labour discipline and rationing

- Workers lost the rights and freedoms given to them by the November 1917 Decree on Workers' Control of Factories. The workers' soviets, which had run the factories, were abolished.
- Strict discipline was re-imposed on workers. Fines were imposed for slackness, lateness and absenteeism.
- Wages were replaced with ration-card workbooks. Rations were given out in accordance with class status. Red Army and factory workers got the most, and the bourgeoisie the least (or nothing at all).

Effects of war communism

War communism helped the Bolsheviks to win the war, but it created as many problems as it solved.

Famine in the countryside

- In the countryside, the **kulaks** (peasants able to hire others to work with them) were the worst hit. Sometimes their entire stocks were seized. Peasants with little or no land of their own were treated slightly better as they were viewed as the allies of the proletariat.

- Harsh requisitioning reduced grain supplies to dangerously low levels. Peasants were forced to eat the animals they used for ploughing and farm work. Peasants also sowed less grain in protest at the requisitions.
- As a result, the harvest of 1921 produced only 48 per cent of 1913's harvest, leading to widespread famine. Millions died of starvation and disease.
- Russia's population in 1913 was 170.9 million. By 1921, war and famine had reduced it to 130.9 million.

Depopulated cities

- By 1921, industrial output was just 20 per cent of pre-war levels. Rations had to be cut.
- Although some workers welcomed state control because it meant their factories were more likely to stay open, others went on strike or fled to the country in the hope of finding food.
- By the end of 1920, the population of Petrograd had fallen by 57.5 per cent and Moscow by 44.5 per cent from 1917 levels.

The Red Terror

- Worsening conditions in the cities and countryside, along with concern over the Bolsheviks' policies, meant the Party lacked popular support. They had to rely on coercion and force to impose their policies. This intensified during the period known as 'the Red Terror'.
- The trigger for the launch of the Red Terror was an assassination attempt on Lenin in August 1918.
- In response, the Cheka rounded up Mensheviks, SRs, anarchists and anyone else considered a threat. Estimates suggest 500,000 were executed.
- The Red Terror also targeted possible counter-revolutionaries. Former bourgeoisie were top of the list, but the regime used the campaign as a general measure to terrify people into compliance.

The Tambov revolt

- The famine and requisitioning in the countryside prompted a series of peasant revolts, the worst of which was in the Tambov province.
- In August 1920, a peasant army of 70,000 men rose up against government forces. The revolt spread over large areas of south-east Russia and lasted until June 1921.
- 100,000 Red Army soldiers were used to crush the revolt, with a brutal approach that destroyed whole villages.

The Kronstadt rising

- In 1921, further reductions in food rationing led to strikes and riots in the cities. In March this promoted 30,000 sailors at the Kronstadt naval base to rebel.
- The Kronstadt sailors had been the Bolsheviks' most loyal supporters in 1917, but by 1921 they opposed the Bolsheviks' one-party dictatorship and use of terror.

- Trotsky sent the Red Army to put down the uprising. 15,000 rebels were imprisoned and the ringleaders were shot.
- The uprising caused divisions within the Bolshevik Party. The Workers' Opposition group was set up under Alexander Shlyapnikov and Alexandra Kollontai to protect workers' rights and oppose the continuation of war communism. The members of this group believed the Bolshevik leadership was becoming too authoritarian and was straying too far from its original mission of 'all power to the soviets'.

The New Economic Policy

In February 1921, **Gosplan** was established to advise on a 'New Economic Policy' (NEP), which was introduced at the Tenth Party Congress in March 1921. It aimed to fix the problems caused by war communism, which had damaged the economic and social state of Russia.

Lenin knew many Bolsheviks would object to the NEP ecause it was an ideological step backwards. Therefore he did not allow a vote on whether it should be introduced or not.

Features of the NEP

In the countryside	• Grain requisitioning ended. • The ban on private trade ended. • Peasants still had to give a quota of grain to the state, but could sell their surplus produce for whatever price they could get for it.
In the cities	• While the state kept control of key large-scale industries (such as coal, oil and steel), small-scale industries became private again. • Rationing ended. • Industries had to pay workers out of their profits. Workers could be paid according to how much work they had done rather than at a centrally set (low) wage.

The economic impact of the NEP

The NEP, along with the end of the Civil War in 1921, helped to stabilise the Russian economy.

- Private businesses reopened and grew quickly. Cities regained services such as shops and restaurants.
- Agricultural production also recovered quickly, as peasants grew more in order to earn more money from private trade.
- However, so much food was grown that food prices dropped. Manufactured products were still quite scarce, so their prices remained high. This risked peasants hoarding their grain again.

- To prevent this 'scissors crisis' from worsening, the peasants' quota became a money tax, forcing peasants to sell grain to pay the tax. The price of industrial products was capped.
- Private traders (known as **Nepmen**) helped to get the economy moving, although they were hated by many Bolsheviks as representatives of capitalism.

Political and social impact of the NEP

To many Bolsheviks, the introduction of the NEP was regarded as a retreat back to capitalism, which put the transition to socialism much further away on the agenda. Lenin knew many socialists would be unhappy about the NEP, and to meet this he ordered a crackdown on any kind of opposition within the Party.

- A 'ban on factions' was introduced in 1921. There could be discussions about policy, but once the Central Committee had made a decision, every Party member had to follow it. Disagreeing (forming a faction) would mean expulsion from the Party.
- The Menshevik and Socialist Revolutionary parties were banned in 1921 and thousands of Mensheviks and SRs were arrested.
- The Cheka (renamed the GPU in 1922) was given more power to root out possible counter-revolutionaries. There was also a crackdown on Nepmen to try to suppress any moves from the NEP towards full capitalism.
- Censorship was increased and the Church came under more pressure. Thousands of priests were arrested.
- The **nomenklatura** system was introduced in 1923. Only those who showed complete loyalty to the Party made it on to the nomenklatura lists, which were the approved lists of people to be considered for promotion in the Party and government jobs.

SUMMARY

- The Bolsheviks introduced state capitalism as a 'halfway house' to socialism. This was replaced with war communism, which went much further towards full socialism.
- War communism reduced food supply and industrial production.
- The Red Terror was a new period of intense political repression intended to remove all Bolshevik enemies (or potential enemies). This provoked uprisings against the harsh rule of the Bolshevik regime, including the Tambov revolt and the Kronstadt rising.
- The New Economic Policy was introduced to aid the failing economy. It was accompanied by a crackdown on any kind of opposition within and against the Bolshevik party.

APPLY

SOURCE ANALYSIS

SOURCE A

From an article by Lenin, published in a pamphlet intended for a wide public readership, written in April 1921.

It was the war and the ruin that forced us into war communism. We are still so ruined and crushed by the burden of war that we cannot give the peasants manufactured goods in return for all the grain we need. That is why we shall take the minimum of grain we require (for the army and the workers) in the form of a tax and obtain the rest in exchange for manufactured goods.

Our poverty and ruin are so great that we cannot restore large-scale socialist state industry at one stroke. So it is necessary to help to restore small industry, which can immediately assist peasant farming by manufacturing equipment for them.

What is to be the effect of all this? It is the revival of the petty bourgeoisie and of capitalism. That much is certain and it is ridiculous to shut our eyes to it.

Is it necessary? Can it be justified? Is it not dangerous?

These questions are evidence of simple-mindedness, to put it mildly.

SOURCE B

From the memoirs of N.V. Valentinov, published in 1956. Valentinov had helped plan the NEP but clashed with Lenin over revolutionary theory. This passage refers to a conversation he had in 1921.

At this point I cannot help recalling a conversation with my old friend Steklov, who had become editor of *All-Russia Central Executive Committee News*. 'Lenin,' said Steklov, 'has brought about an astonishingly bold and decisive political change. "Learn to trade!" – I thought I'd sooner cut out my own tongue than come out with such a slogan. In accepting such a directive we've got to cut out whole chapters of Marxism: they can't give us guiding principles any more. And when someone said as much to Lenin, he retorted, "Please don't teach me what to put in or take out of Marxism! Don't teach your grandmother to suck eggs!"'

When I pointed out that I had the impression that not everyone in the Party was enthusiastically following Lenin, Steklov began to explain that, in fact, the situation was far worse, because virtually nobody agreed with Lenin.

 With reference to these sources and your understanding of the historical context, which of these sources is more valuable in explaining the introduction of the NEP?

a Identify the key elements of the provenance of each source:

- Who is the author? How does this affect the value of the source?
- What is the context of the source?
- What is the purpose and audience of the source?

b Work out what the key message is in each source:

- Highlight the key words or phrases that help to convey the view in each source.
- Summarise the attitude in each of the sources towards the introduction of the NEP. Try to do this in one or two sentences for each source.

c Using your answers to **a** and **b** as a starting point, write a complete answer to the essay question above.

EXAMINER TIP

AS-level questions on source analysis require you to come to a conclusion about which source is more valuable, as well as evaluating the provenance and content of each.

EXAMINER TIP

Make sure you concentrate on identifying what overall view is given in the source, rather than explaining what each sentence says.

APPLY YOUR KNOWLEDGE

a   Write a brief definition for each of the key terms in the table below.

b   Then give one way that each term links to the actions of the Bolshevik government in 1917–21. (One row has been filled in for you.)

Term	Definition	Link
Nationalisation	Placing businesses under state control.	A key feature of war communism; businesses were placed under state control to make sure the Red Army had enough provisions.
Private trade		
Requisitioning		
Nomenklatura system		
Nepmen		

REVIEW

To complete this question you should also review Chapter 11, which covers economic developments through to 1928.

HOW SUCCESSFUL?

 A LEVEL How successful was the NEP in solving the USSR's economic and social problems in the years 1921 to 1928?

a   To assess how successful something was, you first need to identify what its aims were, and then assess to what extent these were achieved. Some of the main aims of the NEP were:

- to revive the economy
- to appease workers in the towns
- to appease peasants in the countryside.

For each of these aims, compile any evidence to show that the aim was achieved, and any evidence to show that it was not achieved.

b   Write a paragraph that could serve as an introduction to the exam question. You could include some of the key aims and measures of the NEP that you are going to examine, and explain how you are going to assess their success.

EXAMINER TIP

A good introduction will contain a judgement that directly answers the question. Check that your introduction does this.

PLAN YOUR ESSAY

 AS LEVEL 'War communism created more problems than it solved.' Explain why you agree or disagree with this view.

a   Copy and complete the table below.

Features of war communism	How it solved a problem	How it created a problem
Nationalisation		
Grain requisition		
Labour discipline		
Rationing		

EXAMINER TIP

Organising an essay into different factors can help you to develop your analysis and come to an overall assessment, instead of simply listing problems and solutions.

b   Use your table to write an essay plan in response to the exam question above.

8 Foreign relations and the attitudes of foreign powers

In March 1918, the Treaty of Brest-Litovsk took Russia out of the war, but at a serious cost to the country. Russia's former allies felt betrayed by the peace negotiations with Germany, and during the next few years relations between the new Bolshevik regime and the outside world were complicated and hostile.

Russia was not invited to the Paris Peace Conference, nor involved in the formation of the League of Nations. Britain, France, Japan and the United States intervened in Russia, often becoming involved with anti-Bolshevik forces in the Civil War. But by 1921, Bolshevik Russia had somehow survived in a capitalist world.

Nobody had expected this outcome. The Allies had hoped to see the threat of Bolshevism strangled at birth; the Bolsheviks had believed that it was only possible for communism to develop in Russia if there was world revolution. Neither of these things happened. From 1921, it was necessary to work out new relationships.

KEY CHRONOLOGY

1918	March	Treaty of Brest-Litovsk
		British naval blockade imposed
	August	Allied forces land in north Russia and the Far East
	November	Armistice to end the First World War
1919	March	Russia is excluded from the Paris Peace Conference
		First Comintern Congress in Moscow
	June	US forces start to withdraw
	August	British naval assault on Petrograd
1920	March	Withdrawal of Allied forces from south Russia
	August	Westward advance of the Red Army halted at the Battle of Warsaw
	November	The Bolshevik state is given recognition by Britain
1921	March	Treaty of Riga ends the Russo-Polish War
1922	April	Treaty of Rapallo moves Russia away from diplomatic isolation

Foreign intervention in the Civil War

Features of foreign intervention

The Allies sent troops to help the Whites in the Civil War between 1918 and 1920. Although foreign forces were spread across Russia, the numbers involved were small.

- In the north, British forces attacked at Murmansk, and the British navy also blockaded trade to Russia through the Baltic Sea.
- In the Far East, 11,000 US troops landed at Vladivostok, and Japanese troops invaded eastern Siberia.
- In the south, Baku was occupied by the British (much of Russia's oil came from here), and British and French navies blocked trade through the Black Sea and the Caspian Sea.

Reasons for foreign intervention

- At first, countries like Britain, France and the USA wanted to help the Whites to win so Russia could be kept in the war and stop Germany moving troops from the Eastern Front to the Western Front.
- The Allies had sent huge amounts of ammunition and weapons to Russia during the First World War, which they did not want the Bolsheviks getting control over.
- After the armistice between Germany and the West was agreed in November 1918, the reasons for Allied intervention changed to combatting Bolshevism.
- However, the Western nations had very confused aims. None of the Allies was prepared to fight a major war. There was little coordination between foreign forces and an uncertainty over which anti-Bolshevik leaders to support.
- In Britain there was strong support for Bolshevism in the trade union movement.
- Public opinion was also divided in France, and in America President Woodrow Wilson was very reluctant to intervene.

Impact of foreign intervention

Foreign intervention did not significantly affect the outcome of the Civil War.

- Most foreign intervention was too small-scale to have an impact.
- Major intervention, like the Japanese invasion of eastern Siberia, was in the Far East and did not threaten Bolshevik control of Russia.
- However, foreign support for the Whites at the start of the war did help them to achieve initial advances.

The Bolsheviks were able to claim they had faced down a major attack by foreign powers. The West's response was to continue to isolate Russia (although there were exceptions to this, such as Britain's reopening of trade talks in November 1920).

Comintern

Comintern (the Communist International) was an international communist organisation that aimed to promote Marxism and spread proletarian revolution around the world. Delegates attended congresses from as far afield as the USA, Australia and Japan.

Comintern Congress	Key issues	Outlook of delegates
Founding Congress of the Communist International, Moscow, March 1919	Lenin promoted the soviet system as the best way of spreading Marxism.	Positive. Despite the Civil War and the suppression of the Spartacist uprising in Germany, delegates were convinced world-wide communist revolution was imminent.
Second Comintern Congress, Petrograd, July–August 1920	Lenin's '21 Conditions': the requirements that must be met to become a member of the Comintern.	Mixed. Some parties broke away from the Comintern because of the 21 Conditions. But Bolshevik victory in the Civil War looked certain.
Third Comintern Congress, Moscow, June–July 1921	The recovery of the bourgeoisie in countries like Poland and Germany.	Disappointed. Expected revolutions had turned instead into support for bourgeois democracies. Germany was ruled by the 'bourgeois-democratic' Weimar Republic. Bolshevik Russia was left alone in a capitalist world.

After the Third Comintern Congress, the focus of the Bolshevik leadership shifted away from world revolution to concentrate instead on rebuilding the economy in Russia.

The Russo-Polish War

In the wake of the Bolshevik takeover in Russia, Lenin had fully expected a proletariat revolution to break out in Poland, in accordance with Marxist theory. When that failed to occur, his plans for the future of communism in Russia (supported by revolution elsewhere) were undermined.

- As the map below shows, Bolshevik Russia faced attacks by non-Russian forces (purple arrows) as well as White forces (orange arrows) during the Civil War.
- Poland emerged as an independent country by the end of the First World War in November 1918.
- The new borders of Poland were contested, and both Poland and Russia hoped to gain more territory.
- The first conflicts between Polish and Bolshevik forces occurred in February 1919.
- In May 1920, the Poles allied with the Ukrainians to take Kiev from the Bolsheviks.
- A Red Army counter-attack pushed the Polish army all the way back to Warsaw, where the Poles mounted a successful defence and the war settled into stalemate.
- Peace terms were agreed in October and formalised by the Treaty of Riga in March 1921.

The scope of foreign interventions
The main areas of intervention were:

- North Russia (Archangel'sk, Murmansk and the Baltic States) – British and French forces; the British navy patrolling in the Baltic Sea; Australian, Canadian and Italian forces at Archangel'sk; 11,000 Estonian troops in the War of Independence
- The Far East – 11,000 American troops at Vladivostok; also 2000 Chinese troops, and a small British force; substantial Japanese forces invading eastern Siberia
- Southern Russia, Ukraine, the Black Sea and the Caspian Sea – French and British naval forces; Turkish troops active in Caucasus (Georgia, Armenia, Azerbaijan)
- Central Siberia – sections of the Trans-Siberian Railway controlled by the Czech Legion

Key
- Russian territorial losses after the Treaty of Brest Litovsk, 1918
- Controlled by Bolsheviks, 1919
- Occupied by Allied troops, 1919
- Attacks by White forces
- Attacks by non-Russian anti-Bolshevik forces
- Boundary of Soviet territory, March 1921

The Russian Civil War

The Rapallo Treaty

- Although other countries disapproved of the Bolsheviks, once revolution seemed less likely to spread in Europe there was interest in opening trade deals with Russia. For example, Britain decided to reopen discussions about trade in 1920.
- Both Bolshevik Russia and Weimar Germany had been excluded from the League of Nations after the end of the First World War.
- However, in 1922 the Soviet Union's deputy commissar for foreign affairs, Georgy Chicherin, was invited to an important international economic conference held in Genoa.
- Chicherin and representatives from Weimar Germany then held talks in nearby Rapallo, leading to the Rapallo Treaty in April 1922.

Key articles of the Rapallo Treaty

- Russia and Germany agreed to waive any claims for compensation arising from the First World War (Articles 1 and 2).
- Formal diplomatic relations reopened (Article 3).
- 'Mutual goodwill' was stressed in commercial and economic relations (Articles 4 and 5).

There was also a secret treaty allowing Germany to carry out military training on Russian territory.

International recognition and the repercussions of the Zinoviev letter

Britain had granted diplomatic recognition to Russia in November 1920 and opened the way for trade agreements, but Russia remained isolated.

In 1923, a Labour government was formed in Britain, which aroused strong opposition from much of the British establishment who loathed socialism. The Zinoviev letter, published in October 1924, was a forgery promoted by right-wingers that was designed to reduce votes for the Labour Party in the British general election.

- The letter was supposed to be from the chairman of the Comintern, Zinoviev, to one of the leaders of the Labour Party.
- The letter called for trade deals and also said it was time to organise a revolution in Britain. The idea was that British people would not vote Labour once they heard how the Soviet Union was giving orders to the Labour government.
- The impact of the letter on the election was small, but it did damage relations between Britain and the Soviet Union, contributing in part to Russia's continued diplomatic isolation.

Lenin's rule by 1924

	Positives	Negatives
The October/ November Revolution, 1917	Lenin masterminded a successful seizure of power.	The Bolsheviks' power grab upset many people, including other socialists.
Single-party rule	Enabled Lenin to enforce his will on the Party, providing strong leadership in difficult times.	A rapidly increasing bureaucracy, a 'dictatorship of the Party', and ruthless repression of any possible opposition.
The Treaty of Brest-Litovsk	Bought the Bolsheviks breathing space to consolidate their hold on Russia.	Enormous territorial losses for Russia. Triggered the Civil War. Russia's allies turned hostile.
War communism	Sacrificed everything to make sure the Red Army had what it needed. This helped the Reds win the Civil War.	Created a famine that contributed to the deaths of millions. Caused a collapse in Russia's economy.
The NEP	Helped the economy to stabilise and reduced food shortages.	Many Bolsheviks saw the NEP as a backwards step on the road to socialism.

SUMMARY

- Various foreign powers intervened in the Civil War, first in the hope it would help Russia to return to the First World War, then to try to stop the spread of Bolshevism.
- The Comintern had to adjust to a realisation that the USSR was alone rather than the first in a rapid chain of socialist revolutions.
- After the war ended, countries such as Britain and Germany began trade talks with the USSR, but the USSR remained diplomatically isolated.
- By the time Lenin died in 1924, he left behind a highly centralised one-party state that had managed to revive the economy, but the USSR still faced problems politically, economically, socially and in terms of its international relations.

APPLY

APPLY YOUR KNOWLEDGE

a Complete the following timeline.

October/November 1917: _____

3 March 1918: _____

November 1918: Fighting ends in the First World War

April 1922: _____

b For each event, explain how it affected foreign relations with Russia.

PLAN YOUR ESSAY

 AS LEVEL 'The Bolshevik regime was unsuccessful in its dealings with foreign powers in the years 1918 to 1924'. Explain why you agree or disagree with this view.

a Complete the following table to assess the success of the Bolsheviks' dealings with foreign powers in the years 1918–24.

	Evidence of success	Evidence of limited success
Ending Russia's involvement in the First World War		
Promoting socialist revolutions in other countries		
Gaining international recognition for Bolshevik Russia/ the Soviet Union as a country		

b Use your completed table to write a conclusion to the essay question above.

EXAMINER TIP

If you simply restate the points from your table, the conclusion will just be a summary. Instead you need to give your judgement on the view in the essay question, providing an overall assessment of the success of the Bolsheviks' dealings with foreign powers in 1918–24.

ASSESS THE VALIDITY OF THIS VIEW

> **A LEVEL** 'By 1924, Lenin had succeeded in solving the major problems that had faced the Bolshevik regime in 1917.' Assess the validity of this view.

a Complete the following table to assess Lenin's success in solving the major problems facing the Bolsheviks after the October/November revolution.

REVIEW

Look back at Chapters 4 and 5 for more information on the problems facing the Bolshevik regime after the October/November Revolution.

Problem	Lenin's actions to solve the problem	How successful were Lenin's actions in solving the problem?
Russia's involvement in the First World War		
Political opposition to the Bolshevik seizure of power		
Food shortages in the towns and cities		
Division within the Bolshevik Party		

b Use your table as a starting point to write a complete answer to this question.

KEY CONCEPT

Marxism and communism are key concepts in the study of revolution and dictatorship in Russia 1917–53.

a After the October/November Revolution, Lenin expected a worldwide communist revolution to follow (in accordance with Marxist theory). How did his policies and actions reflect this expectation?

b As this revolution failed to occur, ideology had to be moderated by the compromises necessary for survival. List the ways in which Bolshevik actions or policies demonstrated these compromises between 1918 and 1924.

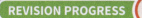

9 The power vacuum and power struggle

 RECAP

When Lenin died in 1924, the Soviet Union faced a leadership crisis. In theory, the Party was controlled by a collective leadership; there was no established process for choosing a single leader.

Lenin's death created a power vacuum that led to a long struggle for leadership of the Party and of the USSR. This struggle was not only about the rivalries between key individuals competing for power; it was also an ideological struggle about the policies that should be implemented in the newly formed Soviet Union.

KEY CHRONOLOGY		
Lenin's last years		
1922	April	Stalin is made General Secretary of the Party
	May	Lenin is incapacitated by a stroke
		The 'Triumvirate' of Stalin, Kamenev and Zinoviev is formed
	December	Lenin suffers a second stroke
		The USSR is formed
1923	March	Lenin is close to death after a third stroke
1924	January	Lenin dies
	May	Lenin's Testament is suppressed at the Party Congress

Ideology and the nature of leadership

Marxist ideology suggested that power should be shared in a collective leadership. However, while ideology pointed in one direction, Lenin's legacy, issues of practicality and individual ambitions pointed in another. In Lenin's state, decisions were supposedly made collectively by voting in the Central Committee, but in practice Lenin had dominated governance.

- Instead of encouraging democracy in the Party, Lenin had introduced the 1921 'ban on factions', which meant it became dangerous to express disagreement with anything proposed by influential Party members.
- Centralised control by the Party had replaced any notion of 'power to the soviets'.
- Leninist government had created a huge state bureaucracy carrying out orders from superiors.

Lenin's Testament

In December 1922, Lenin dictated a 600-word 'Testament', in which he proposed changes to the membership of the Party's Central Committee, to double it from 50 to 100. He also commented on some of its individual members.

- Lenin's Testament criticised almost everyone in the Party leadership, but was especially critical of Stalin. Partly this was because Stalin had been rude to Lenin's wife, Nadezhda Krupskaya, and partly because Stalin had used brute force to suppress Georgian independence, going directly against Lenin's orders.
- Lenin did not endorse anyone as his successor, which could suggest he wanted the Party to return to collective leadership (although the Testament does not say this).

This document was entrusted to Nadezhda Krupskaya, to be read out at the Twelfth Party Congress in April 1923. However, Krupskaya kept it secret in the hope her husband would recover, and did not produce it until after his death in January 1924. She asked for it to be read at the Thirteenth Party Congress in May 1924.

Kamenev, Zinoviev and Stalin had already formed a triumvirate in order to keep Trotsky out of power, and since Lenin's Testament criticised all three they did not want it to be made public, as it would have seriously damaged their leadership chances. Consequently, only a few of the non-damning parts were read to other Party officials.

Divisions and contenders for power

Trotsky initially seemed the most likely person to succeed Lenin. He had played key roles in the Bolshevik seizure of power and the Reds' victory in the Civil War.

→

In 1922–23, a 'Triumvirate' of Stalin, Kamenev and Zinoviev formed to block Trotsky's rise to power. They dominated the Central Committee.

↓

By 1924–25, Stalin was becoming more dominant, so Zinoviev and Kamenev joined Trotsky in the Left Opposition.

←

Bukharin was on the right of the Bolshevik Party, often supported by Rykov and Tomsky. He joined Stalin against the Left Opposition, but Stalin resented Bukharin's popularity.

Stalin

Strengths and weaknesses of Stalin

Character: reasonable (though sometimes rude), patient, jealous, hard-working, violent

Strengths	Weaknesses
His role as General Secretary meant he could appoint supporters to key roles in the Party.	Not very prominent in the October/November Revolution or the Civil War.
His opponents underestimated him because he was very good at concealing his real thoughts and ambitions.	Colleagues saw him as ill-educated, rude and crude. Lenin had criticised his violent methods.
Placed himself close to Lenin in 1922–23, and claimed to know Lenin's wishes.	Seen as boring: 'a grey blur' according to Menshevik Nikolai Sukhanov.
Because he did not seem to be a threat to other contenders, Zinoviev and Kamenev allied with him to isolate Trotsky.	Although Lenin's Testament was blocked, senior Bolsheviks knew Stalin had fallen from Lenin's favour.

Trotsky and the Left

Strengths and weaknesses of Trotsky

Character: energetic, organised, ruthless, arrogant

Strengths	Weaknesses
Recognised as a hero of the October/November Revolution for his leadership of the MRC and his organisation of the seizure of power.	Arrogant and dismissive of people who were not as intellectual as him (e.g. he badly underrated Stalin).
Recognised as a hero of the Civil War for his role in creating and leading the Red Army.	Indecisive and inconsistent, e.g. he allied with Zinoviev and Kamenev after opposing them.
An inspirational speaker and intellectual; the writer of many important books on communist theory.	Many Bolsheviks feared Trotsky, worrying that he would use his Red Army influence to seize power.
Known for his formidable political skills and organisational ability.	He did not seriously try to build a base of followers in the Party, and attacked the Party bureaucracy in 1924 when he needed its help.

Strengths and weaknesses of Zinoviev

Character: intelligent, imposing, vain, inconsistent, compromiser

Strengths	Weaknesses
An 'Old Bolshevik' who Lenin had once called his 'closest and most trusted assistant'.	Opposed Lenin in October 1917, arguing against the timing of the uprising and briefly leaving the Party.
Had a strong power base in Leningrad, where he ran the local Party.	Vain and prone to unpredictable mood swings.
One of the Party's best speechmakers, with a commanding presence.	Underestimated Stalin; he and Kamenev were too late in switching their support from Stalin to Trotsky.

Strengths and weaknesses of Kamenev

Character: thoughtful, loyal, inconsistent, compromiser

Strengths	Weaknesses
An 'Old Bolshevik' who had helped form Party policy and was close to Lenin.	Opposed Lenin in October 1917, arguing against the timing of the uprising and briefly leaving the Party.
Had a strong power base in Moscow, where he ran the local Party.	Viewed as Zinoviev's side-kick; seen as lacking the ambition to be a sole leader.
An effective team player, good at reaching compromises between different people.	Underestimated his opponents, especially Stalin.

Bukharin and the Right

Strengths and weaknesses of Bukharin

Character: brilliant, very popular, eager to please, naive

Strengths	Weaknesses
Popular in the Party; close to Lenin and Trotsky; a close associate of Stalin.	Because he was so cooperative and wanted to avoid Party in-fighting, he had no power base.
Widely regarded as the best theoretician in the Party.	His popularity in the Party made him a target for Stalin's enmity.
An expert on economics and agriculture (key issues for the Bolshevik government).	Underestimated Stalin; left it too late to make an alliance with Zinoviev and Kamenev.

Strengths and weaknesses of Rykov

Character: loyal, moderate, wanted to find common ground

Strengths	Weaknesses
Widely respected in the Party as an 'Old Bolshevik'.	His policy of heavy taxation on vodka was very unpopular.
A good administrator; he had helped implement war communism and the NEP.	Opposed Lenin over the timing of the revolution.
Supported by Sovnarkom; he was chosen as Deputy Chairman in 1923 and Chairman in 1924.	Lacked a power base; too much of a conciliatory moderate, and overshadowed by Bukharin.

Strengths and weaknesses of Tomsky

Character: plain speaker, moderate political views

Strengths	Weaknesses
Widely respected in the Party as an 'Old Bolshevik', with working-class origins.	Hated Trotsky so much that he could not see the threat from Stalin.
Strong base of support from being General Secretary of the Red International of the Trade Unions.	His power base in the trade unions made him a target for Stalin's resentment.
Natural ally of moderates such as Rykov and Bukharin.	His support for the NEP was used against him by Stalin when the grain crisis of 1927 hit.

SUMMARY

- Lenin died in January 1924 without indicating who should follow him as leader.
- Although Marxist ideology suggested that the USSR would need collective leadership, individual contenders jostled for power.
- The USSR was initially ruled by the 'Triumvirate' of Stalin, Kamenev and Zinoviev, until Kamenev and Zinoviev broke away to join Trotsky when they realised how powerful Stalin had become.

⚙ APPLY

APPLY YOUR KNOWLEDGE

The table below contains details about Stalin's character and position in the Party. Complete the table by deciding whether each characteristic is a strength or a weakness in relation to Stalin's bid for power. Explain your answer in each case.

Characteristic	Strength or weakness?
Stalin had a bad temper and was prepared to use violent methods.	
Stalin became General Secretary of the Party in April 1922.	
Stalin was able to conceal his long-term aims and ambitions.	
Stalin was not seen as one of the Party's intellectuals.	

ASSESS THE VALIDITY OF THIS VIEW

 'The main reason why Trotsky did not become leader after Lenin's death was because of his own failings.' Assess the validity of this view.

a Complete the following table. Provide evidence to support each side.

Evidence that Trotsky himself was responsible for failing to become leader	Evidence that other factors prevented Trotsky from becoming leader

b Which of the factors do you consider to be the main reason for Trotsky not becoming leader?

c Write a concluding paragraph which provides a substantiated judgement about whether or not you believe the given view in the exam question is a valid one.

REVISION SKILLS

Create revision flashcards on each of the six contenders for power after Lenin's death (Stalin, Trotsky, Bukharin, Kamenev, Rykov, Tomsky and Zinoviev).

On one side of the flashcard, write the contender's name and add a photo of them if possible.

On the other side, add the following information:

- character
- strengths
- weaknesses.

Test yourself by trying to remember the information for each contender before turning over the flashcard to check.

EXAMINER TIP

Contextual knowledge is important to making successful evaluations, so it is important to build up information about key individuals from which you can select precise details to use as evidence in your answers.

10 Ideological debates and issues in the leadership struggle

In the initial years of its regime, the Bolshevik state only just survived the threats to its existence. In the process there were many compromises between Marxist ideals and political realities.

Many issues remained undecided even after survival had been secured, such as the direction of economic policy, relations with the outside world, and the question of who would succeed Lenin. These issues led to lengthy and complex internal debates and power struggles. It was not until 1929 that these struggles culminated in the emergence of Stalin and Stalinism.

The economy was perhaps the most important issue. In 1921, Lenin had introduced the New Economic Policy so that the reintroduction of private trade could rescue agricultural production and allow smaller-scale manufacturing to recover. However, the NEP was ideologically very difficult for those on the left of the Bolshevik Party to accept; it reintroduced elements of bourgeois capitalism instead of making sure the proletariat was in full control of the state.

Was the NEP merely a temporary compromise in the crisis of 1921? Or did it represent a long-term economic policy?

The NEP and industrialisation

Marxism taught that only an industrialised economy could create the plenty that awaited all of society in a socialist future. However, not all Bolsheviks agreed on how this industrialisation should happen, and how quickly.

The Left	Stalin	The Right
The Left, led by Trotsky, Zinoviev and Kamenev, wanted to abandon the NEP in favour of state-controlled, rapid industrialisation funded by 'squeezing' the peasants.	Stalin's attitude was inconsistent. During his struggle against Trotsky he opposed the Left and supported the NEP. Once Trotsky was no longer a threat, in 1928–29, he shifted to a policy of replacing the NEP with rapid industrialisation and the collectivisation of agriculture.	The Right, led by Bukharin, Rykov and Tomsky, believed the NEP should continue, with the peasants becoming richer and the state using taxes on the peasants to fund gradual industrialisation.

'Permanent revolution' or 'Socialism in One Country'

- All theories of Marxism-Leninism had assumed it was impossible for revolution to survive in a single country, because the capitalist countries would gang together and strangle the revolution at birth.
- Thus it was not just desirable but essential for the Bolshevik revolution in Russia to trigger a chain reaction of other revolutions.
- But Marxist theory was contradicted by real-world events. Revolutions in Germany and Hungary were crushed, and defeat in the Russo-Polish War in 1920 blocked the revolution from extending to the West. In the 1920s, the USSR existed as the only communist state in the world.

Permanent revolution

- Trotsky and the Left argued for '**permanent revolution**'.
- They believed the USSR could not survive on its own without support from other socialist countries, so revolution must be constantly encouraged in Europe to make sure this support was fostered.
- Lenin had made this argument many times, and Stalin had written about it too.

Socialism in One Country

- In 1924, Stalin developed his counter-theory of '**Socialism in One Country**': the USSR *could* build socialism on its own without needing the support of other socialist states.
- Stalin referenced an old article by Lenin that said one country could show the rest of the world the benefits of socialism, and workers would then rush to support that country and rise up in revolutions in their own countries.
- Stalin used his argument to criticise Trotsky for a) contradicting Lenin and b) dismissing the USSR's potential.

How and why Stalin became Party leader

Stalin's rise to power occurred over a long period, and in the context of a Party ideologically committed to collective leadership and to avoiding splits and factions. Stalin occupied a moderate, central position in the power struggle until his position was secure.

Date	Key event	What happened?
January 1924	Lenin's funeral	Stalin used his powers as General Secretary to make the most of Trotsky's absence (who was recovering from the flu). He took charge of arranging Lenin's funeral and styled himself as Lenin's disciple.
May 1924	Lenin's Testament is blocked from being read at the Thirteenth Party Congress	Stalin, Zinoviev and Kamenev were criticised by Lenin in his Testament and so blocked the reading of it. Trotsky chose not to insist on the reading going ahead (possibly to avoid splitting the Party, though Trotsky was also criticised in the Testament).
	Trotsky's criticisms of the Party bureaucracy are rejected at the Party Congress	As General Secretary, Stalin's control over the appointments to the Central Committee meant the Congress was filled with his supporters. Trotsky was voted down.
October 1924	Trotsky criticises Kamenev and Zinoviev for not backing Lenin in 1917	Stalin stayed out of the fight on the Left. The criticism weakened his rivals while he appeared moderate. He brought in more supporters to the Central Committee.
December 1925	At the Fourteenth Party Congress, Kamenev and Zinoviev criticise Stalin for his move to the Right and support for the NEP	Stalin's support meant that every vote at the Congress went against Kamenev and Zinoviev. Stalin's 'Socialism in One Country' theory became very popular. Stalin and Bukharin formed an alliance on the right, known as the 'Duumvirate'. They largely ran the country in 1926–27.
1926	Kamenev, Zinoviev and Trotsky form the United Opposition	When the United Opposition tried to organise demonstrations against Stalin, he was able to accuse them of factionalism (banned by Lenin in 1921).
November 1927	Kamenev, Zinoviev and Trotsky are expelled from the Party	At the Fifteenth Party Congress, Stalin's supporters confirmed the expulsion of Kamenev, Zinoviev and Trotsky, along with a hundred more 'oppositionists'.
Early 1928	The regime faces a grain procurement crisis; food shortages had begun in late 1927 and it was hard for the regime to get enough grain from the peasants	As criticism of the NEP began to increase in the Party, Stalin split from Bukharin and used harsh requisition methods for getting grain from peasants in western Siberia.
April 1928	Bukharin criticises the 'excesses' of officials following Stalin's methods	Bukharin expected some support for his criticism, but he received none. He was now isolated and vulnerable to Stalin's attacks.
November 1929	Bukharin, Rykov and Tomsky are expelled from the Politburo	Stalin's supporters were bolstered by opponents of the NEP from the Left of the Party. They agreed to remove Bukharin from the Politburo (he had made a strong defence of the NEP at the Fifteenth Party Congress in 1927).

The outcome for the other contenders

- After they were expelled from the Party in 1927 for factionalism, Kamenev and Zinoviev criticised their past actions and were allowed to re-join the Party in 1928. However, they lost their high positions and places in the Politburo.
- Trotsky refused to do this and was exiled, first to Kazakhstan, and then deported in 1929. He lived in many countries until, in 1940, he was murdered in Mexico on Stalin's orders.
- Bukharin, Rykov and Tomsky were initially allowed to stay in the Party after admitting their 'mistakes'.
- Bukharin, Kamenev, Zinoviev and Rykov were all executed after show trials were held against them in the late 1930s (see pages 88 and 92).
- Tomsky committed suicide before he could be put through the same ordeal.

SUMMARY

- By December 1929, Stalin's dictatorship was at last fully established after he had outmanoeuvred and marginalised all his rivals.
- Ideologically, Stalin's key themes were now dominant: 'Socialism in One Country', centralised control, Stalin's own role as Lenin's true successor, and the need to rush through the economic transformation of the Soviet Union.
- Internal dissent within the Party (and anywhere else) was largely obliterated. The era of Stalin the despot was underway.

APPLY

SOURCE ANALYSIS

SOURCE A

From a speech by Kamenev to the Fourteenth Party Congress, December 1925.

Our General Secretary is not the kind of figure that can unite the old Bolshevik staff around himself. I have arrived at the conviction that Comrade Stalin cannot fulfil the role of unifier of the Bolshevik staff. *(Voices from the audience)* 'Untrue!' 'Nonsense!' *(Voice from a seat)* 'Long live Comrade Stalin!' *(Stormy, continued applause)*

(Chairman) 'Comrades, I beg you to quiet down. Comrade Kamenev will now finish his speech.'

I began this part of my speech with the words, 'We are against the theory of one individual being more important than others, we are against creating a Chief!' With these same words I end my speech. *(Applause by the Leningrad delegation)*

(Voice from a seat) And who do you propose?

a What is the context of this source?

b Explain what you think the purpose of this source was.

c Write a paragraph explaining the value of this source in understanding the opposition to Stalin during 1924–29.

EXAMINER TIP

Whenever you are asked to think about the value of a source, you should try to remember what was happening at the time it was produced. Showing your knowledge of context is always a requirement in the source analysis question.

ASSESS THE VALIDITY OF THIS VIEW

 'Stalin's victory in the leadership struggle was because of his opposition to the NEP.' Assess the validity of this view.

a Create a timeline of the events contributing to Stalin's victory in the leadership struggle.

- Highlight events that relate to his opposition to the NEP.
- Use a different colour to highlight events related to his support for the NEP.
- Use a third colour to highlight events not related in any way to the NEP.

b Which of these events do you think were most significant in contributing to Stalin's victory? Explain why.

c Use your answers to **a** and **b** to write a complete answer to the essay question.

EXAMINER TIP

Breaking down a process into individual events will help you to stay focused on the question's requirements.

KEY CONCEPT

Communism, Leninism and Stalinism are all key concepts in the study of revolution and dictatorship in Russia 1917–53.

a Write a sentence for each of the following to show what you understand by:

- Communist beliefs about how the economy of a state should operate.
- The Leninist approach to the working of the economy.
- Stalin's approach to the working of the economy.

b Make a chart to show the similarities and differences between these three approaches. Can you explain why there are differences?

APPLY YOUR KNOWLEDGE

EXAMINER TIP

This activity will help you to identify evidence that you can use to substantiate arguments about Stalin's rise to power.

Find evidence from this chapter and chapter 9 to support each of the following statements. Use this to complete the table below.

Statement	Evidence
In 1924, much evidence suggested that Trotsky would succeed Lenin as Party leader	
One of the reasons for Stalin's success in the power struggle was the position he held and the influence he wielded in the Party	
Stalin used his theory of 'Socialism in One Country' to damage Trotsky	
Stalin used debates over industrialisation and the NEP to damage his rivals	
Lenin's ban on factionalism in 1921 was significant in Stalin's rise to power	

11 Economic developments

Lenin had introduced the 'compromise of 1921' – the NEP – because the state did not have the resources to rescue the economy from collapse on its own. Although the state kept control of the 'commanding heights' (large-scale industry), private trade was permitted in agriculture and smaller industries.

While many in the Party were uncomfortable with the ideological implications of the NEP, it helped to create a certain amount of economic stability after the Civil War.

However, by the late 1920s, increasing economic and political pressures were demanding the replacement of the NEP and a radical shift in economic policy. This 'Great Turn' was forced through by Stalin, who had defeated Trotsky and the Left by 1927, and then defeated Bukharin and the Right in 1928–29. The NEP was ended and Stalin emerged from the power struggle as a dominant leader ready to impose Stalinism.

KEY CHRONOLOGY

The Great Turn

1927	October	Start of the grain procurement crisis
	November	Trotsky, Kamenev and Zinoviev expelled from the Party
	December	End of the NEP announced at the Fifteenth Party Congress
1928	January	Stalin demands 'extraordinary measures' to deal with the grain crisis
	October	Launch of the first Five Year Plan
1929	April	Five Year Plan confirmed by the Central Committee
	November	Bukharin expelled from the Politburo
	December	Stalin's declaration of 'war against the kulaks'

The 'Great Turn'

What was the 'Great Turn'?

- The 'Great Turn' was a radical change in economic policy. The Party rejected the NEP and committed to rapid industrialisation under state control, along with the collectivisation of agriculture.
- The 'turn' began in 1925 when the Fourteenth Party Congress committed to industrialisation; the Fifteenth Party Congress in 1927 announced the end of the NEP.
- The 'Great Turn' marked the start of Stalinism.

Reasons for the 'Great Turn'

Reason	Further detail
The slow pace of industrialisation under the NEP	By 1927, the NEP was failing to produce the growth that many leading communists had expected. They were anxious to increase the USSR's military strength and develop its self-sufficiency. Serious weaknesses in industrial management also needed to be addressed. More efficiency was needed to increase production, and to improve the quality (and lower the price) of industrial goods.
The grain procurement crisis in 1927–28	In the winter of 1927–28, the amount of grain purchased by the government was 25 per cent down on the previous year's total. Local Party officials blamed the peasants for hoarding their grain in the hope of higher prices.
Ideological concerns about the NEP	Many in the Party were impatient to revert to 'true' communist ideology to manage the economy. For this it was essential to develop industry, and to not have a state dependent on procuring grain by purchasing it from peasant producers. The state had lost control over the countryside and this control had to be regained in a 'war on grain' so the USSR could get back on the right ideological path.
Stalin's changing attitude	Having previously supported the NEP, Stalin was ready to be more radical. This may have been because economic circumstances pushed him to look for new solutions, or because he now felt secure enough in power to push through the policies he had always wanted. With the end of the NEP, Stalin emerged from the power struggle as a dominant leader ready to enforce his leadership and impose Stalinism.

The launch of the first Five Year Plan

Stalin launched the first **Five Year Plan** in 1928. With this he wanted to:

- catch up with the industrial strength of capitalist countries – Stalin said the USSR was between 50 and 100 years behind
- ready the USSR for a war with capitalist countries – Stalin reminded his people that Russia had often suffered defeats and exploitation because it was backwards and weak

- achieve 'Socialism in One Country' – the USSR's achievements would show workers around the world what a socialist state could achieve
- assert his own authority and dominance over the Party.

The Five Year Plan was not intended to improve living standards for workers and Stalin knew it would cause problems for peasants as investment was pulled out of the countryside.

Key features of the first Five Year Plan

Central planning

- Gosplan (the state planning committee) would set targets for different industrial sectors.
- A **command economy** would bring a top-down, centralised approach to managing the economy.

Rapid industrial growth

- Overall industrial production was planned to increase by 300 per cent between 1928 and 1932.
- Heavy industry (coal, iron, steel, oil and machinery) was prioritised.
- Light industry (such as household products and chemicals) was given a lower priority, but still expected to increase production by 100 per cent.

Investment in infrastructure

- The plan called for a huge increase in the supply of electrical power in order to transform the economy and society.
- There was significant investment in infrastructure, especially the railway network.

New industrial centres

- Thousands of new industrial centres were planned, some on a massive scale.
- E.g. the 'steel city' of Magnitogorsk was built from virtually nothing to a settlement of 175,000 people by 1932, with a huge steel production facility at its centre.

Propaganda and discipline

- Propaganda campaigns were the driving force for achieving the first Five Year Plan.
- Boards were erected outside every factory showing worker output levels and Plan targets. The threat of harsh punishments motivated managers and workers to find ways to hit these targets.

Ideology

- The ideology behind the ambitious targets of the Plan was that socialism could achieve what would seem impossible to bourgeois capitalists.
- Stalin said in 1931, 'there are no fortresses the Bolsheviks cannot capture'.

The use of foreign experts

- Industrial experts were brought in to build the new complexes and to train Soviet workers.
- E.g. Magnitogorsk was planned by an American company (Arthur McKee & Co), which also trained Soviet engineers in how to build it.

Reactions to the first Five Year Plan

Stalin's rush to transform Russia through industrialisation and collectivisation aroused much enthusiasm and high expectations in many sections of society.

- Many Party members were pleased to see a commitment to radical social change and an end to the compromises of the NEP.
- Propaganda had a considerable impact. Urban workers hoped for better employment prospects and higher living standards.
- Many poor and 'middle' peasants were led to hope they would benefit from further land reform and the introduction of more modern methods.

However, there were also serious concerns:

- Stalin authorised higher wages for skilled workers (including the industrial experts). Some worried that this was creating different classes within the proletariat.
- The harsh imposition of collectivisation, and the switch in investment from agriculture to industry, was a worry to many in the Party who feared it would result in less food being produced.
- Many of those managing industrial production were already critical of the adverse impact of central planning. They regarded a huge new emphasis on central planning as a high-risk gamble.

The grain procurement crisis

An important trigger for the decision to push through a massive acceleration of collectivisation was the grain procurement crisis of 1927–28.

- Poor harvests had reduced the supply of grain, but the state had still set a low grain price. There was a shortage of manufactured goods, meaning there was little for peasants to buy. There were few incentives for peasants to sell their grain.
- In 1928 in the Urals and western Siberia, the harvest had generally been good but grain procurement was down a third on the previous year. This convinced Stalin that kulaks were responsible for hoarding grain.
- Stalin closed the free markets and pressured local officials and police to seize the grain by force. He believed his brutal 'Urals-Siberian method' was successful and should be extended throughout Russia.

Features of the decision to collectivise

- There were already some collective farms in the USSR (they had been introduced with the 1917 Decree on Land), but they were not popular with peasants. At the start of 1929, only 5 per cent of farms in the USSR had voluntarily collectivised.
- There were different models for collective farms, but the Central Committee decided on using *sovkhozy* (state farms) and *kolkhozy* (collective farms). The difference was that a *sovkhoz* (state farm) was directly owned and run by the state, while a *kolkhoz* (collective farm) was in principle a voluntary cooperative of farmers pooling their resources and labour.
- The target for collectivisation of the first Five Year Plan was 15 per cent of the USSR's farms. This was expected to lead to a 50 per cent increase in agricultural production.
- Although collectivisation was officially voluntary, the Central Committee sent 25,000 industrial workers into the countryside to promote it. These idealists forced peasants to collectivise and they also worked to remove kulaks.

Reasons for accelerating collectivisation

In November 1929, the Party's Central Committee decided to accelerate collectivisation. There were several reasons for this.

The problem	The solution
The Revolution had broken up the old landlord estates and agriculture was now small-scale peasant farming, using traditional methods. This type of agriculture could never produce enough food for a workforce that needed to build socialism on its own.	Collective farms would combine hundreds of peasant families and their land together. Tractors would enable the land to be worked efficiently and production could be on a large scale. New methods could be introduced by farming specialists to increase production.
Private trading under the NEP had made some peasants richer. Many believed these richer peasants (kulaks) hoarded grain in order to drive up prices.	Collectivisation would be accompanied by dekulakisation. The kulaks were to be eliminated as class enemies.
The grain procurement crisis of 1927–28 had shown that private peasant farming was not reliable enough to provide the grain needed to rapidly industrialise the USSR and carry out the first Five Year Plan.	Collective farms would be set production targets and paid a fixed (low) price for their produce. Private trade in most farm products would be banned. This would ensure the state could plan production reliably and increase grain supplies without having to pay higher prices to farmers.
Private farming was not socialist. It created petty-bourgeois attitudes that were selfish and capitalistic.	Collective farms would bring peasants together, who would work cooperatively for the good of everyone in the USSR.

Collectivisation and Bukharin

- Bukharin was an opponent of the Urals-Siberian method and of accelerated collectivisation. He criticised the use of harsh methods to increase grain supplies because it risked peasants stopping the supply of food. During war communism this had led to food shortages, rationing and protests.
- However, during 1929 the drive for accelerated collectivisation became more popular in the Party. Local Party officials were very enthusiastic and their enthusiasm fed back up the Party hierarchy.
- As a result, Bukharin's political position was weakened. In April 1928, he was outvoted on agricultural policy in the Politburo.
- In November 1928, Stalin attacked Bukharin directly, accusing him of a 'Right deviation' from Marxism-Leninism. In November 1929, Bukharin was removed from the Politburo.

SUMMARY

- The 'Great Turn' of 1927–29 meant the abandonment of the NEP in favour of forced collectivisation and rapid industrialisation.
- The first Five Year Plan, launched in 1928, was an ambitious attempt to increase production and industrialise the USSR through central planning.
- The 'Great Turn' had significant political as well as economic consequences. It enabled Stalin to remove Bukharin as a rival with accusations of 'Right deviationism'.

APPLY

ASSESS THE VALIDITY OF THIS VIEW

EXAMINER TIP

The question is about Stalin's 'Great Turn' rather than the Party's turn away from the NEP. This puts the stress on Stalin's motivations in championing the 'Great Turn'.

A LEVEL 'The 'Great Turn' was motivated by Stalin's desire to reinforce his leadership.' Assess the validity of this view.

a Copy and add to the following spider diagram to give the reasons for the 'Great Turn'.

| The grain procurement crisis of 1927–28 | **Reasons for the Great Turn** | The slow pace of industrialisation under the NEP |

b Write a paragraph assessing the ways in which the 'Great Turn' was linked to the power struggle after Lenin's death.

c Use your answers to **a** and **b** to write a complete answer to the essay question.

REVIEW

It will be useful to recap the ideological debates and issues in the leadership struggle (see Chapter 10) to assess the significance of the leadership struggle in the 'Great Turn'.

APPLY YOUR KNOWLEDGE

The following table gives some of the percentage increases called for by the first Five Year Plan.

Type of output	Electricity	Coal	Oil	Iron	Steel	Machinery
Percentage increase required	335	111	88	203	160	157

a What can historians learn from these figures about the aims of the first Five Year Plan?

b Give five ways in which the targets of the first Five Year Plan were intended to be achieved.

PLAN YOUR ESSAY

EXAMINER TIP

Organising your essay into different factors or reasons will help you to develop your analysis and come to an overall assessment. An essay plan is always a good idea as it allows you to organise your thoughts and information before you commit to writing your answer.

AS LEVEL 'Stalin launched a policy of forced collectivisation in order to eliminate the kulaks.' Explain why you agree or disagree with this view.

a Create a table with the following headings. Provide evidence to support each side.

Evidence that Stalin's main motivation was the elimination of the kulaks	Alternative motives for accelerating collectivisation

b Use this table to help write a plan to answer the essay question.

APPLY YOUR KNOWLEDGE

a Complete this timeline that charts the start of forced collectivisation and Bukharin's downfall:

1927	October	start of the grain procurement crisis
1928	January	_____
	April	_____
	November	_____
1929	Start of the year	only 5 per cent of farms in the USSR have voluntarily collectivised
	April	the first Five Year Plan is launched at a Party conference
	November	the Central Committee decides to accelerate collectivisation
		_____
	December	Stalin gives his 'war against the kulaks' speech

b What does this timeline tell us about Stalin and his commitment to collectivisation?

12 Government, propaganda and foreign relations

RECAP

In the years after Lenin's death, Stalin gradually extended his control over the machinery of the Party and the state until he reached a pinnacle of dictatorial power in 1929. This was achieved by outmanoeuvring political rivals, and by using his central position as General Secretary to manipulate decision-making and to place allies and supporters in key positions.

Stalin's rise to power was unobtrusive. He was underrated by his rivals until it was too late for them to stop him. But Stalin was already building the foundations for the cult of personality that would dominate the USSR from the 1930s. He did this by maximising the cult of Lenin, and by placing himself in the role of Lenin's only, indispensable, true successor.

Stalin's style of government

Bureaucratic centralism

- Under Stalin, the central control of the economy was matched by central control of the government.
- The Party leadership controlled the appointment of key bureaucratic positions down to a local level.

Divide and rule

- Stalin brought people into favour, but if they grew too powerful he encouraged their rivals to bring them down.
- Yezhov's rise and fall (see page 91) is a good example of Stalin's divide-and-rule approach.

Features of Stalin's style of government

Continuing Lenin's legacy

- By positioning himself as Lenin's heir and the chief interpreter of Lenin's wishes, Stalin responded to any challenge by showing how Lenin's words supported him.

Fear

- The role of the secret police (renamed OGPU in 1926) became more pervasive under Stalin than under Lenin.
- Fear permeated the imposition of Stalin's policies. E.g. collectivisation was forced through by the extensive use of the secret police.

Loyal supporters

- Stalin's ability as General Secretary to influence the appointment of Party officials was key to his control over the government.
- The Politburo, filled with Stalin's loyal supporters, made decisions that the Central Committee approved without question.

Propaganda and the beginning of the Stalinist cult

- Stalin relied heavily on propaganda (such as images and slogans) to launch campaigns and boost enthusiasm for his grand schemes for building socialism in one country. For example, the launch of the first Five Year Plan in 1928, and the acceleration of collectivisation in 1929, were both accompanied by images of happy, productive workers.
- Stalin's image was developed as the 'Great Helmsman', skilfully steering the country through all of the dangers surrounding it. For example, one Soviet slogan was 'Forward to socialism under the leadership of Great Stalin!'
- Stalin used propaganda to position himself as Lenin's heir, with slogans such as 'Stalin is the Lenin of today'.
- Stalin boosted the cult of Lenin to add to his own status. For example, Lenin's corpse was embalmed and displayed on Stalin's orders (against the wishes of Lenin's wife) to act as a shrine to the great leader. Lenin was being treated like a god, which gave Stalin, as Lenin's disciple and heir, godlike characteristics.

He who does not work, does not eat!
Forward to socialism under the leadership
Thank you beloved Stalin for our happy childhood
Kulak – a bitter enemy of a hardworking farmer
Away with private peasants!
of Great Stalin!
Stalin is the Lenin of today
Away with private peasants!
Thank Stalin is the Lenin of today
Stalin is the Lenin of today
Forward to socialism under the leadership
you beloved
He who does not work, does not eat!
Stalin for our happy childhood
of Great Stalin!
Away with private peasants!

Stalin's attitude to foreign powers

- Stalin's main aim in foreign affairs was to keep the USSR safe while concentrating on the domestic priority of building socialism in one country.
- However, it was not possible for the USSR to become completely isolated. Pressing concerns included instability in China (the USSR's neighbour), and opportunities in Germany that Georgy Chicherin (the Commissar for Foreign Affairs from 1918 to 1930) was eager to pursue.
- The USSR's main representatives internationally were Chicherin and his deputy, Litvinov. Both presented a moderate diplomatic image that helped reassure foreign powers about doing business with the USSR. Stalin saw them as important in keeping relationships with capitalist foreign powers 'safe', especially Germany.
- While the Comintern had been a low priority for Stalin during the leadership struggle, in 1929 he used it to launch an attack on social democratic parties in Europe, which he believed were diluting the appeal of communism to the working classes.

China

Stalin's policy towards China was strongly linked to the leadership struggle in the USSR.

- The Chinese Revolution in October 1911 saw the overthrow of the emperor.
- Instability in China intensified after the death of President Sun Yat-sen in 1925.
- Rival groups battled for power, including the Chinese Communist Party (CCP) and the nationalist Guomindang (GMD).

- Trotsky supported the CCP, which wanted to lead a proletarian revolution in China.
- He believed another communist state would be a big step forward for permanent revolution.

- Stalin did not think the CCP was strong enough to take control.
- He worried that an unstable China could threaten the USSR's borders.
- The CCP also had unorthodox ideas about peasant revolutionaries.
- He backed a bourgeois revolution led by the GMD, who had good financial backing.

- Stalin urged the CCP to join with the GMD in its bourgeois revolution, after which the CCP could start building up to a proletarian revolution.

- This alliance failed to happen. Instead, using funding and military assistance from the USSR, the GMD built up its army, violently suppressed worker revolts and massacred CCP members.

- While the Party Congress of 1927 criticised Stalin for his actions over China, Trotsky's accusations of Stalin betraying communism in China did not stick.

Stalin's policy towards China shows how far his attitude towards foreign policy was rooted in his determination to eliminate his rivals, and his overriding concern for the security of the USSR. To him this was more important than spreading revolution to other countries.

Germany and the Treaty of Berlin

- After the Rapallo Treaty was signed in 1922 (see page 46), the USSR continued to build good relations with Weimar Germany. The German and Soviet foreign ministers – Gustav Stresemann and Georgy Chicherin – were committed to fostering cooperation.
- In 1926, the Treaty of Berlin was signed. This was aimed at building 'trustful cooperation between the German people and the peoples of the USSR'.

- For example, article 2 stated if one of the two countries was attacked by a third country, the other would remain neutral in the conflict. Article 3 stated that neither country would join in any economic boycott organised against either of them.
- The USSR benefitted economically from the Treaty, receiving large financial credits from German banks in June 1926.
- Stresemann died in 1929. This, along with the development of the world economic crisis, Stalin's more aggressive approach to foreign policy, and Hitler's rise to power, strained relations between the USSR and Germany in the 1930s.

Changes in the Comintern

Before 1929	The Comintern was a low priority for Stalin as he focused on gaining control of the Party. His commitment was to developing socialism in one country; the Comintern was strongly associated with Trotsky and his opposing theory of permanent revolution.
After 1929	Stalin identified a new phase for the Comintern: an all-out attack on anti-communist, social democratic parties in Europe ('**social fascism**'). The Comintern would ready itself for this renewed fight by: • ensuring all foreign communist parties purged themselves of 'weak' elements • imposing strict Party discipline on foreign communist parties • making sure all communist parties followed the line on policy handed down to them by the USSR. Soviet control over the Comintern became tighter as Stalin appointed 'Yes men' to lead it.

Reasons for Stalin's more aggressive approach after 1929 are unclear. It could have been:

- a way to attack Bukharin, who was opposed to the new focus
- a result of Stalin's confidence in having removed Trotsky
- a 'Stalin revolution' in foreign policy
- connected to Stalin's fear of challenges from power bases in other countries.

SUMMARY

- By the end of 1929, Stalin's control over the political system of the USSR was virtually absolute.
- As the personification of ideology, policy and authority, Stalin could put his stamp on the methods of dictatorial government and present himself through the cult of Stalin as Lenin's true disciple and heir.
- In relations with the outside world, Stalin had followed a 'safe' foreign policy, playing down the importance of 'world revolution' in the 1920s in favour of securing internal stability through 'Socialism in One Country'.

⚙ APPLY

SOURCE ANALYSIS

SOURCE A

From a lecture about Stalin's attitude to foreign communist parties by George Kennan, a former US diplomat who had lived in the USSR. The lecture was given at Oxford University in the 1950s.

Stalin was hostile to really spontaneous and successful revolutions by any of the foreign communist parties. He recognised clearly that so long as these parties remained struggling opposition groups they would have a dependence on Soviet support – a dependence he could exploit in order to keep them under his control. If on the other hand they were actually to come into power, this dependence would be lost. From this came Stalin's insistence on rigid disciplinary control of the foreign communist parties, even at the expense of their prospects for coming into power. So long as he could control in this way at least a portion of the foreign communist and socialist movements, he could be sure of preventing the growth of their defiance and unity; and above all of preventing any alliance between them and his rivals at home. This remained until his dying day the greatest of Stalin's fears.

Read Source A carefully. Then complete the following table.

What does the attribution tell us about the author of the source, and how might this affect what he says?	
What is the purpose of the source and how might this affect its value?	
What view is put forward in the source about Stalin's foreign policy?	
In what ways could you support or challenge the view of the source from your own knowledge?	
What are the strengths of the source to an historian studying the change in Stalin's foreign policy in 1929?	
What are the limitations of the source to an historian studying the change in Stalin's foreign policy in 1929?	

EXAMINER TIP 🎯

When assessing the strengths and limitations of a source, remember to take into account both its provenance and its content.

TO WHAT EXTENT?

A LEVEL 'To what extent did Stalin's rise to power rely on forceful methods in the years 1924 to 1929?'

a Complete the table below.

	Examples of the use of forceful methods	Examples of other methods
The power struggle		
The implementation of forced collectivisation		
The implementation of the first Five Year Plan		

b Which method do you think was the most important to Stalin's rise to power? Briefly explain your answer.

c Use your answers to **a** and **b** to write a complete answer to the essay question.

REVIEW

Go back to Chapters 9–10 to review the power struggle, and Chapter 11 to review the implementation of forced collectivisation and the first Five Year Plan.

PLAN YOUR ESSAY

AS LEVEL 'Stalin was always cautious in his foreign policy in the 1920s.' Explain whether you agree or disagree with this view.

a Copy and complete the following table. Provide evidence to support each side.

Evidence that Stalin was cautious in his foreign policy	Evidence that Stalin was bold in his foreign policy

b Use this table to help write a plan to answer the essay question.

EXAMINER TIP

This requires a consideration of what a 'cautious' approach to foreign policy might look like. For example, it might involve trying to strengthen the USSR's security without provoking other countries, rather than pursuing a worldwide communist revolution.

AS Level sources sample answer

REVISION PROGRESS

REVIEW

On these Exam Practice pages, you will find a sample student answer for an AS Level sources question. What are the strengths and weaknesses of the answer? Read the answer and the corresponding Examiner Tips carefully. Think about how you could apply this advice in order to improve your own answers to questions like this one.

> **AS LEVEL** **With reference to these sources and your understanding of the historical context, which of these sources is more valuable in explaining the 'Great Turn' against the NEP in 1927–28?**
>
> 25 marks

REVISION SKILLS

The AS Level exam paper will have one source question that is compulsory; the question will be focused on two primary sources, or sources contemporary to the period. Read page 6 of this revision guide for help on how to master the sources question.

SOURCE A

From the memoirs of Victor Serge, a Bolshevik and Comintern bureaucrat. Serge criticised Stalin and was imprisoned in the 1930s. His memoirs were published in France, 1951, after his death.

The grain crisis broke out in 1927, endangering supplies to the towns and the army. The peasants, having paid off their taxes, now refused to deliver their grain to the State because they were not being paid enough for it. The Central Committee decreed requisitions, applying, quite improperly, Article 107 of the Penal Code on concealment of stocks.

Detachments of young communists scoured the countryside, stripping the fields of their grain. Just as in the years of the Civil War, communists were found at the roadsides with their skulls split open. There was no fodder at all; the country folk besieged the bakeries in the towns so they could feed their livestock with black bread bought at the regulation price.

SOURCE B

From a talk about the grain crisis given by Stalin to university students, May 1928.

It is a fact that the amount of marketed grain in our country is now half of what it was before the war, although the total amount of grain has reached the pre-war level. What then is the way out of this situation?

The way out lies in the transition from the small, backward and scattered peasant farms to amalgamated, large-scale socialised farms, equipped with machinery, armed with scientific knowledge and capable of producing a maximum of grain for the market.

The way out lies in systematically increasing the yield of the small and middle individual peasant farms, helping them to increase their crop yields and drawing them into the channel of cooperative organisations.

Sample student answer

The author of Source A was in the Communist Party during the grain crisis and witnessed Stalin's response to it. His account matches what is known about Stalin's response to the grain crisis. He blamed the peasants for not selling their grain and then sent out brigades to requisition grain and other crops from the peasants, for example in western Siberia.

EXAMINER TIP

The student makes some good points, but needs to develop and explain them further. For example the observation that the author was an eye witness to events is stated but not developed with reference to the value of the source. Similarly, although the student uses some contextual information to support the value of the source content, this is undeveloped.

Serge is critical of the Party's harsh response to the grain requisition crisis and says that Article 107 of the Penal Code was improperly applied, although he doesn't explain how. His disapproval can be seen in the tone he adopts, for example 'stripping the fields' and 'skulls split open' are intended to provoke the sympathy of the reader. However, since Serge wrote this account in his memoirs, after the events it describes, and was also imprisoned as a critic of Stalin, his account is bound to be one-sided. So, while the source is valuable as a description of the negative effects of the Party's return to requisitioning, its value is undermined by Serge's bias against Stalin.

EXAMINER TIP

This paragraph comments appropriately on provenance and tone, but fails to develop these ideas in relation to the source's value in explaining the 'Great Turn'. The comments about Serge's bias could have been developed further, for example, to explain why Serge's political views and experiences at the hands of Stalin might affect his account of the requisition policy of the Central Committee. Further contextual knowledge could also have been used to both support and question the value of the content.

Overall this is a valuable source because it provides a critical viewpoint on the way the Party responded to the grain requisition crisis. This shows that not everyone in the Party was ready to reject the NEP's deal with the peasants and return to Civil War-style requisitioning.

The author of Source B is Stalin himself, speaking after the grain crisis (which ran through the winter of 1927–28) to university students. The purpose of the speech is to show Stalin's argument in favour of the 'Great Turn', which is all about the need to increase the amount of grain reaching the market.

EXAMINER TIP

This is a valid judgement on the value of the source but the source analysis preceding it is quite under-developed. It is not actually necessary to provide a 'conclusion' on each source in this comparative question, and the student would have done better to spend more time looking methodically at provenance and content, and thoroughly evaluating both.

It is likely that the speech would also have been reported in newspapers and would have reached quite a wide audience. This makes it extremely valuable as an indication of the sort of arguments Stalin made at the time and how he won support.

EXAMINER TIP

Some good comments are made about the purpose of the source, supported by a little contextual understanding. It is a shame these ideas are not further developed with more of the student's own knowledge.

Stalin's tone in Source B is clear and authoritative. He states 'it is a fact...' and proceeds to inform his audience that 'the way out lies in...'. He appears to be in no doubt that a 'Great Turn' is needed in order to get more grain sent to the markets. It is significant to note that while he implies that peasants have been hoarding grain, rather than selling it, he does not mention the kulaks by name. This is presumably because his purpose is to win support for his programme as an economic move, rather than a social one (eliminating the higher-ranking, 'capitalist' peasants).

EXAMINER TIP

This paragraph shows some good understanding, but having started with a comment on tone, it turns into a criticism of the content. It would have been better for the student to have combined the comment on authorship, purpose, audience and tone in one paragraph, and support and criticism of the source's content in another. However, it provides a good example of the way that omission can be relevant.

Source B provides valuable content which sets out Stalin's solution to Russia's agricultural problems. He refers to 'amalgamated, large-scale socialised farms', 'producing a maximum of grain for the market', which clearly means collectives. Stalin tries to justify this by talking of 'helping' the peasants to increase their crop yields. He is clearly trying to sound reasonable and caring. However, his mild-sounding approach is very different to what is known of the enforced, brutal grain requisitions and the dekulakisation campaign that Stalin was urging by December 1929, so the source's content is only valuable for understanding Stalin's arguments and plans, not for the actual detail of what was to happen.

EXAMINER TIP

The student evaluated the source detail with reference to contextual knowledge in quite an effective way, but the value could be developed further, perhaps by considering who it was that Stalin needed to convince within the Party.

Overall Source B is limited in value. The mention of the 'small and middle peasants' is the only allusion to the kulaks, who became a target for the most brutal liquidation in 1929. Furthermore, collectivisation is described in purely economic terms as a way of increasing farm efficiency, with hardly any mention of the political need to gain control over the peasants, or the approval that Stalin showed for the return to Civil War-style requisitioning of the Ural-Siberian method in response to the grain crisis. I therefore believe that Source A is more useful for understanding the reasons for the 'Great Turn' against the NEP in 1927–28 because it reveals more about the Communist Party's motivation than Source B, and contains valuable content, such as the information about communist activists being killed in revenge for taking everything peasants had.

EXAMINER TIP

The student substantiates their judgement about Source B's usefulness with reference to their evaluation of it in the main part of the answer. The conclusion also gives a clear reason why the student believes that Source A is more useful, and provides an explanation for this. However, the student's judgement is not fully substantiated by the analysis of Source A in the main part of the answer.

OVERALL COMMENT

The answer shows some good understanding and uses contextual awareness to analyse the sources, especially Source B. Relevant comments are made about the author, date, purpose and emphasis of each source, although, in general, the analysis of provenance is quite superficial.

The answer would also have been more successful had the evaluation of provenance and content been separated more effectively, with a good paragraph on each. The contextual detail also needs to be much stronger and more links need to be made to the question, which is about the ''Great Turn' against the NEP' (the latter is barely mentioned).

A comparative conclusion is given, offering some judgement, but the answer is unbalanced because the evaluation of Source A is weaker than that of B. This answer shows some Level 4 qualities, but its weaknesses would limit it to a high Level 3.

OVER TO YOU

Give yourself 45 minutes to answer this question on your own. Then review the Examiner Tips on these pages to check whether you have avoided the same mistakes as in the sample student answer.

❏ Did you fully explain how the provenance of the two sources might affect their value?

❏ Did you include relevant contextual information, relating to both the provenance and content of each source, and use it to evaluate the sources fully?

❏ Did you focus on the 'Great Turn' against the NEP?

❏ Did you include a conclusion showing your judgement about which of the sources has more value, with an explanation to explain your thinking?

Go back and look at page 58 to help refresh your knowledge of the 'Great Turn' in 1927–28.

4 Economy and society, 1929–1941

 REVISION PROGRESS

13 Agricultural and social developments in the countryside

 RECAP

Stalin's 'Great Turn' was highly political. It was a policy shift through which he defeated the Bukharinists and consolidated dictatorial power over the Party. It also enforced revolutionary changes to the Soviet economy.

The 'Great Turn' committed the USSR to a programme of rapid industrialisation and the mass mobilisation of workers. To facilitate this it was necessary to impose an equally rapid agricultural revolution through forced collectivisation in the countryside.

Collectivisation was not new; it was a key element in Marxist-Leninist theory. But from 1921, the compromise of the NEP meant that collectivisation was slow and patchy in the 1920s. Stalin's 'Great Turn', which forced individual farms into collectives, planned to increase grain production by 50 per cent over the course of the first Five Year Plan. It aimed to:

- eradicate 'class enemies' in the countryside (the kulaks)
- make farming in the USSR socialist rather than capitalist
- replace the NEP with true Marxist-Leninist theory.

KEY CHRONOLOGY

1929	Stalin gives his 'war against the kulaks' speech to the Party Congress
1930	Temporary return to voluntary collectivisation
1931	Resumption of all-out dekulakisation
	Launch of Machine Tractor Stations
1932	Start of the famine in Ukraine
1933	Mass famine in Ukraine, Kazakhstan and North Caucasus

Voluntary and forced collectivisation

Although collectivisation was officially voluntary, after December 1929 peasants were forced into collective farms through a campaign of intimidation. Kulaks were targeted as Stalin announced they would be annihilated as a class.

The methods used to enforce collectivisation included the following:

Expansion of the Urals-Siberian method

In May 1929, the 'Urals-Siberian method' of enforced grain requisitioning was extended to almost all grain-producing regions of the USSR, despite opposition from Bukharin that this risked making the peasants hostile to the state.

Help from the poorest peasants

Local Party officials called on the poorest peasants to help identify the kulaks. These poor peasants had the most to gain from collective farms. They would get to use the richer peasants' land, livestock and equipment, and share in the collective harvests.

Help from the Party activists

In November 1929, 25,000 Party activists (industrial workers) were sent into the countryside to help dekulakisation. They were officially sent to promote the benefits of collective farms and provide technical help, but in reality they searched households for hidden grain, helped identify and round up kulaks, administered the exile process, and enforced the collectivisation of the remaining peasants. They were assisted by local police, the OGPU and the Red Army.

A mixture of propaganda and fear

Although Party officials used propaganda and positive messages to convince villages to join collective farms, the real motivation came from fear of what was happening to the kulaks. People who resisted joining the collective farms were likely to be classed as kulaks too.

The process of collectivisation

The process of collectivisation unfolded as follows:

1929	
	At the start of 1929, only 5 per cent of farms in the USSR had voluntarily collectivised.
	During this year around 15 per cent of all peasant households were identified as kulaks. Those who weren't shot by the OGPU for 'terrorism' (resisting dekulakisation) were forced into exile in Siberia. In 1929, 150,000 kulak families were deported to Siberia.
1930	
March	Stalin announced that 50 per cent of peasant farms across the USSR had been collectivised. He also criticised local Party officials for their overzealousness, and allowed a brief return to voluntary membership of collective farms.
October	The return to voluntary collectivisation meant that by October, numbers had dropped and only 20 per cent of households were still collectivised.
1931	
	Once the spring crop had been sown in 1931, collectivisation was enforced again.
1941	
	All farms were collectivised.

State farms and mechanisation

Differences between kolkhozes and sovkhozes

For communist purists, the ideal type of farm was the sovkhoz: a state-owned farm where labourers were paid a fixed wage. However, peasant opposition to becoming wage-labourers meant that most farms in the 1930s were turned into kolkhozes: collective farms where peasants' earnings varied according to how much profit the farms made.

Differences between the two included the following:

Kolkhozes	Sovkhozes
Created by combining small, individual farms together.	Created on land confiscated from tsarist-era large estates. Usually larger than the kolkhoz, and owned and run by the state.
Created from farms that already existed; members often still lived in their old houses. A typical kolkhoz consisted of around 75 families living in one village.	Members were recruited from landless rural labourers. They were often housed in barracks.
Kolkhoz members were paid by dividing any farm earnings by the number of 'labour days' that members had contributed.	Sovkhoz members were classified as workers, not peasants, and were paid a wage for their work (like factory workers).
Kolkhozes had communal fields in which everyone worked, but members were also allowed small private plots to farm.	Sovkhozes were organised for large-scale production on industrial lines. Here too, though, private plots were still allowed.
All communal land was held in common and tools and livestock were pooled; the peasants farmed the land as a single unit.	Sovkhozes were viewed as the ideal form of socialist farming, as the state owned all the land.

There were also important similarities:

- Both types of farm were required to meet high quotas set by the state.
- The price set for these quotas was low. This meant industrial workers could be fed cheaply, and the state could make big profits on exporting grain in order to finance industrialisation.
- After 1932, kolkhozniks (kolkhoz members) and sovkhoz workers were restricted by internal passports to stop them leaving.

Machine Tractor Stations (MTS)

Machine Tractor Stations were set up from 1931. These hired out tractors and machinery to collective and state farms, as well as distributing seed.

Advantages of the MTS	Disadvantages of the MTS
Provided mechanisation and expertise to modernise farming.	There were far more farms than MTS – by 1940 there was still only one MTS for every 40 farms.
Tractors were the main focus. By the start of 1933, there were 75,000 MTS tractors.	Tractor hire prices were high because the state was squeezing farming for money.
Mechanisation reduced the need for peasant labour, so more peasants could leave the countryside and become industrial workers.	Efficiency was only improved in some areas because the machines often only completed part of a process (e.g. cutting the hay but not bailing it).
Agronomists, vets, surveyors and technicians helped to improve efficiency and advised on how to use the machines.	State farms tended to get the majority of MTS support and access to the best machinery (e.g. combine harvesters); advisers were used to spy on workers and ensure political correctness.

The impact of collectivisation on the kulaks and other peasants, and the famine of 1932–1934

- There was widespread and violent opposition to the process of collectivisation. Many peasants killed their livestock and destroyed their machines, fearing they would be branded as kulaks if they kept them.
- The armed forces responded brutally to the unrest, sometimes burning down whole villages and deporting anyone who resisted.
- Deported peasants were often exiled to remote places in Siberia where they worked in labour camps. Thousands died in the harsh conditions of these camps, run by the OGPU. It is estimated that as many as 10 million people were deported as kulaks under Stalin.
- Peasants in collective farms were treated badly. State targets were set high, with farms receiving nothing if quotas were not met. The state prices were low and farms struggled to cover the cost of production, let alone share profits among members. There was little incentive for peasants to work in the collective fields rather than on their own private plots. Many of those who could leave, did; by 1939 about 19 million peasants had migrated to the towns and cities.
- Many regions experienced a drought in 1931, especially Ukraine. Famine spread through these regions in 1932–33. The government continued to demand grain quotas were met despite the drop in production. It is estimated that 6–8 million people died. This famine resulted from the collectivisation process.

The success of collectivisation

In terms of Stalin's aims, collectivisation had mixed results.

As a way of **increasing agricultural productivity**, it was a failure:

> ✗ During the period of peasant opposition, agricultural production fell dramatically. In 1933, the harvest was 9 million tonnes less than in 1927.
>
> ✗ Grain output did not exceed pre-collectivisation levels until after 1935.
>
> ✗ Livestock numbers fell by 25–30 per cent during collectivisation and did not recover until 1953.

Reasons for this included: the loss of the most successful and knowledgeable peasant farmers through dekulakisation; the destruction of the USSR's livestock herds in opposition to collectivisation; the poor organisation of many farms; and the lack of incentive for kolkhozniks to produce more grain.

In terms of **achieving social aims**, collectivisation had mixed results:

> ✓ Dekulakisation and collectivisation put farming completely under state control. There was no opportunity for farmers to hold back grain in order to benefit from higher prices.
>
> ✓ Capitalism in the countryside was eradicated, except for the peasants' privately owned small plots. By 1941, 100 per cent of peasant households were collectivised.
>
> ✓ The money from grain exports funded industrialisation, while the poor conditions on collective farms fuelled migration to the cities. Between 1922 and 1940, the urban population of the USSR increased from 22 million to 63 million.

> ✗ Living standards fell in both urban and rural areas. In the towns and cities wages also declined.
>
> ✗ Famine across the USSR killed approximately 6–8 million people: an extraordinarily high social cost. However, it was not seen this way amongst the Party leadership.

In terms of **consolidating Stalin's position** in the Party, collectivisation was very successful:

> ✓ Despite declining agricultural production from 1930 until at least 1936, the USSR succeeded in its aim of exporting more grain (grain exports rose from 30,000 tonnes in 1928 to more than 5 million tonnes in 1931). This provided investment for rapid industrialisation, justifying Stalin's 'Great Turn' away from the NEP.
>
> ✓ Bukharin had opposed collectivisation, saying it would endanger food supplies to the towns and cities. Despite Bukharin being proved right about peasant opposition, the Party agreed with Stalin that the peasant opposition to collectivisation was actually class war – kulak counter-revolutionary terrorism – that needed to be brutally exterminated.
>
> ✓ Collectivisation allowed the Soviet regime to extend its political control over the countryside.
>
> ✓ Many Party members had tolerated the NEP long enough and there was great enthusiasm for Stalin's model of building socialism.

SUMMARY

- By the end of the 1930s, most of the countryside was either collectivised or consisted of state farms.
- Collectivisation was brutal: kulaks were identified and deported by force; resistance to collectivisation was repressed violently. Millions of peasants died as a result.
- Agricultural production fell and did not recover for many years. However, the process extracted value from the countryside that funded industrialisation.

 **APPLY**

APPLY YOUR KNOWLEDGE

On 27 December 1929, Stalin gave a speech about exterminating the kulaks as a class. Read extracts from the speech in the table below. Copy and complete this table by deciding, for each of the extracts, whether it is:

a Attacking the kulaks

b Justifying Stalin's turn away from his previous support for the NEP

c Attacking Bukharin and the other 'Right deviationists'

Extract	Aim	Explanation
'In 1927 the kulaks produced over 600 million poods of grain, about 130 million of which they marketed. How much did our collective farms and state farms produce at that time? About 80 million poods, of which about 35 million were marketed.'	**a & b**	**a** because Stalin is saying the kulaks only marketed a fifth or so of all their produce in 1927, so he is blaming them for low grain procurement. **b** because…
'It is now ridiculous and foolish to discourse at length on dekulakization. When the head is off, one does not mourn for the hair.'	**c**	
'An offensive against the kulaks is a serious matter. It should not be confused with a policy of pinpricks against the kulaks, which the opposition did its utmost to impose upon the Party. We must smash the kulaks, eliminate them as a class.'		

 EXAMINER TIP

This activity will help you answer questions about Stalin's aims for collectivisation, as well as develop your skills in interpreting source material.

PLAN YOUR ESSAY

 'Collectivisation was a political success but brought economic and social disaster.' Assess the validity of this view.

a Write some notes to evaluate the economic, social and political effects of collectivisation. What changes did collectivisation bring to these aspects of the USSR?

b Write a conclusion to the essay question that shows your overall judgement.

 EXAMINER TIP

You can use economic, social and political impacts or factors as a framework for analysing most topics in this course. Cultural effects are sometimes worth considering too (especially for topics like culture and society).

 REVIEW

Chapter 11 also included information about the decision to collectivise, which could be useful for this activity.

SOURCE ANALYSIS

SOURCE A

From an article written by Stalin and published in *Pravda* on 2 March 1930. *Pravda* was the official newspaper of the Communist Party.

It is a fact that by 20 February of this year 50 per cent of the peasant farms throughout the USSR had been collectivised. That means that by 20 February, 1930, we had overfulfilled the five-year plan of collectivisation by more than 100 per cent.

But the successes have their seamy side, especially when they are attained with comparative 'ease' — 'unexpectedly' so to speak. Such successes sometimes induce a spirit of vanity and conceit: 'We can achieve anything!', 'There is nothing we can't do!' People not infrequently become intoxicated by such successes; they become dizzy with success.

The successes of our collective-farm policy are due, among other things, to the fact that it rests on the voluntary character of the collective-farm movement. Collective farms must not be established by force. That would be foolish and reactionary. The collective-farm movement must rest on the active support of the main mass of the peasantry.

SOURCE B

From an article written by a British journalist who visited Ukraine in 1933. The article was published anonymously in March 1933 in The *Manchester Guardian*, a left-wing British newspaper.

I told the man that I was interested in collective farms, and he was ready to talk. 'I was a poor peasant,' he said, 'with a hectare and a half of land. I thought that things would be better for me on the collective farm.'

'Well, were they?'

He laughed. 'Not at all, much worse.'

'Worse than before the Revolution?'

He laughed again. 'Much, much worse. Before the Revolution we had a cow and something to feed it with; plenty of bread, meat sometimes. Now nothing but potatoes and millet.'

'What's happened, then? Why is there no bread in Ukraine?'

'Bad organisation. They send people from Moscow who know nothing; they ordered us to grow vegetables instead of wheat. We didn't know how to grow vegetables, and they couldn't show us.'

'Some grain must have been produced. What happened to it?'

'All taken by the government.'

SOURCE C

From a report, marked 'top secret', from a regional health inspector following a visit by the inspector to several kolkhozes in Western Siberia in April 1932, during the famine.

Filipp Borodin has earned 650 work-days working for the kolkhoz, has a wife and five children ranging from one-and-a-half to nine years of age. The wife lies ill on the warming stove, three children sit on the warming stove too, they are as pale as wax with swollen faces, the one-and-a-half year old sits pale by the window, swollen, the nine-year-old lies ill on the earthen floor covered with rags, and Filipp Borodin himself sits on a bench and, continuously smoking cigarettes made of repulsively pungent tobacco, cries like a babe.

In the Borodin home there is unbelievable filth, dampness, and stench, mixed with the smell of tobacco. Borodin swears at the children: 'The devils don't die, I wish I didn't have to look at you!' Having objectively investigated the condition of Borodin himself I ascertain that he (Borodin) is starting to slip into mental disorder due to starvation.

 EXAMINER TIP

Remember that when you are evaluating the provenance of a source you should be asking the following questions: who produced it, when, why and who for.

 A LEVEL **With reference to these sources and your own understanding of the historical context, assess the value of these sources to an historian studying the impact of collectivisation.**

a Copy and complete the table below to identify the strengths and weaknesses of the provenance of each of these sources for an historian studying the impact of collectivisation.

	Strengths	Weaknesses
Source A		
Source B		
Source C		

b Write a few sentences for each extract summarising its value, taking into account the strengths and weaknesses of the provenance of each one.

14 Industrial and social developments in towns and cities

 RECAP

Between 1929 and 1941, state power was used to transform the industrial base of the Soviet Union into a 'command economy' through three successive Five Year Plans. Ambitious targets were set and ruthlessly enforced. This rush to industrialise was costly and often inefficient; the real outcomes were often far less than state propaganda claimed. It also caused great hardship to millions of workers and peasants. But by 1941, the foundations of a modern industrialised state had been put in place.

KEY CHRONOLOGY

The Five Year Plans

1928	The first Five Year Plan is launched
1932	The Dnieprostroi Dam is completed
1933	The second Five Year Plan is launched
1936	There is a new emphasis on armaments production
1937	The Moscow-Volga Canal is completed
1938	The third Five Year Plan is launched
1940	Armaments spending is doubled
1941	The third Five Year Plan is interrupted by the German invasion

Gosplan

Gosplan, the State Planning Agency, organised the process by which industry was transformed under the Five Year Plans.

- It drew up plans and set output targets for every economic enterprise in accordance with Party directives.
- The targets Gosplan set were usually very ambitious. If Party leaders considered they were not ambitious enough, they would be revised upwards.
- The process was difficult because Gosplan did not have reliable statistics about the economy to base its targets on, especially about imports and possible exports.
- There were severe punishments for missing targets, so enterprises falsified their production figures. Over-ambitious planning assumptions never got corrected.
- Regional Party bosses competed for their regions to be given the most resources and to be assigned the most prestigious new projects.

The aims and results of the first three Five Year Plans

	Aims	Successes	Limitations
First Five Year Plan (1928–32)	Develop heavy industry. Boost electricity production. Double the output from light industry, e.g. chemicals.	Electricity production tripled. Coal and iron output doubled. Steel production increased by one third.	None of the extremely ambitious targets were actually met. Improvements in the chemical industry lagged behind. Consumer industries were badly neglected.
Second Five Year Plan (1933–37)	Continue the growth of heavy industry. Boost light industry: chemicals, electricals, consumer goods. Develop communications. Foster engineering.	Some large-scale communication projects. Rapid growth in electricity production and chemicals. New metals (e.g. copper and tin) mined for the first time. Steel output trebled. Coal production doubled. The USSR was self-sufficient in metal goods and machine tools by 1937.	Oil production failed to meet its targets. Consumers were still very short of some products. While overall quantity increased, quality still tended to be very low.
Third Five Year Plan (1938–42)	Renewed emphasis on heavy industry. Promote rapid rearmament. Complete the transition to communism.	Some strong growth in machinery and engineering. Defence industries developed exceptional models, e.g. the T-34 tank. Spending on rearmament doubled between 1938–40.	Other areas stagnated after defence was prioritised. Oil production failed to meet targets, causing a fuel crisis. There was a lack of specialists due to Stalin's purges. The German invasion of 1941 disrupted the Plan, causing it to end early.

- Criticisms of the Five Year Plans should take into account the fact that nothing like them had really been tried before, so there was no obvious example to learn from.
- In addition, the initial successes happened in the context of the 1929 Wall Street Crash and Great Depression.
- The effectiveness of the Third Year Plan was reduced in part because of the growing threat that Nazi Germany presented to the USSR, which diverted funds into defence and rearmament.
- A fundamental problem with the plans was Stalin's increasingly authoritarian and repressive regime, where any criticism of the system was likely to be viewed as treason.

New industrial centres and projects

The plans involved a number of projects that were designed to showcase the modernity and capabilities of the USSR. Here are three examples:

Dnieprostroi Dam

- Constructed between 1927 and 1932.
- A dam generating hydro-electric power, built on the Dnieper river in Ukraine.
- One of the largest power stations in the world at the time.
- Once five extra generators were installed in the second Five Year Plan, the dam increased Soviet electric power by five times.
- The dam powered aluminium and steel production in nearby new industrial centres.

Moscow Metro

- Constructed between 1932 and 1937.
- The first underground railway system in the USSR.
- A second Five Year Plan project, designed to help Moscow deal with rapid industrialisation as peasants moved from the countryside to the city.
- Aimed to showcase the achievements of a socialist state, with chandeliers, marble walls and intricate mosaics.
- Massive recruitment campaigns were organised to find the unskilled labourers who constructed the Metro.

Moscow-Volga Canal

- Constructed between 1932 and 1937.
- A 128 km canal connecting the Moskva River to the Volga River.
- Made the small Moskva River navigable by ships, connected Moscow to five seas, and improved links to the industrial centre of Gorky.
- Built by c200,000 prisoners from the enormous Dmitlag labour camp, of whom c22,000 died.

Completely new industrial cities were also built, intended to showcase socialism in action. Examples included:

- **Magnitogorsk:** a gigantic steel plant and town of 150,000 people, purpose-built in the Urals, away from the USSR's western borders.

- **Komsomolsk:** a heavy plant and several shipyards in east Russia, built to open up this area to development. Constructed by volunteer labour from the Komsomol (the Communist youth organisation), together with prison camp labour.

The involvement of foreign companies

Foreign companies were recruited to provide the expertise needed to develop new industries, and to plan and construct the new industrial centres and showpiece projects. For example:

- The Moscow Metro was designed by British specialists recruited from the London Underground.
- Henry Ford advised the USSR on its car industry, trained Soviet engineers in the USA, and helped to design the car-plant at Gorky.
- The Dnieprostroi Dam project used experience from Canadian and US engineers. Six American engineers were awarded the 'Order of the Red Banner of Labour' in recognition of their 'outstanding work' in the construction of the dam.

While the relatively high wages and prestige of working on these mega-projects attracted Westerners to work in the USSR (especially during the Great Depression), there were dangers. For example, the secret police arrested several British engineers working on the Moscow Metro because of suspicions of spying; the OGPU was concerned about their detailed knowledge of Moscow's geography. Engineers for the Metropolitan-Vickers Electrical Company were given a show trial and deported in 1933, ending the role of British business in the USSR.

Stakhanovites

- Stakhanovites were workers who exceeded their targets and were held up as examples for others to follow.
- They were named after Aleksei Stakhanov, a coal miner who exceeded his mining target by a huge amount. He was declared a Soviet hero and rewarded with a bonus and awards.
- Other miners competed to break Stakhanov's record. This competitive over-achievement of targets spread to other industries.
- The Stakhanovite movement was a propaganda campaign based on improving worker productivity for the good of the USSR, not for individual gain.
- The Party promoted the Stakhanovite movement and introduced Stakhanovite competitions in different industries. Stakhanovites received material benefits from their employers.
- Stakhanovites were not always popular with managers because their efforts meant production targets were raised.
- Stakhanovites were not always popular with other workers, since they made them look bad and meant higher targets.
- In 1988, it was reported in the USSR that Stakhanov's original heroic work effort had been stage-managed. Several others had helped him to achieve histarget.

The working and living conditions of managers, workers and women

Managers

- Managers had to find ways of meeting targets (at least on paper) while avoiding problems with workers.
- Managers received bonuses for exceeding targets, but could be put on trial, imprisoned or even executed for failing to meet targets.
- From 1936, factories had to pay for their own raw materials, labour and fuel out of their profits from sales, which meant careful (or creative) accounting. Bribery and corruption were pervasive within the system.
- Managers were responsible for applying state regulations in the workplace, for example regarding work norms and absenteeism. These were not popular with workers and led to protests.
- Any attempts by managers to reduce the pressure on their workers could lead to accusations of **wrecking** (sabotage).

Workers

Living and working conditions for most were far from a 'socialist paradise':

- Long working hours over six days a week were brought in to help achieve the first Five Year Plan.
- From 1938, labour books (in addition to internal passports) recorded workers' employment, skills and any disciplinary issues.
- Absenteeism or lateness could result in dismissal, eviction from housing and loss of benefits. Measures to toughen up on absenteeism appeared in 1930–33. In 1940, absenteeism became a crime.
- Strikes were illegal and damaging machinery was a criminal offence, as was leaving work without permission.
- Most city workers lived in crowded communal apartments with few amenities and little privacy.
- Although rationing ended in 1935, many food items remained hard to get or afford.

However, some workers did benefit:

- There were far more opportunities for workers to progress than under tsarism.
- Training programmes were widely available to improve skills.
- From 1931, wage differentials were introduced that meant those who worked hard over long hours were rewarded for their efforts.
- Wages increased during the second Five Year Plan (though they were still lower in 1937 than in 1928).
- Stalin's purges removed white-collar workers and intellectuals, creating opportunities for workers to advance their careers.

Women

- By 1940, around 43 per cent of the workforce was female. State provision of nurseries, crèches and child clinics allowed mothers to work.
- As prices increased, women entered the workforce to help earn the income needed to sustain their families.
- Managers who were under pressure to achieve their targets would agree to employ workers' wives and daughters.
- The Party also ordered managers to employ more women in heavy industry for the second Five Year Plan.
- However, managers continued to give the best-paid, highest-skilled jobs to men and were reluctant to allow women to get training to improve their skills.
- From 1936, the Party responded by making it easier for women to enter technical training programmes.
- Although by 1940 women earned around 40 per cent less than men, advances had been made.

The success of the Five Year Plans

Strengths	Weaknesses
• The Soviet economy probably grew at 5 to 6 per cent per year between 1928 and 1940. This was an impressive result, especially in the context of a global recession. • The USSR became a major industrial power as a result of the Five Year Plans. • There were impressive results in heavy industrial growth. Light industry also started to deliver more consumer goods for Soviet citizens. • The Five Year Plans created opportunities for ordinary workers to develop new skills and progress in their careers, increasingly for women as well as for men. • The plans fostered a sense of pride in the communist system and what it could achieve.	• Social downsides included deteriorating living conditions, and working conditions that were dominated by strict labour discipline. • Fear of missing targets created an environment of bribery and corruption, and a focus on quantity rather than quality. • The success of the Five Year Plans in achieving industrialisation was also built on prison-camp labour and the very low prices paid to collective farms for very high quotas of grain – even during times of food shortage and famine.

SUMMARY

- Gosplan oversaw the organisation of the Five Year Plans and set the targets for different industrial sectors.
- The main focus was on heavy industry, switching to defence during the Third Year Plan. Other sectors were comparatively neglected.
- Living and working conditions were harsh, but there was some marginal improvement by 1941 and skilled workers generally did well.

APPLY

APPLY YOUR KNOWLEDGE

EXAMINER TIP

This activity will help you to understand the achievements of the Five Year Plans as well as their limitations.

The following table compares selected targets and actual production figures of the first and second Five Year Plans. Use the table to answer the questions below.

Economic area	First FYP target production	1932 actual production	Second FYP target production	1937 actual production
Coal (million tonnes)	75	64.4	152.5	128
Oil (million tonnes)	21.7	21.4	46.8	28.5
Steel (million tonnes)	10.4	5.9	17.0	17.7
Pig iron (million tonnes)	10	6.2	16.0	14.5
Electricity (m. kWh)	22,000	13,450	38,000	36,000

a This table shows no actual production meeting or exceeding its Five Year Plan target: true or false?

b The impressive second Five Year Plan increase in which economic area would have been aided by the extension of the Dnieprostroi Dam?

c Do these statistics suggest that the first two Five Year Plans had not been properly thought through before they were launched? Why or why not?

d Using the table to support your answer, outline one strength and one limitation of the first two Five Year Plans.

APPLY YOUR KNOWLEDGE

a Use the table to identify three ways in which industrialisation under the Five Year Plans created opportunities for workers, and three ways in which industrialisation made life harder for workers.

Created opportunities	Made life harder

REVIEW

Collectivisation was an important way in which industrialisation was achieved, so your answer might benefit from a review of Chapter 13.

b Use your completed table to write a paragraph in response to this statement: 'Industrialisation under the Five Year Plans was achieved by lowering living and working conditions.'

APPLY YOUR KNOWLEDGE

Add to the spider diagram below to show the factors that contributed to inefficiency and labour shortages during the Five Year Plans.

Absenteeism

Lack of motivation

Factors contributing to inefficiency and labour shortages

TO WHAT EXTENT?

A LEVEL **To what extent did the Five Year Plans achieve Stalin's aims for industrial development?**

a The first column in the table below outlines some of Stalin's aims for industrial development. Complete the second and third columns in the table.

Aim	Example of its success	Limitations to its success
Rapid industrialisation	Within ten years the USSR had become a leading industrial nation capable of winning the war against Nazi Germany.	
A focus on heavy industry		
The development of new industrial centres		Many of these projects relied on prison-camp labour and were achieved at a horrendous cost of human lives and suffering.
Collectivisation to feed the urban workforce and fund industrialisation		

b Use your completed table to help write an answer to the essay question.

REVIEW

Information in Chapter 11 will help with evaluating the success of Stalin's aims.

EXAMINER TIP

Your answer should aim to show a balanced judgement that defines and then balances Stalin's aims with the degree of change that took place.

15 The development of the Stalin cult

The cult of personality

Stalin's personal character was not strongly evident during his rise to power. He had little overt charisma and was often underrated by his rivals in the Party. The cult of personality promoted by Stalin in the 1920s was the cult of Lenin, with Stalin as his 'humble successor'.

However, the Stalin cult grew noticeably after Stalin's fiftieth birthday celebrations in December 1929, when leading Party members each wrote articles praising him in *Pravda*. The Stalin cult was only fully established after 1933 and did not reach its height until after the Second World War.

Stalin was portrayed as:

An infallible leader
Described as 'all-knowing' and a 'universal genius'

A sure guide
He knew how to lead the USSR forward despite dangers on all sides ('the Great Helmsman')

The successor to Marx, Engels and Lenin
Giving the sense of a progression of great men who had brought socialist enlightenment to the Soviet people

A father figure
Described as the 'father of the nation'

A semi-religious leader
Symbolised by titles such as 'the shining sun of humanity'

A true Bolshevik
Living simply with no extravagance

Components of the cult of personality

Stalin's cult of personality was built up in different ways. Stalin's own role in developing the cult is not clear, though he revelled in it and certainly could have stopped it if he had wanted to.

Infallibility
The cult portrayed Stalin as an 'all-knowing', infallible leader

Relationship to Lenin
The cult portrayed Stalin as the heir of Lenin, transferring features of the Lenin cult to Stalin

Components of the Stalin cult

Propaganda
Paintings, poems, posters, slogans and sculptures glorified Stalin, while written works were dedicated to him and prefaced with acknowledgements of his genius

Patronage
Stalin's inner circle were associated with the cult too, with cities and factories named after them

Falsification of history
Stalin's role in the pivotal events of Bolshevism was enlarged, while his rivals were downplayed, reimagined as enemies of the people, or excised from books and photographs completely

Tsarist symbolism
The cult borrowed from the 'little father' image associated with the tsars (the belief that the tsar cared for all his people as he was like a father to them)

Literature, the arts and socialist realism

While Lenin had allowed creativity in the arts, as long as it was not counter-revolutionary, Stalin took a different view. Literature and the arts were only valuable if they supported his view of socialist ideology.

- From 1932, all writers (including journalists, novelists, poets and literary critics) had to belong to the Union of Soviet Writers. All artists and art critics had to belong to the Union of Artists. There were similar unions for musicians, film-makers and sculptors.

- These unions dictated what sort of literature and art were allowed. Anyone not following the guidelines risked exclusion, which meant no chance of their work being published, exhibited, performed or paid for.
- Writers and other artists were required to create works that embodied 'socialist realism'. This meant showing what Soviet life was moving towards in an ideal future. By depicting the 'socialist reality' of the future, people would want to strive towards it.

- The frame of reference for writers was laid down by Andrei Zhdanov in April 1934 at the first Congress of the Union of Soviet Writers. Socialist realist works were expected to glorify the workers, especially communities working together and embracing new technology. Works were expected to be uplifting and optimistic.
- One popular novel was Nikolai Ostrovsky's *How The Steel Was Tempered*. The novel is about the life of a young revolutionary who fights in the Civil War and then overcomes his health issues to inspire others through his writings.
- During the 1930s there was a renewed interest in Russian works from the nineteenth century, such as the authors Pushkin and Tolstoy. These were promoted to all the peoples of the USSR. This was partly to allow Soviet proletarians access to what had been bourgeois culture under tsarism.
- Folk music and dance, and peasant arts and crafts were also celebrated, as Stalin was committed to promoting 'national' values.

Propaganda

Soviet propaganda was seen as a way of educating Soviet workers and peasants about the 'truths' of Stalinism and the importance of building socialism. The state controlled all the media and used it all for propaganda.

- Propaganda started early in life. Nurseries and schools were full of messages about the glories of communism. Pictures of Lenin and Stalin were prominent, there were communist youth groups (for example the Young Pioneers), and textbooks and lessons glorified Soviet achievements.
- Pavlik Morozov is a good example of youth propaganda. He was portrayed as a hero for denouncing his father to the NKVD for helping kulaks, and also for reporting that other peasants had been hoarding grain. He was then murdered by local kulaks. Soviet propaganda portrayed him as a martyr and his example was used to encourage young people to put the state first, even over their families.
- One example of propaganda in education was the use of *History of the Communist Party of the Soviet Union: Short Course* (which Stalin edited), which all students had to read and use in their work as the source of answers to all important questions. Ambitious Party members learned it by heart.
- Stalinist campaigns depended on propaganda to create a buzz of enthusiasm, aspiration and national pride. The Five Year Plans relied heavily on propaganda.
- Propaganda for workers focused on worker-heroes such as Aleksei Stakhanov (see page 75). This propaganda aimed to inspire workers to out-perform their targets. Statues of workers and peasants were erected, for example the 24.5 metre-high 'Worker and Kolkhoz Woman' statue by Vera Mukhina, produced for the 1937 World Trade Fair in Paris. Worker-heroes featured in books, art and film.
- Posters and murals were widely displayed showing achievements of the Soviet state or warnings about the dangers of the USSR's enemies. Cinema and radio gave similar messages.
- 'Talking pictures' (films that included sound) became very popular in the 1930s. Fictional films and newsreels were a perfect vehicle for propaganda.

Despite the state's complete control over the media, there is evidence of people rejecting or questioning its message:

- Despite a huge propaganda campaign that accompanied collectivisation, many peasants resisted the process by slaughtering their livestock. When enforced collectivisation was briefly relaxed in 1930, the percentage of collectivised households dropped from 50 per cent to 20 per cent.
- The Communist Party archives contain many examples of letters from workers expressing their anger at the lack of adequate housing, there being nothing to buy in the shops, and the corruption, favouritism and bribery they saw amongst their managers at work.
- There is evidence that Stakhanovites annoyed fellow workers because targets were increased as a result of their efforts, while managers found Stakhanovites challenging because of the power it gave them to criticise working conditions.
- Jokes, graffiti and popular songs criticised the Five Year Plans. For example, one song talked about 'The Five Year Plan in Ten', i.e. taking ten years rather than the propaganda line of 'The Five Year Plan in Four'.

SUMMARY

- The Stalin cult began to grow in the 1930s as Stalin came out from behind the cult of Lenin.
- The Stalin cult was developed in the 1930s until Stalin was seen as a godlike father-figure to the nation. (This was only a first stage, however – the Stalin cult was greatly enhanced by the Great Patriotic War, and reached ultimate heights in the years of 'High Stalinism' after 1945.)
- Literature and the arts were required to embody socialist realism and glorify Soviet achievements. This was a contrast to the creativity encouraged after the Revolution.
- The Soviet regime had virtually complete control over the media. They used this control to educate young people and workers about their shared communist future.

 **APPLY**

APPLY YOUR KNOWLEDGE

The table below includes extracts from a speech given by the Soviet writer Maxim Gorky (a favourite of Stalin). The speech was made at the Soviet Writers' Congress of 1934, which was dominated by Zhdanov's drive for socialist realism in the arts.

Explain in your own words what each extract tells us about the characteristics of socialist realism.

Extract from Gorky's speech	What it tells us about the characteristics of socialist realism
'As the principal hero of our books we should choose a worker, i.e. a person who in our country is armed with the full might of modern technique, a person who organises labour so that it becomes easier and more productive, raising it to the level of an art. We must learn to understand labour as creation.'	
'When narrating facts which mark the intellectual growth of the factory workers and the transformation of the farmers into collective farm members, we writers should not be mere chroniclers of the bare facts, doing little justice to the emotional process of these transformations.'	
'The Party leadership of literature must be thoroughly purged of all bourgeois influences. Party members active in literature must be the teachers of ideas that will muster the energy of the proletariat in all countries for the last battle for their freedom'	
'Soviet literature, with all its diversity of talents, and the steadily growing number of new and gifted writers, should be organised as an integral collective body, and an instrument of socialist culture.'	

 EXAMINER TIP

Knowledge and understanding of socialist realism will be useful for answering exam questions on culture in Stalin's USSR.

HOW IMPORTANT?

A LEVEL **How important was propaganda in Stalin's Soviet regime?**

a Copy and complete the following table.

Evidence to support the idea that propaganda was important	Evidence to support the idea that propaganda had limited importance

b Use your completed table to write an answer to the essay question.

EXAMINER TIP

You will need to show an overall assessment in your answer, although you could differentiate between different social groups when making your judgement. (For example, you could consider the importance of propaganda to young people, peasants or workers).

KEY CONCEPT

Ideological control is a key concept in the study of revolution and dictatorship in Russia 1917–53.

Ideological control refers to the control or manipulation of citizens so they accept the ideology of the state. Propaganda is one tool used to enforce ideological control.

a Give three examples of how propaganda was used to enforce ideological control in the USSR during the 1930s.

1. _____

_____

2. _____

_____

3. _____

_____

b Explain how socialist realism was used to exert ideological control in the USSR during the 1930s.

_____

_____

_____

_____

_____

_____

_____

16 The social and economic condition of the Soviet Union by 1941

 **RECAP**

The German invasion of Soviet Russia in June 1941 was an unwelcome interruption to the 'Stalin Revolution'. Stalin had hoped to avoid war, or at least to postpone it far into the future, so that the transformation of society and the economy could be completed.

By June 1941, there had been a massive expansion of industrial capacity, but there were also huge inefficiencies and failures. Agriculture had been revolutionised but at the cost of enormous hardship and resentment. A vast propaganda image of a new Soviet society had been created, but this was dependent on terror as much as on persuasion. The extent of the success of the Stalin Revolution was about to be tested by four years of a war for survival.

Economic strengths

Strength	Example
By 1941, the Five Year Plans had transformed the USSR into a highly industrialised nation.	By 1940, the USSR had overtaken Britain in iron and steel production, and was not far behind Germany.
Collectivisation and the Five Year Plans had increased urbanisation, leading to a much larger potential workforce for industries to draw on.	In 1926, 17 per cent of the population lived in urban areas. By 1930 this had increased to 33 per cent.
By 1941, all farms had been collectivised and brought into the Soviet centrally planned economic system.	In 1929, less than 5 per cent of farms were collectivised. This had increased to 100 per cent by 1941.
Military spending increased quickly over the 1930s, and Stalin's push for heavy industry meant the USSR could rapidly develop its military strength.	Military spending increased from 3 per cent of the total budget in 1933 to 34 per cent in 1940.

Economic weaknesses

Weakness	Example
Economic development was uneven. Heavy industry grew rapidly during the Five Year Plans while consumer production was cut back, leading to severe shortages of consumer products.	In 1928, the USSR produced 4 million tonnes of steel, while by 1940 it was producing 18 million tonnes. In contrast, there were lengthy waits and queues for basic consumer goods.
The quality of products was often poor, as Five Year Plan targets emphasised quantity over quality.	Meat targets were set by weight. Fatty meat is heavier than lean meat. So farmers produced fatty meat, even though consumers did not like it.
The central planning system struggled to deal with an increasingly complex economy, and organisation at a local level was often poor.	In the early 1930s there were 300 planning targets for Gosplan to set and monitor. By 1940, there were 2500.

Social strengths

- By 1941, state ownership had been achieved over industry and agriculture. The Soviet regime claimed that state ownership was essentially the same as ownership by the Soviet people, and therefore socialist.
- Stalin had achieved much greater state control over society, notably in the countryside. From 1929, peasants were supervised by Party officials attached to each kolkhoz and secret police units were stationed at each Motor Tractor Station.
- Food rationing ended in 1934. Kolkhozniks were allowed to have their own private plots to farm from 1934, which helped food production to recover (these private plots were producing nearly two thirds of the USSR's food by the late 1930s).
- There were significant benefits available to workers who consistently beat their targets, such as improved wages and living conditions. The state provision of childcare allowed more women to enter the workplace, and training programmes allowed some women to acquire well-paid, skilled positions.

Social weaknesses

- Around 6–8 million people died in the famine of 1932–34, and another 10 million peasants died from the effects of dekulakisation and deportation. Conditions on the collective farms were miserable.
- Rapid urbanisation took place without sufficient expansion of housing. This made living conditions for workers very poor. Shanty towns developed on the outskirts of big cities, with no facilities for washing or sanitation.
- Working conditions were harsh and discipline was strict. For example, being late for work three times in a row could result in a sentence of ten years' hard labour. In 1940, a decree was issued making poor-quality production a criminal offence, adding further to the pressure put on managers.
- The benefits available to Party bureaucrats began to produce social inequalities. Around 50,000 senior Party officials were rewarded with far better living conditions, better food and better clothes than ordinary workers, while industrial workers had access to better pay, opportunities and leisure activities than kolkhozniks.

The situation on the outbreak of war in 1941

- Central control of the 'command economy' helped the USSR to organise its war effort in 1941.
- Rapid industrialisation, especially of heavy industry, gave the USSR the basis for its victory against Germany.
- It is possible that the harsh labour laws and severe working conditions helped to build resilience among the Soviet workforce, enabling them to cope with the hardships of war.
- However, by 1941 the economy was still producing less grain than under the NEP. Enforced collectivisation had weakened the USSR's food production.
- The advent of war left Stalin in a state of panic.

> **SUMMARY**
> - Economic strengths by 1941 came from the successes of the Five Year Plans in rapidly industrialising and urbanising the USSR. However, weaknesses included the lack of consumer products for Soviet citizens.
> - Social strengths by 1941 included the opportunities for ordinary people to access better jobs and living conditions. However, for most people living and working conditions remained very poor.

 APPLY

APPLY YOUR KNOWLEDGE

Complete the following table by deciding whether you think the changes in the USSR by 1941 strengthened and/or weakened the USSR. Explain your reasoning.

Change	Strength or weakness?
Industrialisation	
Urbanisation	
Collectivisation	
State ownership of the means of production	
Centralisation	

PLAN YOUR ESSAY

A LEVEL **Was central planning the most significant factor in the Soviet Union's economic development during 1929 to 1941?**

a Unpack the question using these four prompts. Write one or two sentences to answer each one.

- What was central planning in the Soviet Union?
- What was the relationship between central planning and economic development?
- What was the Soviet Union's economic development in the years 1929 to 1941?
- How important was central planning to this economic development?

b How could each of the following points be used to argue against central planning being the most significant factor in driving economic development in the years 1929–41? Write one or two sentences for each one.

- Propaganda
- Prison camp labour
- Collective farm private plots
- Foreign expertise
- Fear

c Use your answers to **a** and **b** to plan out an answer to the exam question.

REVIEW

Look back at Chapters 13 and 14 to help you answer this question.

EXAMINER TIP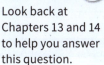

You may want to use the same supporting evidence in different ways to support different comments, but make sure examples are precisely relevant to the focus of the question.

ASSESS THE VALIDITY OF THIS VIEW

 'The USSR in 1941 was still not a communist state.' Assess the validity of this view.

a The first column of this table contains extracts from Marx and Engels' *The Communist Manifesto* (1848). Complete this table by firstly deciding what the extract means and then deciding whether this feature of communism was present in the USSR in 1941.

Features of a communist state	Meaning	Present in the USSR in 1941?
'The proletariat alone is a really revolutionary class'	Only the proletariat can lead a socialist revolution (the key step to communism).	
'The theory of the communists may be summed up in the single sentence: Abolition of private property'		
'The communists abolish countries and nationality' 'The working men have no country'	Communism would be international with no countries or nationalities	Not present. Instead, Stalin had rejected permanent revolution in favour of Socialism in One Country.
The proletariat will 'increase the total productive forces of the state as rapidly as possible'		

b Use the table above to write a definition of what a communist state should look like, according to Marx.

c Use your answers to **a** and **b** to write a complete answer to the exam question.

EXAMINER TIP

Think carefully about what the term 'communist state' means. If you are not clear about this then you will not be able to answer the exam question convincingly.

IMPROVE AN ANSWER

 To what extent had Stalin's Five Year Plans improved the lives of Soviet citizens by 1941?

Consider the following paragraph from a mediocre answer to the essay question above:

Answer

The Five Year Plans were accompanied by forced collectivisation. The conditions on the collective farms were often very poor and many in the countryside died from famine. Others were deported for being kulaks or showing resistance. They were sent to prison camps in Siberia where many of them also died from the harsh conditions. This shows that the Five Year Plans didn't improve living conditions for peasants in the countryside.

a Assess the strengths and weaknesses of this paragraph.

b Write an improved version of this paragraph.

EXAMINER TIP

A good paragraph will begin with an argument, linked to the question, which is then supported by precise and specific information.

REVISION PROGRESS

17 Dictatorship and Stalinism

 **RECAP**

State terror permeated the Soviet Union in the 1930s. The Stalinist dictatorship imposed a brutal repression that affected every aspect of politics, culture and society – partly in order to force through Stalin's policies and destroy any opposition, and partly because of Stalin's paranoid fears for his own survival.

The machinery of terror and show trials was already operating in the early 1930s, but was taken to new depths of intensity after the murder of Kirov in 1934. In 1936, there were show trials against key figures such as Kamenev and Zinoviev. The scale of the terror was masked by the benign constitution of 1936, but terror was the driving force of the regime.

The machinery of state terror, the NKVD and the early purges

- The USSR was already a police state by the end of the 1920s, with the Soviet people under strict surveillance by Party activists and informers.

- Purges of the Party had taken place under Lenin, but these generally led to people losing their Party membership, not to their arrest, imprisonment or execution, as occurred on a large scale under Stalin.
- Lenin had established the Cheka, the secret police, in December 1917. From 1922 to 1934 this became the OGPU (the Department of Political Police).
- In 1934, the OGPU's functions were transferred to the NKVD: the People's Commissariat for Internal Affairs. The NKVD carried out normal police duties and secret police work.
- The NKVD took over the supervision of the Gulag: a network of forced labour prison camps.
- In the early 1930s, the population was not only repressed through arrests and show trials. The enforced famine in Ukraine was also as much an aspect of the Terror as the political arrests. It was an 'economic terror' intended to bring about submission.

Early purges and trials

The following are five early purges and trials carried out under Stalin's regime.

Date	Event	Who was targeted?	Likely explanation for the purge or trial
1928	Shakhty trial	Managers and technicians of the Shakhty coal mine who had questioned the rapid pace of industrialisation. Five were executed and others imprisoned.	To warn others not to criticise the Five Year Plans
1929	Trotsky expelled from the USSR	While others from the Left Opposition had admitted their 'mistakes' to Stalin, Trotsky had never done so.	To remove the leader of the Left Opposition
1930	The 'Industrial Party' trial	A group of senior industrialists and economists accused of planning a coup and plotting to wreck the Soviet economy.	To link the Five Year Plans' economic problems to 'wrecking'
1932	Martemyan Ryutin imprisoned; Zinoviev and Kamenev expelled from the Party	Ryutin criticised Stalin and collectivisation in a long document known as the 'Ryutin Platform'. Stalin said Ryutin intended to assassinate him and wanted him executed. Kirov and others argued against this. Ryutin was imprisoned for ten years instead. Kamenev, Zinoviev and 14 others were expelled from the Party for not reporting Ryutin's document earlier.	To remove Ryutin and purge those suspected of supporting him
1933	Party purge	In 1933, the Communist Party had 3.2 million members, many of whom had joined after membership rules were relaxed in 1929. Over 570,000 'Ryutinites' were expelled in the 1933 purge.	To try to restrict Party membership to Stalin's supporters

Kirov's murder

- Stalin's policies came under attack at the Seventeenth Party Congress (January–February 1934). Some members of the Politburo wanted a slower pace of industrialisation and an easing-off of grain requisition.
- This followed serious economic problems since 1932, including protests over low wages and long working hours. Famine was also killing millions.
- Sergei Kirov, who had previously been one of Stalin's closest allies, now sided with those opposing him. His speech at the Congress received a standing ovation. Kirov was the leader of the Leningrad Party and had a strong power base there; his popularity was a threat to Stalin.
- Stalin's position of General Secretary was abolished and Stalin, Kirov, Zhdanov and Kaganovich were all made 'Secretaries of Equal Rank'. This may have happened with Stalin's approval as a way to share around the blame for the USSR's problems.
- The Seventeenth Party Congress was a major challenge to Stalin. Many of those attending were targeted in the purges that followed.

On 1 December 1934, Kirov was shot by a man called Nikolayev, whose wife Kirov may have been having an affair with.

Stalin blamed the murder on a Trotskyite threat to overthrow the Party.

A day after the murder, Yagoda (head of the NKVD) was given powers to arrest and execute anyone found guilty of 'terrorist plotting'.

Over 100 Party members were shot and thousands were arrested and sent to prison camps.

In January 1935, Zinoviev, Kamenev and 17 others were arrested, accused of causing terrorism, and sentenced to between 5 and 10 years imprisonment.

In June 1935, the death penalty was extended from applying to those engaged in subversive activity to applying to anyone aware of subversive activity who did not report it.

Kirov's assassination was used as a reason (or an excuse) for the regime to begin widespread purges.

The show trials

- Show trials emphasised the threat to the regime from 'enemies of the state', helping to justify the harsh and repressive methods used by the regime to subdue such enemies. They were also used to shift the blame for economic and social problems.
- In the months leading up to a show trial, the NKVD made sure that the accused made a signed confession. Sleep deprivation, beatings, starvation and torture were common.
- In April 1935, it was made legal for those 12 and over to be punished in the same way as adults, including the death penalty. The NKVD used this to extract confessions by threatening to charge the defendant's children.

The Trial of 16, August 1936

The first major show trial was held in August 1936. It featured Kamenev and Zinoviev (along with 14 others). Both accepted responsibility for Kirov's murder (as well as pleading guilty to planning Stalin's murder), and both were executed. For Stalin, this show trial eliminated his old rivals and provided scapegoats for Kirov's murder.

The Stalin constitution

The new constitution, drafted by Bukharin, was introduced in 1936. It was intended to celebrate the triumphs of previous years, and declared that socialism had been achieved in the USSR.

The constitution proclaimed the USSR to be a federation of 11 Soviet Republics. Each republic had its own 'supreme soviet', which met together in the new 'Supreme Soviet' that replaced the Congress of Soviets.

Each republic had some rights of jurisdiction, including primary education. Other rights set out in the constitution included the following:

Ethnic groups were promised autonomy within the Union, with support for national cultures and languages.

Soviet citizens were promised elections every four years, with voting rights for everyone over 18 – including 'former people' (the old bourgeois elites).

Civil rights were set out in the new constitution, such as freedom from arbitrary arrest, freedom of the press, freedom of religion, and the right to free speech.

Citizens were expected to work and were guaranteed work, plus the right to education and social welfare.

There was a contrast between the political freedoms set out for Soviet citizens in the constitution and the reality of state control and repression.

- The promised rights of the constitution were largely ignored in practice. For example, although republics were allowed to leave the Union according to the constitution, Stalin did not allow this to happen.
- However, Soviet citizens did make use of the constitution when making complaints. For example, citizens protesting about anti-religious discrimination referred to their constitutional right to freedom of religion.

> **SUMMARY**
> - The machinery of state terror had been in place since 1918, including purges. But the scope of state terror became much greater in the 1930s.
> - Kirov's assassination triggered a new wave of purges, many aimed at Stalin's old rivals.
> - Stalin's constitution was democratic in theory, but largely ignored in practice.

 **APPLY**

APPLY YOUR KNOWLEDGE

The following table gives selected articles from the 1936 Stalin constitution. What points can you make to challenge or support the idea that these articles were only propaganda? Draw on your own knowledge of Stalin's rule in making your assessment.

> ARTICLE 17. To every Union Republic is reserved the right freely to secede from [to leave] the USSR.

> ARTICLE 122. Women in the USSR are accorded equal rights with men in all spheres of economic, state, cultural, social and political life.

> ARTICLE 125. The citizens of the USSR are guaranteed by law: freedom of speech; freedom of the press.

> ARTICLE 127. No person may be placed under arrest except by decision of a court.

REVIEW

Review Chapter 18 as well as Chapter 17 to help you complete this activity. Chapter 15 may also be useful.

HOW SIGNIFICANT?

A LEVEL **How significant was Kirov's murder in the development of Stalin's use of terror in the 1930s?**

a Complete a table like the following one to provide examples of Stalin's use of terror before and after Kirov's murder. One has been provided for each to get you started.

Examples of Stalin's use of terror between 1929 and December 1934

- One of the many purges before Kirov's death was the Party purge of 1933, where 570,000 Party members were expelled following Ryutin's criticism of Stalin's policies.

Examples of Stalin's use of terror after December 1934 until 1939

- A decree was published a day after Kirov's murder giving the NKVD powers to arrest and execute anyone found guilty of 'terrorist acts'.

b Use your table to write a conclusion to the essay question above.

SOURCE ANALYSIS

SOURCE A

From an account of Kamenev and Zinoviev's show trial, by Denis Pritt, published in Britain in 1936. Pritt, a Labour Party MP, was present at the show trial.

The trial of Zinoviev, Kamenev and other persons accused of participation in terrorist conspiracies against the Government of the Soviet Union, resulting in all the accused being sentenced to death and executed, has given rise to a good deal of criticism in Great Britain. A great deal of this criticism was based on unjustified assumptions that the Soviet authorities had been guilty of abuse.

It seems plain to me that anything in the nature of forced confessions is intrinsically impossible. It must be remembered that we are considering the case of stubborn and infinitely experienced revolutionaries, men who knew most kinds of prisons and most kinds of investigations. If it were the practice of the People's Commissariat for Home Affairs to extract confessions by violence (which I do not think any competent observer believes) no one would be better able than these men to support the violence and subsequently to expose it before the world in the sure hope of discrediting their enemies and gaining sympathy for themselves.

SOURCE B

A note sent by Stalin to his loyal supporter Molotov, about preparations for an early show trial. The note was written on 2 September 1930.

It makes sense to publicise the Kondratev* 'case' in the papers only if we intend to put this 'case' before a court. Are we ready for that? Do we think it necessary to turn this 'case' over to the courts? It would certainly be difficult to get by without a trial.

By the way, cannot the accused gentlemen consider admitting their *mistakes* and generally humiliating themselves politically, at the same time admitting the stability of Soviet power and the correctness of our collectivisation methods? That would not be bad.

About prosecuting communists who assisted the Gromans** and Kondratevs, I agree, but what is to be done about Rykov (*who unquestionably helped them*) and Kalinin (who has clearly been implicated in this 'affair' by the *scoundrel Teodorovich*)? We need to think about this.

* Kondratev, a former Menshevik, was an economist who supported the NEP and had travelled widely in the West. He was arrested and sentenced to 8 years in prison in 1930.
** Groman, a former Menshevik, was a senior member of Gosplan and a statistician who opposed forced collectivisation and rapid industrialisation policies.

SOURCE C

Extracts from speeches by Zinoviev and Kamenev at their show trial in August 1936.

Gregory Zinoviev

I would like to repeat that I am fully and utterly guilty. I am guilty of having been the organiser, second only to Trotsky, of that block whose chosen task was the killing of Stalin. I was the principal organiser of Kirov's assassination. The Party saw where we were going, and warned us; Stalin warned as scores of times; but we did not heed these warnings. We entered into an alliance with Trotsky.

Lev Kamenev

I, Kamenev, together with Zinoviev and Trotsky, organised and guided this conspiracy. My motives? I had become convinced that the Party's – Stalin's policy – was successful and victorious. We, the opposition, had banked on a split in the Party; but this hope proved groundless. We could no longer count on any serious domestic difficulties to allow us to overthrow Stalin's leadership. We were motivated by boundless hatred and by lust of power.

 A LEVEL **With reference to these sources and your own understanding of the historical context, assess the value of these sources to an historian studying the show trials of the 1930s.**

a These are three different types of sources. Explain how the value of each source might be affected by its type. Think about the purpose and audience of each source.

b Think about who wrote each of these sources. Explain how the value of each source might be affected by its author.

c Choose one of the sources and, with the inclusion of your own knowledge about its context, write a full evaluation of its value to an historian studying the show trials of the 1930s.

 EXAMINER TIP

In the exam you will need to do this with all three sources. You are advised to spend about an hour on this question, so each source evaluation should only take around 20 minutes.

18 The Yezhovshchina

RECAP

By 1936, mass terror and repression were already enveloping the Soviet Union in fear, but after the death of Kirov the intensity of terror increased. From July 1937, the **Yezhovshchina** began.

Nikolai Yezhov, who had replaced Yagoda as the head of the secret police in 1936, started the ruthless implementation of NKVD Order 00447. Mass purges followed: of ordinary people, of state bureaucrats, of high-placed Soviet leaders, and of the Army. Countless people were imprisoned by the Gulag (the government agency in charge of the prison camps), or executed. Yezhov himself was shot in 1940. Nothing stopped the reign of terror until the German invasion of Russia in June 1941.

KEY CHRONOLOGY

Stalin and Terror

1929	Expulsion of Trotsky from the Party
1930	Industrial Party show trial
1933	Party purge; mass famine in Ukraine
1934	Seventeenth Party Congress; murder of Kirov
1936	Show trial of Kamenev, Zinoviev and others
1937	The Yezhovshchina and start of the Army purge
1938	Show trial of Bukharin and others; Yezhov replaced by Beria
1940	Assassination of Trotsky

Mass terror and repression at local levels

Stalin gave the NKVD (led by Yezhov between 1936 and 1938) the power to unleash mass terror through a top-secret directive: NKVD Order 00447.

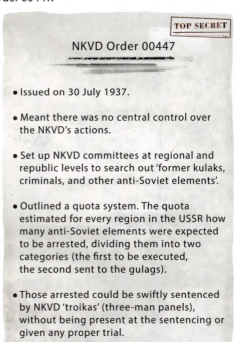

TOP SECRET

NKVD Order 00447

- Issued on 30 July 1937.

- Meant there was no central control over the NKVD's actions.

- Set up NKVD committees at regional and republic levels to search out 'former kulaks, criminals, and other anti-Soviet elements'.

- Outlined a quota system. The quota estimated for every region in the USSR how many anti-Soviet elements were expected to be arrested, dividing them into two categories (the first to be executed, the second sent to the gulags).

- Those arrested could be swiftly sentenced by NKVD 'troikas' (three-man panels), without being present at the sentencing or given any proper trial.

The impact of Order 00447

- Within one month, around 100,000 people had been arrested and 14,000 sent to the gulags. By the start of 1938, around 575,000 people had been sentenced, and 258,000 of them executed. All executions were carried out in secret, as were the disposals of the bodies.

- The NKVD targeted people who were considered dangerous to the regime, such as former members of other political parties, but many 'innocent' people were also caught up in the arrests.

- Pressure to meet and exceed arrest quotas was so great that people started to be arrested randomly. For example, the NKVD picked names out of telephone directories, while people living near factories where there had been a lot of accidents were targeted as wreckers.

- People were encouraged to root out 'hidden enemies'. People denounced their colleagues, friends and family members in the hope of saving themselves.

Mass terror and repression at a central level

The spread of mass terror through the USSR coincided with the Great Purges: a series of show trials of senior Party members and the military.

The Trial of 17, January 1937

Who was targeted?	Likely explanation of purge or trial
17 senior Party members, including Karl Radek and Gregorii Sokolnikov. All confessed and 13 were sentenced to death, accused of plotting with Trotsky, spying and sabotaging industry.	To eliminate potential rivals.

From exile, Trotsky asked 'who can believe such accusations' of these Old Bolsheviks, who were condemned in 'monstrous, impossible, nightmarish trials'.

Military purge, May–June 1937

Stalin feared that the military might try to force him from power after several officers were caught up in the show trials. He decided to purge the military before this could happen.

Who was targeted?	Likely explanation of purge or trial
Marshal Mikhail Tukhachevsky and seven other top military commanders, accused of spying and plotting with Trotsky. All confessed and were executed in June 1937.	Stalin's fear of a military coup.

The 'Great Purge' of the Red Army followed.

- This included some of the most senior officers but also spread throughout the Army ranks. Between 1937 and 1939, over 30,000 army leaders were sacked, with thousands arrested and executed.
- The reason given for the purge was a 'military-fascist' plot with the USSR's enemies in Germany and Japan, as well as a plot to overthrow Stalin.
- Anyone objecting to the trials and purges was arrested too. 74 military officials were shot for refusing to approve the execution of their colleagues.
- Stalin's purge destroyed the Red Army's command structure at the very time that the USSR was increasing military spending against the threat from Nazi Germany.

The Trial of 21, March 1938

Who was targeted?	Likely explanation of purge or trial
Bukharin, Rykov and 19 others. (Tomsky would also have been put on trial, but committed suicide first.) The charge was that Bukharin and the others had plotted to assassinate Stalin and to overthrow the Soviet Union on the orders of Germany and Japan. The accused were all found guilty and executed.	To eliminate potential rivals.

Similar trials were held throughout the USSR, at which Party members were often denounced by their colleagues. As a result, by 1938 a third of all Party members had been purged.

The gulags and the treatment of national minorities

The gulags

- More gulags had been built during the 1930s to house political prisoners and class enemies, and to provide prison-camp labour for Stalin's huge industrial projects.

- The Great Purges from 1937 caused a huge surge in the gulag population, from c800,000 in 1935 to between 5.5 and 9.5 million by 1938, according to some estimates.
- The aim was no longer to re-educate class enemies; prisoners were worked to death or murdered outright.
- Mortality rates in the camps were between four to six times higher than those in the rest of the USSR, as a result of meagre rations, long working hours, and harsh conditions.

The treatment of national minorities

- Stalin was suspicious of minorities from other countries living in the USSR, for example Koreans living in the USSR's Far East and Germans living in the Volga region.
- When war with Japan became a threat in 1937, Stalin had the Korean minority deported to Central Asia. In 1941, over 400,000 Volga Germans were deported to Siberia and Central Asia.
- Stalin also purged the Party leadership of the non-Russian republics. Between 1937 and 1938, virtually all were replaced by those more likely to accept central rule from Moscow.
- Anti-Semitic persecution occurred after 2 million Jews were incorporated into the USSR in 1939–40, following the invasion of Eastern Poland and the Baltic republics. Many rabbis and religious leaders were arrested in these areas.

The end of the purges and the death of Trotsky

The end of the purges

- The pace of the purges slowed after the end of 1938, although Stalin continued to target possible opponents into the Second World War.
- The Yezhovshchina had destabilised the Soviet state and economy, and Stalin pushed the blame for this on to Yezhov.
- The Eighteenth Party Congress declared that 'mass cleansings' were no longer needed.
- Yezhov was secretly tried and executed in 1940; he was replaced by Lavrentii Beria.

The death of Trotsky

In August 1940, Ramon Mercado – a Stalinist agent – assassinated Trotsky. Trotsky had been living in a fortified house on the outskirts of Mexico City.

With Trotsky's death, Stalin ensured that the last of the old Bolsheviks who might have had a greater claim to leadership than him, and who could act as a figurehead for other Stalinist opponents, was no longer a threat.

Responsibility for the Terror and purges

There are different interpretations about the extent to which Stalin or others were responsible for the scale of the Terror, as shown in the diagram below.

Stalin

- The suicide of Stalin's wife in 1932 may have been a trigger for the start of the Terror.
- Stalin's vindictive and even paranoid nature meant he was determined to eliminate potential rivals and seek revenge against old opponents.
- Stalin was personally responsible for promoting the purges. He also had the power to end the purges sooner, but chose not to.

Bolshevik leaders

- The Bolsheviks had always used terror to consolidate and maintain power.
- The Bolsheviks believed all means were justified to defend the revolution.
- Stalin simply escalated this, applying terror on a more ruthless and larger scale.

Who was responsible?

Local Party activists

- Some over-zealous local officials acted on their own agendas.
- Some local Party activists promoted terror but knew their actions would not be checked.

Ordinary individuals

- Terror escalated out of control as individuals chose to denounce others, who in turn denounced others, and so on.
- Individuals denounced others for a variety of reasons, such as out of self-preservation, to settle scores or to remove rivals.

The impact of the Terror and purges

- There are no exact figures on the numbers executed during the Terror. According to figures released from KGB archives in 1995, nearly 650,000 people were executed in 1937–38. The vast majority were ordinary people who had done nothing 'anti-Soviet'.
- According to the same source, the prisoner population of the gulags increased by 1 million between 1937 and 1938. Other sources put the figure much higher (an increase of 8 million is suggested by some).
- The families of those executed or imprisoned for anti-Soviet crimes were punished as well. They lost their jobs, were evicted from their homes, often exiled or sent to the gulag for being 'a member of the family of a traitor to the Motherland'. Children were discriminated against as 'a child of an enemy of the people'.
- 850,000 Party members were expelled between 1936 and 1938. By 1939, less than 10 per cent of the Party had joined before 1920.
- The military purges meant the loss of around 23,000 experienced officers. Many new officers had to be recruited as the Red Army increased in size (it grew from under 1 million in 1936 to 5 million by 1941).
- The military failures of the first months of the war must have had some link to the loss of these experienced officers from throughout the military administration.
- Skilled personnel (such as engineers, planning specialists, teachers and academics) were purged at the time when rapid industrialisation depended on their skills.

- On the other hand, the purges created a lot of opportunities for others to progress their careers. The fear of denunciation also made bureaucrats and managers do their jobs more carefully.
- By the end of the purges, Stalin was in a position of supreme power. He was a dictator with absolute control over the Party and a subservient populace.

SUMMARY

- The Yezhovshchina brought mass terror to all levels of society, from the centre to local levels and from Moscow out to all republics of the USSR.
- The Party, the military and national minorities were a focus of the Yezhovshchina.
- Denunciations and the quota system led to indiscriminate arrests at a local level.
- The gulag system changed and became more extreme. Instead of being 'class enemies' who needed re-education, prisoners were seen as 'anti-Soviets' to be starved and worked to death.
- From the end of 1938, the scale and pace of the purges was slightly reduced due to the damage being done to industry and administration, but mass repression continued right up to the German invasion of Russia in June 1941.
- Stalin's personal responsibility for the Terror and purges is open to debate, as is the impact they had.

 **APPLY**

APPLY YOUR KNOWLEDGE

Copy and complete this timeline by adding any key events or developments you regard as important to the unfolding of the Terror. Use Chapter 17 as well as Chapter 18 to help you.

1928 The Shakhty Trial
1929 Trotsky expelled from the USSR
1934 The Seventeenth Party Congress, where support was given for Kirov's more moderate line
1937 NKVD Order 00447 starts the Yezhovshchina
1940 Trotsky assassinated

TO WHAT EXTENT?

 To what extent was Stalin personally responsible for the mass terror of the 1930s?

a The following boxes name different individuals or groups of people who could be considered responsible for the mass terror of the 1930s. For each group, fill in supporting evidence concerning their responsibility.

Stalin	Bolshevik leaders
Local Party officials and activists	**Ordinary individuals**

b Write a few sentences to explain your judgement on the extent to which Stalin was personally responsible.

c Use your answers to **a** and **b** to write a complete answer to the essay question.

APPLY YOUR KNOWLEDGE

Use your knowledge of the machinery of state terror and the Yezhovshchina to answer the following questions.

Question	Answer
What were the gulags?	
What connects Yagoda, Yezhov and Beria? Add dates to your explanation.	
Who killed Kirov in December 1934?	
Who claimed responsibility for Kirov's murder in August 1936?	
Who was the target of NKVD Order 00447?	
Which of the following was not executed after the Trial of 21 in March 1938: Bukharin, Rykov or Tomsky? Why?	

REVIEW

Some exam questions will require you to draw on more than one chapter. Doing activities that require you to look at different chapters of this book will help you prepare for this. There are particular pairs of chapters that it would be helpful to revise together: chapters 17 and 18 are one example.

EXAMINER TIP

Part **b** of this activity will help you to sustain a line of reasoning from the beginning of your answer all the way through to your concluding paragraph.

REVISION SKILLS

You could prepare a similar list of revision questions on this or any other topic and use them to test yourself. If you are revising in a group, every person could prepare a list of questions and use them to test each other.

KEY CONCEPT

Dictatorship is a key concept in the study of revolution and dictatorship in Russia 1917–53.

Complete the spider diagram below to identify the different elements of dictatorship in the Stalinist regime during the 1930s. Add one or two supporting details to each element.

The cult of personality

Ideological control

Elements of Stalin's dictatorship in the 1930s

Propaganda

EXAMINER TIP

Key concepts in this option include: Marxism, communism, Leninism, Stalinism, ideological control and dictatorship. This option is also designed to allow you to explore issues of political authority, the power of individuals, and the inter-relationship of governmental and economic and social change.

PLAN YOUR ESSAY

A LEVEL **How significant was mass terror and repression in Stalin's political dominance of the USSR in the late 1930s?**

a   Write a sentence or two to explain how each of the following factors contributed to Stalin's political dominance of the USSR in the late 1930s.

EXAMINER TIP

Make sure you include specific details and examples, as depth examination papers will expect these at the highest levels.

Factor	How did it contribute to Stalin's political dominance?
Stalin's 'Great Turn'	
The growing threat of war from Germany and Japan	
Collectivisation and the Five Year Plans	
Stalin's cult of personality	
Mass terror and repression	

b   Which factor or factors do you think were most significant to Stalin's political dominance? Explain your reasoning.

c   This table could serve as an essay plan for the exam question above. Write an introduction and a conclusion that would fit with this plan.

19 Culture and society

Culture had a significant place in the USSR. It was used to promote and instil the propaganda ideals of the Soviet system, and was part of the transformation of mass society. On the one hand, culture was seen a positive force, providing education, moral guidance and entertainment for the people, as well as legitimacy for the Soviet state and its ideology. On the other hand, culture was also a weapon of repression and enforced conformity.

The impact of Stalinism on the Church

Under Stalin, the Church came under more sustained attack:

- Religious schools were closed down and the teaching of religious creeds was forbidden. By 1941, nearly 40,000 churches had been destroyed.
- Sunday was abolished as a religious day of rest. Workers worked for six days a week, with one-sixth of all workers having their day off on any one day of the week.
- Many priests were victims of the purges. For example, 4000 priests were imprisoned.
- However, while the power of the Church as an institution was broken, religious faith continued to be important to many Soviet citizens.

Other religions

Other religions were also targeted:

- Soviet Muslims suffered as their property and institutions (land, schools and mosques) were seized and their Sharia courts were abolished. Pilgrimages to Mecca were forbidden from 1935 and the frequency of prayers, fasts and feasts was reduced. This led to a backlash in Central Asian regions where some traditionalist Muslims murdered those who followed the Soviet orders. Many Muslim priests were also imprisoned or executed.
- Jewish schools and synagogues were closed down, and there were attacks on Buddhist institutions.

The impact of Stalinism on women

Trotsky called Stalin's social policies the 'Great Retreat', as they were seen as a retreat from the radical social experiments of the 1920s, which aimed to liberate women and men from bourgeois traditions and roles. A new 'family code' became law in June 1936, which:

- made abortion illegal
- banned contraception

- gave tax breaks to mothers with six or more children
- made divorce more difficult to obtain and more expensive
- made adultery a criminal offence.

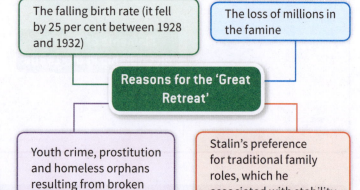

The falling birth rate (it fell by 25 per cent between 1928 and 1932)

The loss of millions in the famine

Reasons for the 'Great Retreat'

Youth crime, prostitution and homeless orphans resulting from broken families

Stalin's preference for traditional family roles, which he associated with stability and discipline

Impact of the 'Great Retreat'

The 'Great Retreat' had a limited effect:

- The number of abortions dropped sharply from 1.9 million in 1935 to 570,000 in 1937, but then began to increase again, reaching 755,000 in 1939. This was despite abortions becoming a criminal offence in 1936.
- After a slight rise, the birth rate fell again from 1938 and never reached pre-revolutionary levels.
- Although women were encouraged to give up paid work when they married, the numbers of women working in factories and on collective farms continued to increase. In 1928 there were 3 million women working in the USSR; by 1940 this had increased to 13 million.
- Encouraging traditional marriage meant that in 1937, 91 per cent of men and 82 per cent of women in their thirties were married, but the divorce rate remained high (37 per cent in Moscow in 1934).
- Working women were still expected to do housework and childcare rather than these tasks being shared by both men and women.

The impact of Stalinism on young people

In the 1920s, education prioritised ideology over knowledge. Stalin saw the 1920s' education policies as a disaster, failing to produce the skilled workers, scientists and technicians that the country needed. In the 1930s the USSR returned to more traditional education, emphasising technical subjects and practical skills.

- In 1935, the quota system was abandoned and selective secondary schools now accepted only the most able, with no preference for children of proletariats.
- Selective secondary schools had a rigid academic curriculum, which also promoted nationalism and military training in the pre-war years. Discipline was reintroduced. Exams, which Lenin had banned, were reintroduced.
- Higher education was put under the control of Vesenkha. The emphasis was on producing industrial specialists though courses in maths, science and technology.
- There was a USSR-wide focus on improving literacy. From around 65 per cent of people being literate before 1917, by 1941 around 94 per cent of the population in towns were literate, and 86 per cent in the countryside.

Komsomol

Komsomol (the Soviet youth organisation) increased in importance under Stalin.

- Komsomol was for 10–28 year olds, with 10–15 year olds being 'Young Pioneers'.
- Komsomol encouraged socialist values (for example by organising voluntary work) and discouraged selfish or unhealthy behaviour (such as drinking alcohol).
- There were special 'palaces' for Young Pioneers, and free summer and winter holiday camps.
- Komsomol had always had close links to the Communist Party, and became directly affiliated in 1939.
- Members took an oath to live, study and fight for the Fatherland. They helped carry out Party campaigns and assisted the Red Army and police.
- Many Komsomol members were enthusiastic about fulfilling the Five Year Plans. For example, many volunteered for building mega-projects like Magnitogorsk and Komsomolsk.
- Komsomol membership was a big commitment but offered a chance for social and political advancement.

The social disruption caused by collectivisation and rapid industrialisation contributed to a large rise in the numbers of orphaned and abandoned children. The regime linked these children to 'hooliganism'. This was one reason why children 12 or older who committed violent crimes were to be tried as adults.

Although a minority of youths did not conform to the Party's expectations and were interested in (largely forbidden) Western culture, direct confrontation between young people and the Soviet system was rare, despite the regime's preoccupation with 'hooliganism'.

The impact of Stalinism on working men

The Revolution had promised 'all power to the soviets', but while skilled working men generally did well, Stalinism hit the unskilled workers badly.

Skilled working men	Unskilled working men
• Improved opportunities from training and education. • Wage differentials from 1931 meant skilled workers were paid more. • The Stakhanovite movement from 1935 gave some workers some power over managers. • A skills shortage in the 1930s meant good workers were in high demand.	• Many former peasants, escaping collectivisation, found harsh labour discipline difficult to manage. • Many unskilled workers moved from place to place to avoid getting a bad working record. • Living conditions for the unskilled were poor and overcrowded, with little or no privacy.

Urban and rural differences

Overall, life in the 1930s was better in urban areas than in the countryside. This changed after 1941 as rationing was reintroduced, as rural inhabitants could grow some food for themselves.

Life in the USSR under Stalin

	Positives	Negatives
Urban areas	• Regulated hours and wages • Workplace canteens and shops • Some public transport • Free education • Opportunities for skilled workers	• Overcrowded living conditions • Practically no privacy in communal apartments • Denunciations from neighbours • Often a lack of basic services, e.g. sewage • Water was rationed • Problems with crime • Food shortages (especially in 1933 and 1936)
Rural areas	• Better access to food • Collective farms often had health clinics and schools • Access to private plots • Free education	• State control over the countryside • Trauma from collectivisation • Fear of purges and continued focus on 'kulaks' • State requisitioning of most produce • Grinding poverty • Low status

The socialist man and woman

Building socialism was partly about building a new type of citizen: the **socialist man** and woman, or *'homo sovieticus'* ('Soviet human'). This was linked to the pseudo-science of Trofim Lysenko, who believed that socialist qualities developed in one generation could be inherited by the next.

'Party-minded': dedicated to the Party and its needs

Educated in socialism and science

Works for the good of everyone, not for themselves

Qualities of the socialist man and woman

Urban and modern, not rural and traditional

Part of a community; not independent or private

Self-sacrificing: putting the Party above family or friends

Enthusiastic campaigners for socialism and against bourgeois values

The impact of cultural change

- Stalin's insistence that Soviet culture must help build socialism was taken up enthusiastically by Komsomol members and some creative figures, who produced 'socialist realist' works or attacked those creating 'bourgeois' art .
- However, many of the artists and writers of the time who are valued today were targeted by the regime or realised it was best to remain silent, such as the poet Anna Akhmatova, the novelists Boris Pasternak and Mikhail Bulgakov, and the composer Dmitri Shostakovich.
- Historian Dr John Barber suggests that only one-fifth of workers fully supported the regime, with others not persuaded by the regime's propaganda.

Similarities and differences between Lenin's and Stalin's USSR

Lenin's USSR by 1924	Stalin's USSR by 1941
Old Bolsheviks carried authority	Old Bolsheviks had gone; the new generation owed everything to Stalin
Secret police (Cheka) established	Secret police (NKVD) had wide powers over society
Terror used against real or potential enemies	Widespread terror and purges used in a seemingly arbitrary way (although the worst had passed by 1940)
Censorship and control but some opportunity to experiment in the arts; freedom in schools and limited Party influence in rural areas	Strong elements of totalitarianism in all aspects of society and culture; little opportunity for independent thought and action

SUMMARY

- Stalin's 'Great Retreat' reversed the radical social experiments of Bolshevism after the Revolution, especially in regard to women's roles in society, education, cultural expression (including religion), and the role of workers.
- The effect of Stalinism on Soviet society had mixed results. The birth rate continued to fall, despite bans on contraception. Women continued to work, despite propaganda about traditional family values. Skilled workers made the best of their opportunities, but few truly believed in building socialism. Religion came under sustained attack, but religious faith remained important to many people throughout the USSR.
- The repression and totalitarianism of Stalinism was on a larger scale to that of Lenin. However, there was continuity between Lenin and Stalin, as well as change.

 **APPLY**

APPLY YOUR KNOWLEDGE

Copy and compete the table below, by listing the main qualities of the socialist man and woman, and explaining how these qualities were expressed or encouraged in the USSR during the 1930s.

Quality of the socialist man and woman	How this was expressed or encouraged in the USSR during the 1930s
Educated in socialism and science	• Komsomol, which increased in importance under Stalin, had close links to the Communist Party and encouraged socialist values in young people. • Courses in maths, science and technology were given more importance in higher education. • Skilled scientific workers were paid more and had better working conditions.

 **EXAMINER TIP**

Always think carefully about the words used in exam questions. In this case, reflect on the word 'equal'; this can be examined from many angles, such as political equality, social status, working opportunities and pay, educational opportunities and legal rights.

ASSESS THE VALIDITY OF THIS VIEW

A LEVEL 'Women and men were equal in the USSR during the 1930s.' Assess the validity of this view.

a Copy and complete the table below to give evidence for and against the statement in the exam question.

Evidence to support the statement	Evidence to counter the statement

b Use this table to write a conclusion to the exam question, in which you give a judgement and support this with reasoning.

REVIEW

You might find it useful for this activity to look back at page 76.

PLAN YOUR ESSAY

A LEVEL 'The skilled workers were the only social group to benefit from Stalinist policies in the 1930s.' Assess the validity of this view.

a Make a list of the benefits gained by skilled workers under Stalinism (link to specific policies if you can). Then add any ways in which this group suffered under Stalin.

b Make a list of other social groups and note the ways they benefited or suffered under Stalinism (again, link to specific policies where possible).

c These lists could form the plan for your answer to the essay question above. Write an introduction that would fit with this plan.

20 Stalin and international relations

After the 1917 Revolution, Soviet Russia was internationally isolated. The West feared being 'infected' by the spread of communism and was wary of the role of the Comintern. The USSR feared counter-revolution.

However, the USSR needed trade with other countries to pay for industrialisation. At first only Germany would deal with the USSR. The Treaty of Berlin in 1926 built on the foundations of the 1922 Treaty of Rapallo, and had significant economic benefits for both countries. It also opened the way for the USSR to join the League of Nations.

Stalin's rapid industrialisation depended on foreign expertise, especially from Germany and the USA. However, the early purges turned against foreigners and the USSR became gripped by fears of an imminent invasion by the capitalist countries, and increased threats from Japan.

Cooperation with Germany

The most intensive period of Soviet cooperation with Germany was from 1929 to 1932.

- German expertise helped industrialisation in the USSR (of the 9000 foreigners working in the USSR in 1930, around 70 per cent were German; most of the rest were American).
- The USSR benefited from German military training; the Germans benefited from access to areas in the USSR in which they could carry out military developments banned under the Versailles Treaty.
- Germany was the USSR's biggest export market, while the USSR was a major customer for German manufacturing.
- In 1931, Germany and the USSR negotiated the continuation of the Berlin Treaty.

Stalin may have welcomed Hitler's rise to power as a sign of weakness and division between the capitalist countries. When Hitler became Chancellor in 1933, however, Stalin moved away from cooperation with Germany towards a greater emphasis on collective security.

Soviet entry into the League of Nations

The USSR was invited to join the League of Nations in September 1934.

Benefits to the West	Benefits to the USSR
Bringing the USSR into the League strengthened collective security against aggression from Germany or Japan (both of whom had withdrawn from the League in 1933).	Offered the potential for international cooperation against the anti-communist Hitler. Gave the USSR the opportunity to influence the actions of Britain and France.

Pacts with France and Czechoslovakia

Despite the obvious threat to the USSR from Hitler's regime, Stalin was slow to react, even when the German Communist Party (KPD) was severely repressed by the Nazis. Possibly, Stalin may have hoped for Germany, Britain and France to weaken each other in a war while a neutral USSR grew stronger.

However, Stalin did seek new alliances with other countries threatened by German aggression:

November 1932	Non-aggression pact with France
December 1932	Non-aggression pact with Poland
May 1935	Mutual assistance pacts with France and Czechoslovakia

The pact with Czechoslovakia said that the USSR would intervene militarily if Czechoslovakia was attacked by another country (i.e. Germany) as long as the French did the same. However, the pacts were not followed by any serious military planning.

The Comintern's policy switch

Stalin's willingness to form alliances encouraged a complete reversal in the Comintern's policy, which was officially announced at the Comintern Congress in 1935. Instead of targeting democratic socialists, foreign communist parties were encouraged to form 'popular fronts' with the socialists in order to fight fascism.

Soviet intervention in the Spanish Civil War

Civil War broke out in Spain in July 1936, as fascist-supported nationalists aimed to overthrow the socialist Republic.

- Stalin decided to intervene in the war in September 1936. Soviet support (consisting of military equipment and Soviet 'advisors') was significant in helping the Republic to hold off the nationalists in the first part of the war.
- In 1937, Stalin moved to a strategy of prolonging the Spanish Civil War in the hope of wearing down German and Italian forces fighting on the nationalist side.
- Stalin was disappointed by the weak response to the Civil War from France and Britain in the opportunity to fight fascism in Spain. This signalled to Stalin that the Western powers might continue to be weak against the threat from Nazi Germany.
- Soviet intervention exacerbated fear and dislike of Soviet communism in the West, weakening the prospects of future collaboration.

Reaction to Western appeasement and Japanese aggression

Western appeasement and the Munich conference

France and Britain protested against the German annexation of Austria in March 1938, but took no other action. Britain's prime minister, Neville Chamberlain, believed that the appeasement of Hitler was the best way to achieve peace in Europe.

At the Munich conference (September 1938), Germany, France, Britain and Italy discussed how to deal with Germany's claims to the Sudetenland. However, Czechoslovakia itself and the USSR were excluded from the conference. (The Sudetenland was the German-speaking region of Czechoslovakia that bordered Germany. Hitler claimed it should be 'protected' by becoming part of Germany, and used this as the reason for Germany's subsequent invasion of Czechoslovakia in March 1939.)

This approach sent a clear signal to the USSR that it should not expect any robust opposition from the West to stop further German aggression, or expect the West to join Soviet Russia in an anti-Hitler alliance.

The Soviet response to Japanese aggression

In the 1930s, Stalin was very concerned about Japanese aggression; Japan's military dictatorship had built up a powerful war machine.

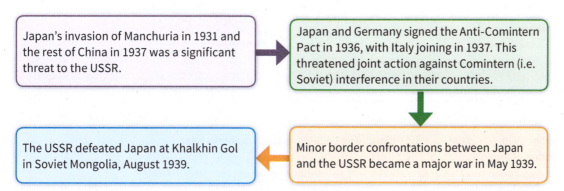

Japan had seriously underestimated Soviet military strength and tactics. 75 per cent of its forces at Khalkhin Gol were killed. Japan very much left the USSR alone afterwards, although the war confirmed to Stalin the need to remain militarily strong in the Far East.

The Nazi-Soviet Pact and its outcome

- The Nazi-Soviet Pact (signed on 23 August 1939) agreed that Germany and the USSR would respect each other's territories, increase trade and settle disputes peacefully.
- A secret part of the Pact divided eastern Europe into a German sphere of influence and a Soviet sphere of influence.
- Even after the Nazi-Soviet Pact, Stalin still kept up a dialogue with Western democracies and the USSR continued anti-Nazi propaganda campaigns.

Reasons for the Pact

On the one hand, Stalin's policy towards Germany can be seen as inconsistent, veering from cooperation to conflict. On the other hand, it can be seen as utterly consistent, always focused on keeping the USSR safe from war.

The Pact came as a shock to contemporary observers but could be interpreted as a 'delaying measure' on the part of the USSR. Stalin was well aware that Hitler planned a Soviet invasion at some point, yet the Red Army was not ready for war in 1939, following the purges and administrative confusion over rearmament.

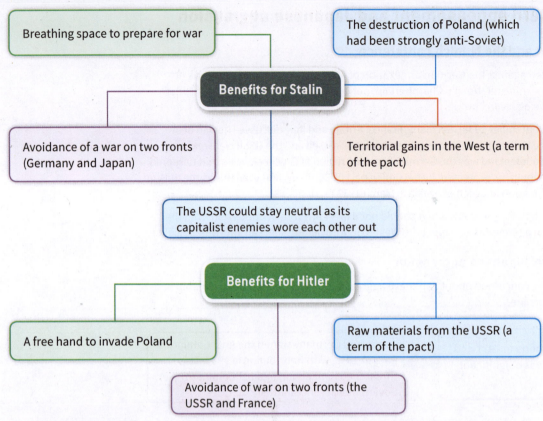

Outcome of the Pact

- At the start of September 1939, Germany invaded Poland. The USSR invaded two weeks later, leading to the destruction of Poland.
- The Pact meant Hitler was free to send his armies westwards without fear of Soviet reprisals in the East. He defeated France in May 1940.
- The USSR seized control of the Baltic States (Estonia, Lithuania and Latvia) in 1940.

The USSR also invaded Finland in November 1939. This 'Winter War' of 1939–40 showed how weak the Red Army was following Stalin's purges. A peace was agreed in March 1940, and Finland gave up 10 per cent of its territory to the USSR.

Stalin's mistakes

Although the Nazi-Soviet Pact brought the USSR some time to prepare and rearm, it provided only temporary safety for the USSR:

- Stalin had calculated that Hitler could not invade the USSR until May 1942 at the earliest, buying the USSR plenty of time to get ready. However, it took the Germans just six weeks to defeat most of Western Europe (by June 1940). Nor was the German war machine exhausted: it was stronger and more motivated than ever.
- Stalin thought he could trust Hitler. He ignored warnings from the USSR's extensive spy network that suggested Hitler had, by October 1940, already begun preparations for the invasion of the USSR.
- As a result, when the invasion came on 22 June 1941, the USSR was still a long way from being fully prepared.

SUMMARY

- From 1924, Stalin attempted to avoid foreign entanglements while concentrating his attention on the internal transformation of the USSR; but avoiding foreign dangers often involved tactical changes of policy.
- In the late 1920s and early 1930s there was cooperation with Germany; this changed with the rise of Hitler.
- The USSR joined the League of Nations in 1934 and was open to mutual defence pacts with other countries, but lost faith in this approach after the Munich conference in 1938.
- Stalin's actions in 1939, the war against Japan and the Nazi-Soviet Pact showed his defensive mind-set and concern for survival.
- The fall of France in 1940 removed the protection offered by Stalin's pact with Hitler and left the USSR exposed to invasion.

APPLY

APPLY YOUR KNOWLEDGE

a   Complete the table below, which identifies possible turning points in Stalin's relations with Germany. Think about what happened and the effect each one had.

Potential turning point	How did it change relations between Germany and the USSR? What effects did it have?
The Treaty of Berlin, 1926	
Hitler becomes Chancellor of Germany, 1933	
Japan and Germany sign the first Anti-Comintern Pact, 1936	
The USSR is excluded from the Munich conference, September 1938	
The German invasion of Czechoslovakia, March 1939	

REVIEW

Go back to page 63 to read about the Treaty of Berlin.

ASSESS THE VALIDITY OF THIS VIEW

 A LEVEL 'Stalin's foreign policies in the 1930s were contradictory.' Assess the validity of this view.

a   The entries in the second column below are mixed up. Put them in the right order so each one provides a contrast to one of the foreign policies in the first column.

b   Complete the third column of the table by explaining why each policy in the second column is a contrast to the one in the first column.

Foreign policies of the 1930s	Contrasting foreign policies	Why was it a contrast?
From 1928, the Comintern aimed to purge foreign communist parties of democratic socialists.	Soviet intervention in the Spanish Civil War (1936–39).	
In the Berlin Treaty between Germany and the USSR, both sides promised neutrality in the event of any attack on the other.	From 1934, the Comintern encouraged communist parties to cooperate with democratic socialists.	
The USSR joined the League of Nations in September 1934. The League aimed to solve disputes through negotiations rather than conflict.	The Nazi-Soviet Pact (August 1939).	
The USSR signed a non-aggression pact with Poland in December 1932. This banned alliances that 'damaged' the other country.	The Franco-Soviet Pact of Mutual Assistance (May 1935).	

c   Consider counter-arguments to the view that Stalin's foreign policies in the 1930s were contradictory. In what ways were some policies consistent? Try to give at least three specific examples.

d   Use your answers to **a**, **b** and **c** to write a conclusion to the exam question.

EXAMINER TIP

A good conclusion will state the view you have adopted in relation to the exam question, and summarise the evidence you have considered to reach this judgement. It should not introduce new information, nor should it be too long.

IMPROVE AN ANSWER

 To what extent was the Nazi-Soviet Pact the result of Western policies and actions towards the USSR during the years 1929 to 1939?

The following paragraph is an introduction to the question above. Read it carefully.

Answer

Western policies and actions in the years 1929 to 1939 were not very favourable towards the USSR. The West disapproved of communism, and Stalin's purges and show trials made them very suspicious. They were not ready to fight Hitler and felt Germany had been badly done by at Versailles anyway. Western policies meant that the USSR was not invited to the Munich Conference and it was this action that drove Stalin to make the Nazi-Soviet Pact.

This introduction addresses the key factor that prompted Stalin to sign the Nazi-Soviet Pact, but it is narrow in scope and does not recognise other factors that influenced the signing of the Pact. Rewrite the introduction so it presents a view but shows an awareness of other factors too.

A Level sources sample answer

REVISION PROGRESS

 REVIEW

On these Exam Practice pages you will find a sample student answer for an A Level sources question. What are the strengths and weaknesses of the answer? Read the answer and the corresponding Examiner Tips carefully. Think about how you could apply this advice in order to improve your own answers to questions like this one.

REVISION SKILLS

The A Level exam paper will have one source question that is compulsory; the question will be focused on three primary sources or sources contemporary to the period. Read page 6 of this revision guide for help on how to master the sources question.

A LEVEL With reference to these sources and your understanding of the historical context, assess the value of these sources to an historian studying the Stalinist Terror in the 1930s.

30 marks

SOURCE A

From an interview in 2004 with Viacheslav Kolobkov about his memories of mass terror in the 1930s. He recalls the impact of the terror on his father, a factory worker.

Every night he would stay awake – waiting for the sound of a car engine. When it came he would sit up rigid in his bed. He was terrified. I could smell his fear, his nervous sweating, and feel his body shaking, though I could barely see him in the dark. 'They have come for me!' he would always say when he heard a car. He was convinced he would be arrested for something he had said – sometimes, at home, he used to curse the Bolsheviks. When he heard an engine stop and the car door slam, he would get up and start fumbling in panic for the things he thought he would need most. He always kept these items near his bed in order to be ready when 'they' came for him. I remember the husks of bread lying there – his biggest fear was going without bread. There were many nights when my father barely slept – waiting for a car that never came.

SOURCE B

From a private diary entry for 29 November 1937 by a writer, Mikhail Prishvin. Prishvin used microscopic writing in the hope no one else could read the diary.

Our Russian people want so much to talk to one another. But as soon as someone gives in, he is overheard by someone else – and he disappears! People know they can get into trouble for a single conversation; and so they enter into a conspiracy of silence with their friends. One of my dear friends was delighted to spot me in a crowded train compartment, and when at last a seat was free, he sat down next to me. He wanted to say something but was unable to say it in such a crowd. He became so tense that every time he prepared himself to speak he looked around at the people on one side of us, and then at the people on the other side, and all he could bring himself to say was: 'Yes.' And I said the same in return to him, and in this way, for two hours, we travelled together from Moscow to Zagorsk:

'Yes, Mikhail Mikhailovich.'

'Yes, Georgii Eduardovich.'

SOURCE C

From a speech by Nikita Khrushchev to the Congress of the Soviet Communist Party in 1956, in which Khrushchev, the then Communist leader, criticised Stalinism.

By fighting the Trotskyists and Rightists, the Party was strengthened so it was able to organise the working class and build socialism. But once the Party's opponents were defeated, repression against them began. Stalin's concept of 'enemy of the people' made cruel repression possible against anyone who disagreed with him or those merely suspected of hostile aims. Stalin was convinced that the Terror was necessary for the defence of the interests of the working class against its enemies' plotting and against attacks by foreign imperialist countries. He saw this from the position of the working class and the interests of the victory of socialism and communism. We cannot say that these were the deeds of a reckless dictator. He considered that this should be done in the interests of the Party, of working masses, and in the name of defence of the revolution's gains.

Sample student answer

Source A is an interview with someone about his memories of his father's behaviour during the mass terror. If Kolobkov was interviewed in 2004 about something he experienced in the 1930s, he must be quite elderly. That could affect the reliability since he might have added elements to his memory based on other people's experience of mass terror. This could limit the value of this source. However, this is only surmised and clear memory in old age often reflects the impact of events at the time, so the source remains valuable.

The source describes how Kolobkov's father was afraid of being taken by nameless persons (the secret police) every night, because he was frightened that someone had heard him 'curse the Bolsheviks'. The source is vivid, with Kolobkov remembering not just what his father said and how he behaved in general (sitting up rigid in bed, shaking and fumbling in panic), but also the smell of his father's fear and the details of what his father had prepared in case he was taken (the husks of bread). This vivid and emotive tone is useful in conveying the oppressive and fearful atmosphere of the mass terror.

It is also useful to know that Kolobkov's father feared being denounced for cursing the Bolsheviks at home, as this suggests that he was frightened of having being overheard by neighbours, or possibly by his own family members. Either was possible, in fact likely. For example, a common form of denunciation was the 'apartment denunciation', when one family sharing a communal apartment would denounce the other family in order to get them evicted. Or there was the propaganda about the boy who denounced his family and was murdered.

The Soviet state was supposed to be a dictatorship of the proletariat, and previous purges and terror had been directed at 'class enemies', Trotskyites, and 'wreckers'. Workers in underperforming factories or factories with a lot of accidents were often targeted by the NKVD. Overall, the source has some value for understanding more about the mass terror at the local level, but mainly its provenance limits its value – the source is probably too distant from the events it describes for an historian to be sure of its reliability.

The author of Source B was a writer, which means he was probably observant and interested in how people expressed themselves, but also may mean he had a tendency to fictionalise elements of his diary. A private diary is valuable, especially as Prishvin took steps to make it difficult to read (in case it was seized by the secret police).

This primary source is from the height of the mass terror, adding to its value to historians. The Yezhovshchina intensified with the issue of NKVD Order 00447 in July 1937, which set up regional-level quotas for criminals, 'anti-Soviet elements' and 'former kulaks'. Within a month of the Order, 100,00 people had been arrested and 14,000 sent to the gulags. The pressure to fill (and overfill) the quotas was so great that in some places the NKVD selected people almost at random. Because Source B is from this particular period of mass terror, it is useful for understanding the impact at the level of ordinary life.

Source B is critical of the purges ('as soon as someone ... is overheard by someone else – and he disappears'), which is valuable as it helps with the question of whether people at the time believed they were surrounded by 'anti-Soviet elements', or whether they instead recognised that anyone could 'disappear' if they were overheard saying 'a single sentence'. Prishvin clearly does not think that he and his friend are 'anti-Soviet elements', because like everyone else they just 'want so much to talk to one another' but were 'unable to say it in such a crowd'.

Overall, however, the authorship of Source B by a writer undermines its value to the historian because the story that it tells is not very believable; a two-hour journey in which two people only say 'yes' and each other's names would be a good scene from a novel, but it seems likely that the author has exaggerated the incident.

Source C is from a speech by Nikita Khrushchev. As he was the Communist leader when he spoke, he would have authority and also direct experience of Stalinist rule. However, his desire to criticise Stalin may reflect his personal ambition to establish himself as a different type of leader. He spoke to the Congress of the Soviet Communist Party which would mean he was trying to convince the ruling body of the USSR of his views, which could well encourage exaggeration. He gave this speech in 1956, three years after Stalin's death, which suggests that he had spent some time preparing this attack. This would have given him time to assemble facts and ensure his argument was secure. Overall the provenance adds to the value of the source for the historian studying the Terror, although readers would have to take into account Khrushchev's own position and ambition.

The tone and emphasis in Source C are critical of the excesses of the Stalinist Terror. Khrushchev seems to accept the early actions against 'Trotskyists and Rightists', which he says helped to strengthen the Party, but he condemns later repression. He talks of 'cruel repression', emphasising his hostility to Stalin's actions when almost anyone could be deemed an 'enemy of the people'. The tone is authoritative as he is trying to set out his case as hard fact to his

EXAMINER TIP

The student demonstrates excellent context knowledge here, but more could have been done to link this context explicitly to the source and to the focus of the question.

EXAMINER TIP

The student selects some relevant material from the source to show how the tone of the source demonstrates the author's criticism of the justification for mass terror, and is able to link this to the source's value.

EXAMINER TIP

This judgement about Source B needs to be developed further to be more effective. Judgement should comprise the evaluation of both provenance and content, and should not be based on supposition that something might be true, even though there is no evidence to confirm it.

EXAMINER TIP

The student makes a number of interesting points about provenance here, linking to author, audience and purpose and date. However, none of the observations are developed and little own knowledge is employed.

EXAMINER TIP

This is a short but direct paragraph. It addresses tone and emphasis, and shows an understanding of the main message of the source (although it does not refer to the final two sentences of the source, which show that Khrushchev did not wish to take his criticisms too far). With a little more development and contextual own knowledge, this paragraph would have offered some very good evaluative comment.

audience. The source therefore provides a valuable view of the Terror, seen with hindsight, and indicates some of the strong feelings it roused.

Source C is also valuable for its content. It is interesting to observe that Khrushchev made it clear that 'anyone who disagreed with' Stalin or 'those merely suspected of hostile aims' were liable to persecution. Details of those detained in gulags or placed under house arrest would support such claims. The motivation for the Terror is also addressed, and Khrushchev suggests that Stalin believed the Terror was necessary for the defence of the working class against its enemies' plotting and 'against attacks by foreign imperialist countries'. This is useful information coming from a man who had been close to Stalin, but we cannot be sure whether it was Stalin's 'excuse' or a real belief. Much of Stalin's behaviour seemed quite paranoid at this time and there is little actual evidence of plotting having taken place.

The final part of Source C is of value because it shows that even critics of Stalinism, like Khrushchev, did not entirely condemn him for the excesses of the Terror. It is suggested that it was all in a 'good cause' ('the victory of socialism and communism'). Khrushchev believes that the Terror was carried out in the interests of the Party, the workers and the revolution. This comment would be valuable in understanding the Terror from a different, ideological perspective.

EXAMINER TIP

This extends the evaluation to the content and makes some good observations. However, the contextual own knowledge is thin.

EXAMINER TIP

The student could have used contextual knowledge here to back up the points made, but this paragraph shows a good understanding, linked to both the source and the question.

OVERALL COMMENT

The student shows an (often very good) understanding of all three sources. The key points of provenance – author, date, purpose and audience, as well as tone and emphasis – are addressed although they are not always developed fully. There is some attempt to put the sources into their historical context, but this is the weakest part of the answer, particularly for Source C. This answer is likely to reach a mid Level 4.

OVER TO YOU

Give yourself 55 minutes to answer this question. Then review the Examiner Tips on these pages to check whether you have avoided making the same mistakes as the sample student answer.

❏ Did you write about all three sources separately and avoid making comparative comments?

❏ Did you comment on the author, date, purpose and tone of each of the sources?

❏ Did you comment on both the value and limitations of each source?

Go back and look at pages 87–93 to help refresh your knowledge on Stalinist Terror.

6 The Great Patriotic War and Stalin's dictatorship, 1941–1953

REVISION PROGRESS

21 The Great Patriotic War and its impact on the Soviet Union, 1941–1945

 **RECAP**

Stalin had signed the Nazi-Soviet Pact in 1939 believing that it would buy his under-prepared country more time before any Nazi invasion of the USSR. Stalin continued to trust in the Pact, despite intelligence reports warning him about German preparations for invasion, months before it began.

The war, which Stalin had tried so hard to avoid, nearly destroyed the USSR; but fighting the war, and ultimately achieving victory, transformed the Soviet Union into a military-industrial superpower.

KEY CHRONOLOGY

The Great Patriotic War

1941	June	German invasion of the USSR
	December	German offensive pushed back from Moscow
1942	June	New German offensive towards the Caucasus oilfields
	October	German advance halted at Stalingrad
1943	February	German surrender at Stalingrad
	July	New German offensive defeated at Kursk
	November	Kiev liberated by the Red Army
1944	January	Siege of Leningrad ends
	December	Soviet forces reach Budapest
1945	January	Warsaw captured by the Red Army
	February	Yalta summit meeting to plan post-war world
	May	Final defeat of Germany
	August	Surrender of Japan

Operation Barbarossa and the Stalinist reaction

Operation Barbarossa

- Operation Barbarossa (the codename for the German invasion of the USSR) was launched on 22 June 1941. It was intended to win a decisive victory in a matter of weeks, well before the onset of winter.
- The invasion was originally planned for 1 June, but was delayed until 22 June following the Nazi invasion of Yugoslavia.
- The invasion forces were split between three huge army groups, one heading towards Leningrad, one into Ukraine, and one towards Moscow.

Stalin's immediate reaction

- Stalin had taken no direct action in the spring to prepare for a German invasion, either because he did not believe it would happen or because he worried that if he increased Soviet defences, this would provoke attack.
- When the German attack came on 22 June 1941, Stalin did nothing. It was nearly two weeks before he spoke publicly about the invasion. Molotov, Stalin's foreign minister, made a radio broadcast in his place on 22 June.
- Stalin's speech on 3 July stressed themes of patriotism, religion and unity. He called on all the peoples of the USSR to join a patriotic war against fascism.

Poor leadership was an issue in the early stages of the war:

- Stalin was indecisive (for example, preparations to move the capital from Moscow to Kuybyshev (Samara) were cancelled at the last minute on Stalin's orders).
- The Soviet army had inexperienced commanders (Stalin had removed the most experienced officers in his military purges of 1937).
- Stalin refused to allow his southern armies to retreat from Kiev until it was too late. This brought a massive defeat in the south in September 1941.

The course of the war

There were three main stages in the Great Patriotic War.

	Stage 1	Stage 2	Stage 3
Dates	June 1941 to summer of 1942	1942 to summer of 1943	1943 to summer of 1945
Summary	Soviet Russia struggled to survive against successive German offensives, suffering massive losses of people and territory.	Soviet Russia stabilised its war effort, built a powerhouse war economy, and halted German advances.	Soviet armies moved on to the offensive, recapturing vast areas that had been occupied, and finally defeating the Germans.
Key dates	• 8 Sept 1941: siege of Leningrad begins • 5 Dec: German advance on Moscow halts; the first sign of German hesitation in the war • 23 Aug 1942: bombardment of Stalingrad begins	• 2 Feb 1943: Surrender of German Sixth Army at Stalingrad • 12 July: Battle of Prokhorovka • 13 July: Kursk offensive called off	• 6 Nov 1943: liberation of Kiev • 28 Nov: Tehran summit • 4 Jan 1944: Soviet troops enter Poland • 27 Jan: siege of Leningrad ends
Key details	• 3 million German troops invaded the USSR in June 1941. • The German advance was swift and there were huge losses for the Soviets (e.g. 665,000 troops were captured at Kiev). • On 15 October the Soviets attempted peace negotiations but Hitler ignored their offer.	• The war was turning into a war of attrition and Hitler did not have the resources to compete. • Mass production of the T-34 tank was central to Soviet success in the Battle of Prokhorovka.	• From August 1943 onwards there was a chain of Soviet victories across Eastern Europe, but the Germans were resilient defenders and it took until April 1945 for the Red Army to reach Berlin.
Turning points	18 October 1941: Intelligence reports from Japan allowed Stalin to bring troops back from Siberia to defend Moscow. This, plus bad weather conditions, meant German capture of Moscow was avoided.	2 February 1943: Hitler made a major error in refusing to pull his troops out of Stalingrad. The defeat of his Sixth Army was a military and psychological disaster for the Germans.	12 Jul 1943: The Soviet victory at Prokhorovka was a springboard for Soviet counter attacks. This was the start of the Soviet offensive that eventually won the war.

The USSR under occupation and the fight back

- The Soviet Union was ravaged by the war, first by the huge destruction caused by the German advance, then by the Soviet 'scorched earth' tactics as the Red Army retreated.
- Life for civilians on the Home Front was unrelentingly harsh. Food, fuel and shelter were all in short supply. Many factories, hospitals and houses were destroyed.
- Approximately 12 million civilians died in the war. Of those alive in the USSR when the war started, one in eight were dead by 1945. 1700 towns and cities and 70,000 villages were also destroyed in the war.

German and Soviet brutality and repression contributed to the suffering:

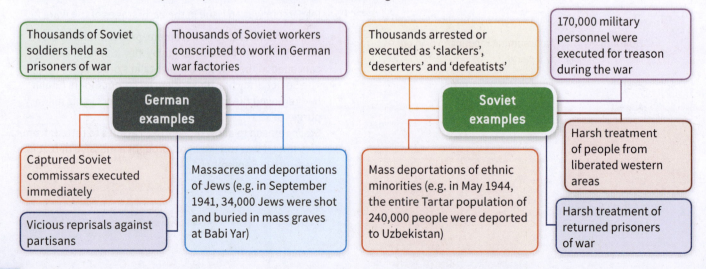

The fight back

The experience of total war, shaped by massive propaganda campaigns, brought Soviet people together. While some criticised the war and Stalin's leadership (and were punished if caught), huge sacrifices were made by millions to defend their country. Powerful unifying factors included:

- fear and hatred of the Germans (helped by German repression and cruelty)
- deep patriotism in defending the Motherland
- an underlying faith in Stalin and the defence against fascism.

The Soviet war economy

Mobilisation and evacuation of industry

Rapid mobilisation

In the early stages of the war, Stalin's errors lost millions of Red Army men and equipment. However, Stalin increased mobilisation rapidly.

In 1941, the Red Army had 4.8 million soldiers. Conscription to the Red Army over the course of the war added 29.5 million.

This rapid and massive conscription was a major strength for the USSR.

The evacuation of industry

The German invasion and occupation of the western regions of the USSR destroyed the basis of the Soviet economy, in both industry and agriculture.

Soviet industry was relocated from western areas to the Urals and further east, beyond the reach of German bombs.

Whole factories were dismantled and moved, together with equipment and workers, via 20,000 trains to the east. For example, 500 factories were moved from Moscow.

Improved military resources

During 1942, the USSR began to build a huge industrial base for war production, especially guns, tanks and aircraft.

The centrally controlled command economy proved to be particularly effective during wartime, helping the USSR to produce the resources it needed.

Huge improvements were made to military vehicles (such as tanks and aircraft) and to military tactics. The T-34 tank, for example, was equal to the German Tiger tank in close-up fighting but was also quick to manufacture and easy to repair.

The USSR could withstand the loss of thousands of T-34 tanks in battle because it had the capacity to build thousands more in its factories hidden away from German attack in the Urals mountains.

Foreign aid

- The scale of foreign aid given to the USSR was vast. Huge quantities of armaments, industrial goods and foodstuffs were transported to the USSR from the USA. For example, 300,000 American trucks were supplied through the US Lend-Lease scheme (a US policy in which the USA supplied its allies, including the USSR, with food, oil and military equipment between 1941 and 1945).
- The USSR downplayed the scale of foreign aid, but it is clear that it was an important factor in the USSR's ability to mobilise for total war, and vital in the winter of 1942 to 1943, when the USSR was recovering from heavy losses earlier in the war.

SUMMARY

- Stalin nearly lost the war during its early stages, but the experience of eventually defeating Germany turned the USSR into a major superpower.
- The war left its mark on the entire population, but also created a great national myth of shared heroism and sacrifice.
- By 1945, the Red Army had liberated the Soviet people and the defeat of Germany looked imminent.

APPLY

ASSESS THE VALIDITY OF THIS VIEW

> **A LEVEL** 'The Soviet victory in the Great Patriotic War was the result of Stalin's command economy.' Assess the validity of this view.

a Copy and complete the first column of the following table by identifying links between factors in the Soviet victory and the Soviet command economy. One has been done for you.

b Copy and complete the second column of the table by adding reasons for the Soviet victory that were not linked to the command economy. One has been completed for you.

Factors in the Soviet victory	Links to the Soviet command economy?	Ways in which the command economy was not significant
Geographical reasons	The command economy helped plan and organise the movement of factories and workers from the west to safety in the east.	The vast size of the Soviet Union meant that the supply lines to the advancing German armies became dangerously overstretched.
Military reasons		
Other reasons		

c For each factor, decide whether you think the reason(s) linked to the command economy was more significant than the reason(s) without a link to the command economy. You could show this by ticking the reason you consider more significant in each case.

d Use your answers to **a**, **b** and **c** to write a complete answer to the essay question.

EXAMINER TIP
This activity will help you to answer questions that require you to assess the extent of one factor in the Soviet victory against other factors.

REVIEW
Chapter 22 also covers reasons for the Soviet victory, so review that chapter as well when completing this activity.

REVISION SKILLS

On a piece of A3 paper, draw a timeline to chart the key events in the Great Patriotic War. Annotate the timeline with key pieces of information, to help you jog your memory when you revise.

You could add colour to your timeline by highlighting Soviet advances or victories in one colour and German advances or victories in another. This would help you to see how the course of the war changed in favour of the Soviets.

SOURCE ANALYSIS

SOURCE A

From Stalin's radio broadcast to the Soviet people, 3 July 1941.

It is a matter of life and death for the Soviet state, life and death for the peoples of the USSR. Are the people of the Soviet Union to be free or fall into slavery? The Soviet people must cease to be carefree; they must mobilise themselves and restructure all their work on a new wartime basis, showing the enemy no mercy.

We must organise every kind of help for the Red Army, ensure its ranks are replenished more intensively, ensure it is supplied with everything it needs, organise the rapid movement of troop and materiel transports and fully assist the wounded.

We must organise a merciless struggle against all disorganisers on the home front, against deserters, scaremongers, rumour-mongers, spies and saboteurs. Anyone at all who gets in the way of our defence with their scaremongering and cowardice must immediately face a military tribunal.

SOURCE B

From Order Number 270, an order written by Stalin on 16 August 1941 and read to all of the USSR's armed forces.

There have recently been a number of shameful acts of surrender into enemy captivity. Certain generals have given bad examples to our troops.

My orders are as follows:

1. Commanders and political workers who rip off their badges of rank in battle and desert to the rear or surrender to the enemy are to be considered malicious deserters. Their families are to be arrested as the families of deserters who have violated their oath and betrayed their Motherland. Commanders and commissars are obliged to shoot such deserting officers on the spot.

2. Units and subunits who are surrounded are to fight selflessly as long as possible, guarding material as the apple of their eye, fight their way back through enemy lines, inflicting defeat on the fascist dogs.

SOURCE C

From secret NKVD reports from November 1941 on public morale in Arkhangel'sk, in the far north of Russia.

This was the mood in the Arkhangel'sk region: 'Everyone was saying that we'd be fighting the enemy on his territory, but just the opposite… Our government's been feeding the Germans for two years when they should've saved the food for our army and people, and now we'll be going hungry.' Such sentiments are not confined to ordinary workers and peasants. Party member and former Civil War partisan declared, 'The Germans are giving us what for, but our people don't have the enthusiasm that was there in the Civil War, especially amongst us partisans. We went out and inspired them ourselves. The present leaders aren't able to organise the masses and raise their spirits.'

Party secretary of the Arkhangel'sk transport administration, declared, 'Our government made loads of boastful speeches, saying we had massive stocks of everything, about how we'd be fighting the enemy on his territory, but in fact it's turned out quite the opposite'.

 With reference to these sources and your own understanding of the historical context, assess the value of these sources to an historian studying the reaction to Operation Barbarossa.

a Copy and complete the following table.

	What does the source tell us about the reaction to Operation Barbarossa?	Why might this source be valuable for an historian studying Operation Barbarossa?	What are the limitations of the source to an historian studying Operation Barbarossa?
Source A			
Source B			
Source C			

b Give an example from your knowledge of historical context that helps you to understand each of these sources.

c Use your answers to **a** and **b** to write a complete answer to the essay question.

 EXAMINER TIP

In your answer remember to evaluate both the provenance and content of the sources.

22 The defeat of the Germans

 **RECAP**

By the end of 1944, the tide of war had turned decisively against Germany. The Red Army had overrun much of East Central Europe and millions of refugees were fleeing to the west. But the final defeat of Germany took many months and cost millions of lives.

Victory over Germany was a huge Soviet achievement, but the rewards of victory did not come quickly or painlessly. Abroad, relations with the Western Allies were difficult. Within the USSR, more sacrifices were demanded of the people to carry through post-war reconstruction.

The defeat of the Germans

- The Germans fought to the bitter end, partly because the Allies insisted on an unconditional surrender. This slowed the Red Army's advance but could not stop it. By early 1945, the USSR had a huge superiority in men, weapons and war production.
- Stalin wanted the Red Army to gain control of as much of Central Europe and Germany as possible by the end of the war. This was because he wanted a buffer zone against any future threats to the USSR. Stalin was willing to accept huge casualty rates in the Red Army in order to advance westwards as fast as possible.
- US General Eisenhower agreed to slow the Allies' advance into Germany from the west to allow the USSR to win the 'race to Berlin'. This was partly to reduce Allied casualties and partly to prevent a confrontation with Soviet forces.
- In April 1945, the Red Army reached Berlin. The final battle for Berlin saw huge losses on both sides (80,000 Soviets and 150,000 Germans). This was partly because Stalin insisted on speed rather than careful planning.
- Germany surrendered unconditionally to the USSR on 9 May 1945. Hitler had committed suicide on 30 April, and the Red Army won the final battle for Berlin on 2 May 1945.

Reasons for the defeat of the Germans

German weaknesses

- Hitler's strategy was based on securing a rapid victory. Once this failed the odds were against Germany.
- From December 1941, Germany had to fight a two-front war.
- Germany lacked self-sufficiency in raw materials. By 1943–44, resources became a problem.
- Hitler made crucial strategic mistakes. He replaced experienced generals with 'yes men'.
- Harsh German repression in occupied countries increased resistance movements and partisans.

Soviet strengths

- The USSR's vast geographical size:
  ○ German supply lines were stretched too far by the end of 1941.
  ○ The size of the USSR enabled whole new armies, and a whole new industrial base, to be built up in the east, beyond Germany's reach.
- Population size (171 million in 1941, three times the size of Germany's): the USSR could replace losses in a way that was impossible for the Germans.
- Natural resource wealth (such as oil): from 1942 the USSR could out-produce German war industries.
- The Soviet 'command economy': well-suited to total war and the emergency mobilisation of workers and resources.
- Military leadership: after a bad start, Stalin's Stavka (military command) became ruthlessly effective.
- Propaganda and patriotism motivated the armed forces and civilians to fight and endure (for example, 4 million people volunteered for citizens' defence in 1941).

The contribution by the Allies

- Stalin's allies meant Hitler was fighting on two fronts.
- Mass bombing campaigns by the British and Americans from 1943 inflicted huge damage on Germany's war effort.
- Allied secret intelligence, gained by code-breaking, undermined Germany's war effort at crucial times.
- Enormous amounts of vital military and economic aid poured into the USSR (see page 111).

The results of victory for the USSR

The USSR became a superpower

- The war unleashed the USSR's economic potential
- The war badly weakened other European powers

Communist ideology was vindicated

- Communism was seen to defeat fascism
- This increased the attraction of a 'socialist road' to development

Stalin was held up as the USSR's saviour

- The cult of Stalin was strengthened

There was a massive territorial expansion of the USSR and its 'sphere of influence'

- The Baltic States became Soviet republics
- Pro-Soviet regimes were established in Eastern European countries

There were devastating costs for the USSR

- At least 20 million Soviet citizens were killed
- Much of the economy and infrastructure were destroyed

Cold War tensions developed

- Stalin feared the USA's influence in Europe
- There were disagreements over the future of Germany

Post-war reconstruction: industry

Stalin promised in 1945 that the USSR would be the world's leading industrial power by 1960. Gosplan worked on a fourth Five Year Plan in 1945, launching it in March 1946. Reconstruction of Ukraine was a particular focus, as it was an important industrial and agricultural region that had been devastated by the war.

Soviet industry faced major problems in adjusting back to peacetime conditions:

- In 1945, mining production, electricity generation and steel production were around half of 1940 levels.
- The transport infrastructure was badly disrupted.
- The workforce was exhausted and depleted by wartime sacrifices.
- The end of foreign aid added significantly to pressures on industry.
- A high investment in military production (25 per cent of total expenditure by 1952) as a result of the **Cold War** meant less investment in other areas.

However, industrial recovery under the fourth Five Year Plan was rapid and successful:

- Many of the Plan's targets were met or exceeded. For example, more coal, oil, steel, cement and electricity were all being produced in 1950 compared to 1940.
- By 1950, Ukraine's industrial output was also higher than before the war.
- There was also some improved production of consumer goods under the fourth Five Year Plan, for example cotton fabrics, wool fabrics and sugar were back to pre-war production figures by 1950. (However, production of shoes, clothes and furniture lagged

behind pre-war levels, which had already been inadequate to meet demand.)
- As early as 1948, average Soviet incomes were back to 1938 levels.

Reasons for the rapid recovery included:

War reparations transferred masses of material from Germany to the USSR

Central planning was able to enforce the mass mobilisation of people and resources

The people were proud of the USSR's victory and willing to make further sacrifices

A 'rebound effect' (recovery from a low base) enabled rapid rebuilding of essential services

Post-war reconstruction: agriculture

Agriculture in 1945 faced major challenges:

- Large numbers of farms had been destroyed in the war (98,000 collective farms were ruined according to official statistics).
- Large quantities of farm machinery had been destroyed and livestock numbers were also seriously depleted.
- Food production in 1945 was at 60 per cent of 1940 levels.
- Deaths and injuries from the war meant a major shortage of farming labour.
- 1946 was also the driest year since 1891, and famine hit parts of Ukraine and central Russia in 1946–47, killing an estimated 1.5 million people.

While other parts of the economy recovered quickly, agriculture's recovery was slow and patchy.

- The fourth Five Year Plan brought some increases but failed to reach most of its targets.
- Famine in 1946–47 highlighted the serious problems faced in agriculture.
- Stalin's writings on the Soviet economy (*Economic Problems of Socialism in the USSR*) blocked reform in agriculture. For example, payments for farm products were still kept very low, taxes were increased, and in 1948 a ban on selling food grown on kolkhozniks' private plots was reintroduced.

SUMMARY

- Victory in the Great Patriotic War was achieved at a great cost, but turned the USSR into a global superpower.
- The USSR was able to win a war of attrition once Hitler's strategy for rapid victory had failed.
- The Soviet industrial economy recovered rapidly after the war, though agriculture continued to struggle.

APPLY

APPLY YOUR KNOWLEDGE

a Add the reasons for the USSR's victory in the Great Patriotic War to the following table.

Geographical reasons	Military and strategic reasons	Political reasons	Contributions by the Allies	Other reasons

REVIEW

Chapter 21 also includes reasons for the USSR's victory.

b Write a paragraph in which you show how some of these reasons link together and influence each other.

Here is an example to illustrate:

The USSR was able to build up its economic resources in the east (*economic reason*), and output soared because the political command structure was able to demand huge sacrifices from the Soviet citizens (*political reason*), whose patriotism had been whipped up by propaganda and who were accustomed to obey without question even before war began (*social reason*).

EXAMINER TIP

This activity will help you to develop your understanding of causation and show your awareness that historical factors do not exist in isolation.

PLAN YOUR ESSAY

A LEVEL **How successful was post-war industrial and agricultural reconstruction in the years 1946 to 1953?**

a Write one or two sentences to set out what you understand by 'success' for post-war industrial and agricultural reconstruction.

b Complete the table below.

	Evidence for success	Evidence for limited success
Industrial reconstruction		
Agricultural reconstruction		

EXAMINER TIP

Including a consideration of the meaning of terms like 'success' in your planning will help you to write answers that fully engage with the question's focus.

c Use your answers to **a** and **b** to write an introduction to the essay question.

23 'High Stalinism', 1945–1953

 RECAP

During the Great Patriotic War, many aspects of Stalin's dictatorship were softened, as the regime sought to mobilise the patriotism of the people. After victory was achieved, however, Stalin turned back to repression, authoritarianism and paranoia. In these years of 'High Stalinism', the cult of personality reached even greater heights. Both the rulers and the ruled lived in a climate of fear until the death of Stalin in March 1953.

Dictatorship and totalitarianism

'High Stalinism' was the culmination of Stalin's regime, lasting from 1945 to 1953. It was the most extreme expression of Stalinism.

Key features of High Stalinism included:

> Unchallenged leadership by Stalin

> An extreme form of dictatorship

> Stalin as the heroic leader of the Great Patriotic War

> The Stalin cult portrayed him as god-like and apart from others

> A secret police state: renewed terror

> Cultural purges in the name of ideological 'purity'

> The Party and its institutions weakened or ignored

> Rivalries and plots amongst Stalin's inner circle

> Stalin increasingly withdrawn and paranoid

> Deep suspicion of any influences from outside the USSR

> A lack of policy reform due to stagnation and inertia at the top of the governmentat

During the war some aspects of Stalin's dictatorship had been relaxed. For example, religion was tolerated and churches were reopened. But after the war, Stalin's dictatorship became even stronger than before.

- The Party was sidelined; there were no Party congresses between 1939 and 1952. The Politburo and Central Committee did only what Stalin ordered.
- The Red Army and its heroes were downgraded, so they would not challenge Stalin. For example, in 1946 war hero Marshal Zhukov was sent to faraway Odessa to a lower-level command.
- Stalin's inner circle were kept divided by Stalin's schemes and their own rivalries. For example, Malenkov and Beria plotted against Zhdanov and engineered his downfall in 1948.
- Terror was renewed to ensure people gave their absolute obedience to the state (**totalitarianism**).

Renewed terror

Stalin ruthlessly enforced the USSR's isolation from the non-socialist world. This was partly for security reasons as the Cold War intensified, but also for fear of Soviets losing their ideological commitment, for example if they saw how much better people lived in other countries.

- Around 15 per cent of 1.8 million returned prisoners of war were sent to the gulags. (It was an offence for any Red Army soldier to surrender, and there were also suspicions that they might have collaborated with the Germans.)
- Any contact with foreigners could get a person denounced and arrested. A 1947 law outlawed marriage to foreigners.
- Foreign travel by Soviet citizens was tightly controlled. Few were allowed to leave the USSR.
- The sense of terror was pervasive and tens of thousands of Soviet citizens continued to be arrested during Stalin's last years, sometimes for no more than a careless few words. In total, around 12 million wartime survivors were sent to the gulags.

The NKVD under Beria

After the war, Lavrentii Beria was not only NKVD chief, but also deputy prime minister, a full member of the Politburo, and the head of the USSR's atomic weapons programme.

The NKVD under Beria was strengthened and reorganised as two separate ministries:

- the MVD (Ministry of Internal Affairs), which controlled domestic security and the gulags
- the MGB (Ministry of State Security), which handled counter-intelligence and espionage.

Zhdanovism and the cultural purge

- Andrei Zhdanov was appointed to lead cultural policy in 1946.
- He insisted that Soviet artists and writers followed Party lines: socialist realism, the praise of Stalin and Soviet achievements, and criticism of American commercialism and inequalities.
- Those whose work did not embody socialist realism had to publicly apologise in order to continue working.

Zhdanovism began with the purge of two literary works: Zoshchenko's *The Adventures of a Monkey* (which seemed to be mocking the difficulties of Soviet life) and a collection of poems by Anna Akhmatova (which were criticised for lacking ideological content). The writers were expelled from the Union of Soviet Writers.

In music, Shostakovich and Prokofiev were two of the composers criticised for 'rootless cosmopolitanism' and 'anti-socialist tendencies'. They were removed from their teaching posts and Prokofiev's wife was imprisoned.

Western cultural influences were blocked. It was impossible to get non-communist foreign newspapers, and only a few approved foreign books were translated into Russian.

Soviet scientific development was hampered by Trofim Lysenko's dominance over the Academy of Sciences; new theories or lines of research were suppressed if they somehow contradicted Marxist principles.

Stalin's cult of personality

- Building on his reputation as the saviour of the USSR, Stalin was portrayed as the world's greatest living genius, equally superior in all areas of philosophy, science, military strategy and economics.
- For example, it became customary for all books and articles to start and end with a paragraph acknowledging Stalin's genius on the subject.
- Stalin's victory in the Great Patriotic War replaced Lenin's October/November Revolution as the greatest event of Soviet (and Russian) history.
- Stalin was portrayed as a man of the people, who was instinctively in touch with what the average worker was thinking, but in fact he was increasingly isolated and often misled by his own propagandists.
- Towns and cities competed for the honour of being named after Stalin; there was even a movement for Moscow to be renamed Stalinodar.
- Stalin prizes were launched in the USSR after it was felt that Soviets were being excluded from winning as many Nobel prizes as they deserved.

The Leningrad affair; purges and the Doctors' Plot

The Leningrad affair

- Stalin was suspicious of the Party's base in Leningrad because his rivals had often built up a power base there (including Trotsky, Zinoviev, Kirov and, by 1948, Zhdanov).
- Stalin also did not like the way Leningraders glorified their heroic struggle to survive their 872-day siege during the Great Patriotic War. There had been accusations that Stalin could have done more to help the city, such as airdrops of food or large-scale evacuations.
- In 1948, Zhdanov appeared to be out of favour with Stalin. When Zhdanov died of a heart attack in August 1948, Stalin launched a purge of the Leningrad Party.
- Leading Party officials, such as Nikolai Voznesenski, were arrested, interrogated and executed in 1950. Most of these people had owed their positions to Zhdanov.
- By 1950, 2000 Party officials had been dismissed and replaced by pro-Stalin communists.

Purges

The Leningrad affair was the first major Party purge since 1938. More followed, increasing the climate of fear.

- The next was the 'Mingrelian Case' in 1951, targeted at Party officials in Georgia who were mainly from the Mingrelian ethnic group.
- Beria was a Mingrelian, and the accusations were mainly against followers of Beria. Many were also accused of conspiring with 'Jewish plotters'.
- Stalin was using the accusations to contain Beria's power. The accusations were still being made at the time of Stalin's death.

The Doctors' plot

- A doctor (and police informer) called Lydia Timashuk accused the doctors who had treated Zhdanov of contributing to his death in August 1948.
- In 1952, Stalin used this complaint as a reason to arrest many Jewish doctors for participating in a 'Zionist conspiracy' to harm the USSR on behalf of Israel and its ally, the USA.
- Other Jewish people were caught up in the purge, including the Jewish wives of Molotov and Kalinin. Thousands of ordinary Jewish people were also arrested and deported to the gulag.
- Nine senior doctors were condemned to death, but Stalin's own death saved them from execution.

SUMMARY

- High Stalinism meant renewed terror, a heightened cult of personality and unchallengeable dictatorship by Stalin.
- Stalin used rivalries between members of his inner circle to stop anyone getting too powerful, together with purges and false accusations to get rid of possible challengers.
- By 1953, Stalin's total control had paralysed the USSR. Everyone was too terrified of Stalin's disapproval to suggest anything new or challenge his ideas.

APPLY

APPLY YOUR KNOWLEDGE

SOURCE A

From a translation of Zoshchenko's *Adventures of a Monkey*, which was first published in a children's magazine in 1945, then in a Leningrad journal called *Zvezda* in 1947.

Now at this time a certain old man was walking along the street. The retired soldier Gavrilich. He was going to the public bath. And he was carrying in his arms a small basket, which contained soap and clean underwear.

He saw the monkey and at first didn't believe his eyes that it was a monkey. He thought he was seeing things, since he had just had a mug of beer. He looked at the monkey in astonishment. And the monkey looked at him. Maybe the monkey thought, What kind of a scarecrow carrying a basket is that?

Gavrilich finally realised that it was a real monkey and not an imaginary one. Then he thought, Why don't I just catch him? I'll take him to the market tomorrow and sell him for a hundred roubles. And with that money I'll drink ten mugs of beer in a row.

a Write a definition of socialist realism, and explain why it was important for writers to follow socialist realist principles in their work.

b Read the extract above carefully. Zoshchenko's story was criticised by Zhdanov for not providing a more inspiring vision of Soviet life. Give an example from this extract of something you think Zhdanov would not have approved of.

c One of Zhdanov's criticisms of Zoshchenko was that his work suffered from 'individualism'. What do you think being called an 'individualist' meant in the USSR, and why was it a bad thing?

EXAMINER TIP

This activity will help to give you a better understanding of the type of writing that was frowned upon in Zhdanovism. You could use Zoshchenko's work as an example when writing about Zhdanov's cultural purge.

REVIEW

Review pages 79–80 to remind yourself about the meaning of socialist realism and its importance in Stalin's USSR.

REVISION SKILLS

a Create a timeline for the period of 'High Stalinism' (1946 to 1953).

b Colour code your timeline to distinguish political, economic, military and social/cultural themes.

KEY CONCEPT

Dictatorship is a key concept in the study of revolution and dictatorship in Russia 1917–53.

Add to the spider diagram below, to complete the picture of Stalin's dictatorship between 1945–53.

Key features of Stalin's dictatorship, 1945–53

The Party was sidelined

Emphasis on terror and control

IMPROVE AN ANSWER

A LEVEL 'In the years 1945 to 1953, the Soviet Union was a one-man dictatorship, but it was not a totalitarian state.' Assess the validity of this view.

Read the following conclusion from a student's answer to the exam question.

Answer

The USSR under Stalin definitely was a totalitarian state. Totalitarianism was at its height in the years of High Stalinism between 1945 and Stalin's death in 1953. When his cult of personality was so strong, it was not possible for anyone to ignore Stalin's orders or say (and perhaps even think) anything contrary to the wishes of the ruler. Even Stalin's inner circle lived in fear. Terror and purges such as the Doctors' Plot and the Leningrad Affair ensured that no one dared do anything other than conform. Cultural figures were closely controlled by Zhdanov who made them practise socialist realism. Workers and peasants were expected to devote themselves to the state without question.

a In your own words, write a sentence to explain the main difference between life in a one-man dictatorship and life in a totalitarian state.

b Create a table with two columns to record the ways in which the USSR was and was not a totalitarian state between 1945 and 1953.

c Rewrite the conclusion to support the view that 'the USSR was more a one-man dictatorship than a totalitarian state in the years 1945 to 1953'.

EXAMINER TIP

Understanding key terms like 'dictatorship' and 'totalitarianism' will help you to use them meaningfully in essays. While a dictatorship can be defined as government by a ruler with total power over his people, 'totalitarianism' suggests a system of government in which all aspects of individual life are subordinated to the authority of the ruler.

APPLY YOUR KNOWLEDGE

Complete the following table. What evidence is there to support the view that the following aspects of Stalinism underwent: a change after 1945; continuity after 1945?

Aspects of Stalinism	Evidence for a change after 1945	Evidence for continuity after 1945
Use of terror	The Doctors' Plot showed a new focus on anti-Semitism and is evidence that Stalin's paranoia and isolation increased after the war.	Stalin's use of terror after 1945 had the same aims: a focus on possible enemies of the state, which also allowed Stalin to weaken possible opponents (e.g. the Leningrad Affair).
Dictatorship		
Personality cult		
Command economy		
Industrialisation as a priority		
Cultural control (socialist realism)		

24 The transformation of the Soviet Union's international position

 **RECAP**

In 1941, the USSR had been hopelessly unprepared for war, in danger of being overrun by the German invasion. By 1945, Stalin presided over a victorious superpower.

Victory in the Second World War enabled Stalin to establish a wide sphere of influence in East Central Europe, but Soviet expansion led to a breakdown in relations with the West and the onset of the Cold War. By the time Stalin died in 1953 there were huge pressures for change in the USSR, both in foreign and domestic policies.

KEY CHRONOLOGY

The Soviet superpower

1944–45	Advance by the Red Army into East Central Europe
1945	Summit conferences at Yalta and Potsdam
1947	US Marshall Plan and 'Truman Doctrine'
1948	Communist coup in Czechoslovakia
	Start of the Berlin Blockade
1949	End of the Berlin Blockade
	Successful test of the Soviet atom bomb
1953	The death of Stalin

The emergence of a 'superpower'

By the end of the Great Patriotic War the USSR had emerged as a global power. Its status as the world's only other superpower (to rival the USA) was confirmed when, in 1949, it successfully tested an atomic bomb.

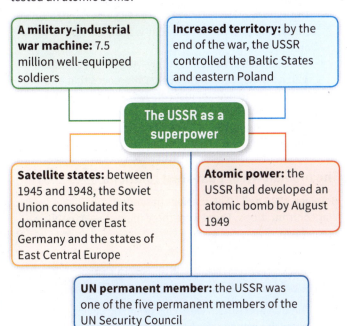

A military-industrial war machine: 7.5 million well-equipped soldiers

Increased territory: by the end of the war, the USSR controlled the Baltic States and eastern Poland

The USSR as a superpower

Satellite states: between 1945 and 1948, the Soviet Union consolidated its dominance over East Germany and the states of East Central Europe

Atomic power: the USSR had developed an atomic bomb by August 1949

UN permanent member: the USSR was one of the five permanent members of the UN Security Council

The formation of a Soviet bloc

- By 1948, most of the Eastern European countries had either been absorbed into the USSR or turned into **satellite states**, governed by parties closely linked to the USSR.
- In some cases this involved 'salami tactics', in which communist parties joined with socialists and liberals to gain power, but then isolated and eliminated their rivals 'slice by slice'.
- Stalin hoped that this buffer zone of satellite states would help to protect the USSR from a future invasion by the West.

A provisional government was set up in Lublin in 1945, dominated by pro-Moscow communists

Eastern Germany became a Soviet zone of occupation in 1945; Moscow-trained communists took political control in 1946

'Salami tactics' enabled pro-Soviet governments to control Hungary (1947) and Czechoslovakia (1948)

The Baltic States were occupied by the USSR in 1940 under the terms of the Nazi-Soviet Pact

Eastern Poland was annexed by the USSR in 1939 under the terms of the Nazi-Soviet Pact

Communists led by Josip Tito gained control of Yugoslavia

Key
- Part of the Soviet Union
- Soviet sphere of influence

Eastern and Southern Europe by 1948

Conflict with the USA and the capitalist West

The wartime summit conferences reflected the latent disagreements between the USA, Great Britain and the USSR.

- At Tehran in 1943, the Allies agreed to demand unconditional surrender from Germany. But there were ideological differences, and Stalin was very critical of his Western allies not opening a 'Second Front' in the European war, to relieve the pressure on the Red Army.
- The meeting between Stalin and Churchill in Moscow, late in 1944, was plagued by disagreements over the future of Poland.
- The Yalta conference in February 1945 was dominated by conflicting ideas about the post-war borders of Germany and Poland.
- The Potsdam conference in July–August 1945 ended with no final peace agreement. Differences that had been papered over, or just delayed, at Yalta became more urgent. By this time, it was clear how the USSR was asserting political control over the countries it had liberated.

The breakdown of East-West relations

Between 1946 and 1949, tensions hardened into Cold War confrontations. There were three main stages to this breakdown.

Stage 1: 1946

- The USA and Britain were concerned by Soviet expansionism and the USSR's demand for its right to have a 'buffer zone' against future aggression.
- This was exacerbated by 'The Long Telegram': a report from Moscow by the American diplomat George Kennan in 1946, urging the USA to contain the spread of communism in Europe.
- The former British prime minister, Winston Churchill, gave a speech in March 1946 warning of an 'iron curtain' dividing Europe, advising that 'strength' was needed to deal with the USSR.

Stage 2: 1947–48

- By 1947, Western Europe was plagued by economic decline and political instability, with strong communist parties in Italy and France.
- The announcement of the Truman Doctrine in March 1947 committed the USA to a policy of **containment** (containing the spread of communism).
- In June 1947, the Marshall Plan – providing US aid for European economic recovery – received a hostile Soviet response, as Stalin believed it would extend US influence.

Stage 3: 1948–49

- After the war, the USSR and the West had disagreed over the control of Berlin (which was located in the Soviet zone of Germany).
- In the Berlin Blockade of 1948–49, Stalin cut off all road and rail links between Berlin and the Western zones of Germany. This hardened the division of Germany.
- The North Atlantic Treaty Organisation (NATO) was formed in 1949. The establishment of this Atlantic alliance for the defence of Europe was seen by the USSR as a hostile act.
- The first successful test of the Soviet atomic bomb in August 1949, and victory for the communist party in the Chinese Civil War in 1950, also increased Cold War tensions.

The death of Stalin

By 1953, Stalin was 73 years old and in poor health. His inner circle knew that change was necessary for the USSR, but they also knew that change was not possible until Stalin died.

- Stalin had a massive stroke on 28 February, and died on 5 March.
- Stalin's inner circle gathered at his bedside, but delayed calling doctors as many felt under threat of a new purge; Stalin's increasingly unpredictable and menacing behaviour in early 1953 suggested a new wave of repression and terror might be on its way if Stalin recovered.
- Soviet citizens grieved Stalin's death. His funeral united the country in mourning.

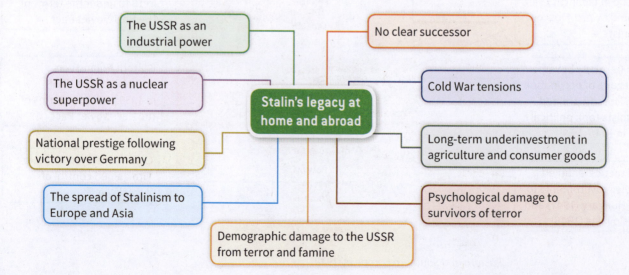

Diagram: Stalin's legacy at home and abroad
- The USSR as an industrial power
- The USSR as a nuclear superpower
- National prestige following victory over Germany
- The spread of Stalinism to Europe and Asia
- No clear successor
- Cold War tensions
- Long-term underinvestment in agriculture and consumer goods
- Psychological damage to survivors of terror
- Demographic damage to the USSR from terror and famine

Problems for Stalin's successors

Stalin's legacy created serious problems for his successors:

Who should take over as leader of the Party	There was no clear successor and at first there was a return to collective responsibility, until a tense power struggle led to Nikita Khrushchev eventually emerging as the new Soviet leader.
How to tackle the legacy of terror	Beria was executed, but perhaps as much for what he knew about the other leadership contenders as for his own crimes.
How to 'de-Stalinse' the USSR	Khrushchev denounced Stalin's 'crimes and errors' in his 'Secret Speech' in February 1956, and people were released from the gulags – but the gulags themselves did not disappear.
How to improve agriculture	The state could pay kolkhozes more, but that would either mean less money for industry or higher prices for food.
How to centrally plan for consumers	Meeting consumer needs continued to be too complex to plan with a command economy.
How to keep people believing in a socialist future	This was especially difficult for the new satellite states of the Soviet 'empire', with unrest spreading through East Germany, Poland and Hungary.

SUMMARY

- The USSR emerged from the Great Patriotic War as a military-industrial superpower, and by 1948 Stalin presided over an extensive Soviet bloc.
- Tensions between the former allies, including over the USSR's spreading influence in Europe, developed into the Cold War.
- Stalin's legacy included both superpower status and the problem of finding an alternative to Stalinist terror to hold Soviet society and the Soviet 'empire' together.

 APPLY

ASSESS THE VALIDITY OF THIS VIEW

 'Fear of the West was the most important factor shaping Stalin's foreign policies in the years 1945 to 1953'. Assess the validity of this view.

a Write a list or create a spider diagram to record Stalin's foreign policies and actions in the years 1945 to 1953.

b For each of these policies and actions, note any factors that might have shaped what happened. For example, 'need to rebuild the Soviet economy after the war', 'desire to show the USSR's superpower status', etc. Add 'fear of the West' whenever you feel a policy or action may have been at least partly motivated by this.

c Use your answers to **a** and **b** to write a complete answer to the exam question.

REVISION SKILLS

Draw a timeline to chart the development of Stalin's dictatorship. Include the key events or developments that helped to consolidate his position.

For each event or development, add a brief note to explain how it increased Stalin's power over the Party or the USSR.

IMPROVE AN ANSWER

> **A LEVEL** **'In 1953, the USSR deserved to be called a superpower.' Assess the validity of this view.**

The following paragraph is an introduction to the question above. Read it carefully.

Answer

In 1953 the USSR was a very powerful country. It had just won a war and had an enormous and well-equipped army. It also possessed an atomic bomb, making it the equal of the USA. The USSR was also powerful because it had a large number of satellite states in Eastern Europe – and it was a huge country itself too. However, it had its problems. Stalin had just died and no one quite knew what the future would bring. Agriculture was not doing well and industry was unbalanced with too few consumer goods. In the Soviet satellite states there were a good number of resentments too. These factors weakened the USSR.

In many respects this is a good introduction, but it has two main limitations:

- there is no definition or consideration of what 'superpower' means
- it is not clear what the writer's judgement on the question is.

Rewrite this introduction to improve it and address these weaknesses.

APPLY YOUR KNOWLEDGE

Read the following extracts from Kennan's 'Long Telegram' of February 1946.

a   In your own words, explain the meaning of the extract in the second column of the table.

b   How did comments such as the ones given below from the 'Long Telegram' influence Western attitudes to the USSR in the years 1946–53?

Extracts from Kennan's 'Long Telegram'	Meaning
'Soviet leaders… put forward a dogma that pictures the outside world as evil, hostile and menacing'	
'This dogma provides justification for that increase of military and police power in the Russian state… and that constant pressure to extend Russian police power'	
'[The USSR believes that] everything must be done to advance the relative strength of the USSR as a factor in international society'	

EXAMINER TIP

Understanding Western attitudes in the late 1940s will help you to write meaningfully about the USSR's foreign relations in the early years of the Cold War.

A Level essay sample answer

 REVIEW

On these Exam Practice pages, you will find a sample student answer for an A Level essay question. What are the strengths and weaknesses of the answer? Read the answer and the corresponding Examiner tips carefully. Think about how you could apply this advice in order to improve your own answers to questions like this one.

 A LEVEL 'The emergence of the Soviet Union as a great world power in the years 1943 to 1953 was due to Stalin's leadership.'

Assess the validity of this view.

25 marks

Sample student answer

Although the USSR only just survived the early stage of the German invasion in 1941, the patriotic resistance that was whipped up against the Nazis, and the USSR's ultimate victory, helped the Soviet Union to emerge as a world superpower in the post-war years. The drive to great world power status was, in many respects, due to Stalin. He was the figurehead for all anti-German activities during the war years. His leadership united the nation and his status over the Party and country grew so strong in the post-war era that nothing could have been achieved without his approval. However, Stalin made some disastrous decisions early on in the war, and Soviet victory was more due to his generals rather than Stalin's own military decisions. Similarly much of the praise that was given to Stalin after 1945 was more the result of an effective propaganda machine than Stalin's own leadership.

Stalin's leadership meant Russia was unprepared for war. Stalin was convinced that the terms of the 1939 Nazi-Soviet Pact had brought the USSR plenty of time to prepare for war, and he was not, at first, prepared to believe stories of the German invasion in 1941. He disappeared from public view, leaving Molotov to speak to the people, and seemed to be in a state of disbelief and panic. Stalin's insistence that the Red Army defend Kiev at all costs led to a massive defeat, and between June and December 1941 the Red Army lost 2.6 million troops killed in action and 3.3 million taken prisoner.

However, once Stalin was roused from his lethargy, he very much acted as the great war leader. He reorganised his war cabinet as well as the army command, and took control of the economy to ensure

 REVISION SKILLS

A Level essay questions may contain a quotation advancing a judgement, in which case the quotation will be followed by 'assess the validity of this view'. Read page 7 for details on how to master the essay question.

 EXAMINER TIP

This is a well-focused introduction, which shows a generally good understanding of the question. It provides some excellent balance and shows some conceptual depth in its comments about Stalin's leadership being the product of an 'effective propaganda machine'.

 EXAMINER TIP

This introduction could be criticised for equating 'emergence as a world power' with military success in the war, but its main fault lies in its failure to express a definite view in relation to the question.

 EXAMINER TIP

Despite some good detail, this paragraph addresses events in 1941, which predates the question. It would have been better to have begun with 1943, both to save time and to avoid irrelevance.

 EXAMINER TIP

This paragraph is more relevant to the period and covers an important area – Stalin's wartime leadership in relation to the government, the army and the economy.

the Soviet Union was able to survive the economic consequences of war. He was ruthless in his demands, both from workers and soldiers. For example, in order to win the Battle of Stalingrad he gave the order (number 227) that the Red Army soldiers must take 'Not One Step Back'. Ruthless attitudes to desertion and any failure to meet economic demands contributed towards the eventual Soviet victory.

The emergence of the Soviet Union as a great world power was also seen in Stalin's participation in international conferences, in particular Tehran in 1943, as well as Yalta and Potsdam in 1945. At these, Stalin was recognised as one of the 'big three' alongside Churchill and Roosevelt, and by the time of Potsdam he was the elder statesman following Roosevelt's death and Churchill's replacement by Attlee. It was thanks to Stalin's tough negotiating stance at these conferences that Eastern Europe remained in the Soviet sphere of influence, becoming a communist Soviet bloc after 1945. Stalin refused to budge on the issue of Poland's borders, and insisted on continued control of Eastern Germany. He even tried to force the Western allies out of West Berlin by setting up a blockade in 1948–49, and although this failed in its immediate objective, the desperation of the West in providing an airlift shows how much they recognised the power of the USSR.

The USSR emerged from the war as a military-industrial superpower and this led to the beginning of the Cold War. Soviet power frightened the West, as seen in Kennan's 'Long Telegram', Churchill's 'Iron Curtain' speech, and the offering of Marshall aid to extend US influence in Western Europe. In 1949 the USSR even succeeded in testing an atomic bomb, which was a clear sign of its new world power status.

However, it wasn't just Stalin's leadership that made the USSR a great power in the years 1943 to 1953. Stalin was never more than a figurehead in the war years, and although he later downplayed the role of men like Zhukov, it was the army generals that led the USSR to victory. Other factors, such as the enormous size and vast resources of the USSR together with its huge population, were also major contributors to Soviet status. Hitler's mistakes and the severity of the Russian winter all helped military victory, and while Stalin was hailed as the great war hero, he could have done nothing without his people's patriotism. The USSR also benefited from the USA entering the war after Pearl Harbour, and gained from the Lend-Lease scheme and the West's need of Soviet support, which led the West to grant concessions that became the foundation for the USSR's expansion.

By the time of Stalin's death in 1953, the USSR was recognised as a great world power by both its own people and Western countries, which formed NATO to combat any further attempts at the expansion of Soviet influence. Before the war Stalin had favoured 'socialism in one country' and had tried to avoid unnecessary foreign entanglements. However, the war completed the transformation of the Soviet economy that had begun in the 1930s. It allowed the USSR to acquire an 'empire' in Eastern Europe, and its world status also benefited from French and British losses as a result of war. With its huge army and atomic bomb, it can certainly be said that Stalin's leadership had transformed the USSR, giving it world power status by 1953.

EXAMINER TIP

This conclusion raises some good points in relation to the position of the USSR by 1953 – again showing some conceptual awareness – and it makes some links to the question and to Stalin's leadership.

EXAMINER TIP

The conclusion never offers a definite view on who or what was actually responsible for the USSR's 'transformation'.

OVERALL COMMENT

The essay has some strengths: there is generally a good understanding of developments, some conceptual awareness, and a good range of well-chosen evidence. It also has some balance. However, some of the supporting material is limited in development, and the points challenging the importance of Stalin's leadership are largely limited to one paragraph. For this reason, this answer would be unlikely to receive more than a low Level 4.

OVER TO YOU

Give yourself 55 minutes to answer this question yourself. Consider this checklist when reviewing your answer.

Did you:

❑ Identify a range of factors that were important to the USSR's emergence as a great world power in the years 1943 to 1953?

❑ Ensure that your supporting evidence is both precise and explicitly related to your arguments?

❑ Achieve a balanced answer that is analytical rather than descriptive in every paragraph?

❑ Provide a well-substantiated judgement?

Go back and look at chapters 21 and 22 to refresh your knowledge of the Great Patriotic War and the defeat of the Germans.

Activity answers guidance

The answers provided here are examples, based on the information provided in the Recap sections of this Revision Guide. There may be other factors which are relevant to each question, and you should draw on as much own knowledge as possible to give detailed and precise answers. There are many ways of answering exam questions (for example, of structuring an essay). However, these suggested answers should provide a good starting point.

Chapter 1

Apply Your Knowledge

Rasputin's position at court: the Tsar's court; because Rasputin (a peasant) became more powerful than many ministers.

Nicholas' relationship with the State Duma: those hoping for a more democratic approach to Russia's government; because Nicholas refused to share any real power with the Duma.

Nicholas' refusal to share responsibility for the war effort: the zemstva and the Progressive bloc; because Nicholas rejected their demands for a civilian government.

Russia's involvement in the First World War: those who were conscripted/faced food shortages/faced soaring rises in the cost of living/were made unemployed; these all made life very hard at a time when the government seemed to be failing in its war effort.

Apply Your Knowledge

a Other challenges could include: workers' harsh working and living conditions; revolutionaries plotting to overthrow the Tsar; Nicholas' lack of political authority/personal failings; the First World War; discontent at the government's running of Russia's war effort (and its refusal to share power with others in doing this); food shortages; cost of living rises.

b This answer will depend on your own views. Remember to explain your reasoning.

Plan Your Essay

a **Nicholas personality:** Nicholas was stubborn and unwilling to accept advice; this prevented his ministers from dissuading him from the unpopular decisions he made, which contributed to the discontent in Russia.

   Alexandra and Rasputin: Rasputin's influential position at court, and his closeness to Alexandra (a German), undermined Nicholas' authority and increased discontent against him at court.

   Nicholas and the State Duma: Nicholas refused to share any real power with the State Duma, increasing discontent amongst those hoping for a more democratic approach.

   Nicholas and Russia's problems: Nicholas' faith that God would solve Russia's problems increased discontent as it meant Nicholas was less active than he could have been in trying to improve the situation.

b Counter-arguments could refer to: food shortages in the cities; rising unemployment as non-military factories were forced to close; the soaring cost of living; Russia's disastrous military failures in the First World War; the experiences of under-supplied soldiers at the Front.

c There is no right answer, as such, as long as you are able to justify your argument. You might think that because Nicholas was the one person in Russia with the power to make real changes, his failings and inaction were the main cause of discontent. However, you might argue instead that economic and social problems were the main reason for discontent – the Tsar and his family were not that significant to most people's everyday existence. Or you might think that all the problems facing Russia were intensified by the war, without which it might have been possible for Nicholas to reduce some of the discontent.

Key Concept

a **Industrialisation and terrible living and working conditions:**
   - *Role of individuals*: tsars had permitted unregulated industrialisation to take place in Russia. Individual factory owners did little to improve working conditions.
   - *Other factors*: rapid industrialisation and the movement of people from peasant villages to big cities is likely to cause social problems regardless of leadership. The war made living conditions unbearable in Russia because of its impact on inflation and unemployment.

   Inflation and food shortages:
   - *Role of individuals*: the Russian government raised taxes and took out enormous loans in order to pay for the war. These measures led to inflation. Some of the decisions taken by Russia's leaders – such as diverting food supplies to the warfront – also contributed to the food shortages.
   - *Other factors*: the huge costs of the war led to inflation and food shortages. Individual actions might have had a small influence, but would not have been able to stem these problems.

   Rising opposition to autocracy:
   - *Role of individuals*: the Tsar's personal failings increased opposition to autocracy. E.g. Nicholas refused to give the Duma a bigger role in Russia's war effort.
   - *Other factors*: the war, inflation and food shortages increased resentment against Nicholas' rule.

b There is no right or wrong conclusion to come to; what is important is the reasoning you use to substantiate (back up) your conclusion. E.g. one argument that highlights the importance of individual actions could be that mismanagement in the distribution of supplies in wartime exacerbated economic problems and caused social discontent.

Assess the Validity of This View

a The Tsar's divine right to rule over all his people in an autocracy.

b Nicholas' decision, which was made against the advice of all his advisors, took him away from Petrograd, leaving Alexandra to govern. It also meant anything that went wrong in the war was now directly Nicholas' fault.

   You could compare this to other factors such as: Rasputin's influence and its damaging effect on support for the royal family amongst the aristocracy and Army leadership; the illness of Nicholas' son Alexei, which meant the royal family was distracted and easily influenced; anti-German sentiment, which influenced perceptions of Alexandra (a German); political challenges to royal authority from within the Duma, and from the zemstva movement; social and economic problems which made people indifferent to the royal family.

c This answer will depend on your own view about the main factor(s), and what order of importance you ascribe to them. You may agree that Nicholas' decision was a disaster, but you might also consider that the loss of royal authority happened at the point when the military stopped obeying Nicholas and instead told him to abdicate.

d Your answer to **c** will inform your overall view of validity, while your answers to **b** will give you alternative viewpoints to assess. Remember that your answer should sustain an argument from the introduction through to the conclusion of your essay.

Chapter 2

Apply Your Knowledge

Other causes could include: workers' harsh working and living conditions; Nicholas II's lack of political authority/personal failings; the First World War; discontent at the government's running of Russia's war effort (and its refusal to share power with others in doing this); the rising cost of living.

Source Analysis

a **Source A:**
   - *Who produced it*: Mikhail Prishvin, a writer. *Type of source*: diary entry. *Date*: 3 March 1917. *Purpose*: to record Prishvin's private observations. *Audience*: possibly intended for readers after his death, but probably mostly for himself.
   - *How the provenance affects the value*: the source is valuable as it was written at the time of the Revolution, rather than recalled later. It is a private diary, so likely to include Prishvin's real views. Prishvin is a writer, so used to describing and expressing vividly. However, the source is restricted to his views only, so it is subjective.

   Source B:
   - *Who produced it*: the Petrograd Soviet (its executive committee). *Type of source*: an official order. *Date*: 1 March 1917. *Purpose*: intended to stop attempts by the Provisional Government to put the soldiers and sailors who had mutinied back under the same heavy discipline and control as before. *Audience*: especially for the committees of soldiers and sailors who had elected deputies to the Soviet, and for the Provisional Government (to make it clear what was going to be allowed and what wasn't).
   - *How the provenance affects the value*: a source directly from the Petrograd Soviet at the time of the Revolution is valuable, but we don't know if the purpose was specific to the Provisional Government's command or more general. It is not clear what the underlying aims of the source were.

   Source C:
   - *Who produced it*: the Provisional Government. *Type of source*: a manifesto – an official document. *Date*: 3 March 1917. *Purpose*: to justify the formation of the Provisional Government and to set out its aims. *Audience*: the Russian people and the rest of Europe.
   - *How the provenance affects the value*: we don't know exactly who wrote the source or what their underlying aims were (e.g. were its authors committed to continuing the war?). However, a source directly from the Provisional Government the day after it was founded is valuable in understanding its intentions.

b **Source A** suggests the February/March Revolution was very popular in Petrograd ('a real great victory's being celebrated'). It also suggests that it was not a good idea to criticise the Revolution or socialism ('a huge angry crowd followed one soldier').

   Source B says that soldiers and workers will only obey the Provisional Government if its orders don't contradict the Soviet, i.e. the Soviet is the main authority of Russia ('except those which run counter to the orders and decrees issued by the Soviet'). It suggests that the soldiers and sailors who made the Revolution a success are not about to give up their new freedom and return to being under the command of the same officers that they mutinied against in the first place.

Source C says that the Provisional Government has been created by the February/March Revolution, by the 'revolutionary enthusiasm' of all the Russian people together with the 'determination of the State Duma'.

c The points you have made in **a** and **b** about the provenance and content of the sources should be included in your answer. You should also apply further contextual own knowledge and include some judgement about the value of each source to an historian studying the February/March Revolution.

For **Source A** you may conclude that the source is valuable in providing an eyewitness account of how people celebrated the revolution, but that it is a subjective account that gives only a partial picture of events.

For **Source B** you may conclude that the source is valuable in helping an historian understand the determination of the Soviet to defend the rights of soldiers and sailors who had mutinied against their tsarist officials. However, the purpose of the source is not clear: was this just a response to the Provisional Government's command to the soldiers and sailors, or was it setting out the basis of dual authority from the start?

For **Source C** you may conclude that the source is valuable in helping an historian understand the Provisional Government's justification for taking power. However, the source's value is possibly limited in that we do not know what other purposes lay behind the manifesto, or how the manifesto was received.

Chapter 3

Apply Your Knowledge

a Ten events or developments could include:
- 3 March: formation of the Provisional Government
- 3 April: Lenin returns to Russia in a sealed train
- 7 April: Lenin's April Theses is published
- 3 June: Petrograd Soviet passes a vote of confidence in the Provisional Government by 543 votes to 126 votes
- 2 July: Trotsky joins the Bolsheviks
- 3–5 July: The 'July Days'
- 3–7 July: Lenin flees to Finland; other Bolshevik leaders are arrested
- 26–30 August: Kornilov's coup fails; the Red Guards are formed
- 26 September: Trotsky becomes Chairman of the Petrograd Soviet
- 10 October: in an all-night meeting, Lenin convinces the Central Committee to support an armed uprising
- 16 October: a Military Revolutionary Committee is set up under Trotsky and Dzerzhinsky

b Your answer will depend on your own views, but a suggested answer is: Lenin's April Theses (as these won support for the Bolsheviks); the Kornilov coup (as this armed the Bolsheviks and weakened the Provisional Government); and the vote on 10 October (as this allowed the rising to go ahead).

Improve an Answer

a
- Most of what the student has written is not relevant to the question.
- It is not easy to tell what the student's judgement is – whether they agree with the view in the question or disagree with it.

b Your answer should focus on the question, which is not about Lenin's influence over the Central Committee of his own Party, but whether he was personally responsible (e.g. through speeches, slogans, or

decisions made) for the Bolsheviks' 'growing appeal' (it would be good to be specific about what you take this to mean), or whether other factors (e.g. the Bolsheviks' response to Kornilov, or the problems of the Provisional Government) were the reasons.

Assess the Validity of This View

a There are various ways this phrase could be defined; the Bolsheviks' influence is likely to be a key factor in your answer.

b Reasons for the increase in the Bolsheviks' 'strength' could include: Lenin's return on 3 April 1917, which changed Bolshevik policy; Lenin's April Theses, which set out his ideology and formed the basis of slogans that became popular amongst Petrograd workers and soldiers; Lenin's leadership strengths (e.g. persistence, flexibility, appearance of being in control); Trotsky becoming Chairman of the Petrograd Soviet; the Bolsheviks' control (by September 1917) of both the Petrograd and Moscow soviets; the Bolsheviks' response to Kornilov and their reputation as the saviours of the revolution; the Bolsheviks' military strength following the arming of 10,000 Red Guards; ==the Provisional Government's failure to improve food supplies to the cities or to control prices; the failure of the June offensive; the continuing failure of the Provisional Government to fix a date for the Constituent Assembly elections; the apparent complicity of Kerensky in Kornilov's attempted coup;== Trotsky's creation of the MRC, giving him access to central control of Petrograd's military forces.

c See the highlighted answers above.

d Your answers to **b** and **c** should have clarified for you the extent to which the weaknesses of the Bolsheviks' rivals were significant in the increased strength of the Bolsheviks, while your answer to **a** will give you a clear focus for your answer. Your answers to **b** can also help to provide alternative views for why the Bolsheviks' strength increased. Combined, this should enable you to plan and deliver an effective and balanced answer to the exam question.

Plan Your Essay

a Other reasons could include: failure to hold elections for a Constituent Assembly (though these were planned for November); Petrograd Soviet's Order No. 1, which undermined the Provisional Government's control of the military; failure to provide land for the peasants; the appointment of Kornilov; the Kornilov coup; Lenin's return to Russia.

b Factors due to Provisional Government mistakes should include anything it had a choice over, e.g. the June Offensive, delaying the elections for the Constituent Assembly, Kerensky's appointment of Kornilov, etc.

c Your plan will be individual to you, but remember that you need to support your judgement with evidence.

Chapter 4

Apply Your Knowledge

Events of the February/March Revolution: the government announces bread rationing; there is a lock-out at the Putilov factory; the International Women's Day march; the Provisional Committee is set up by the Duma; the Petrograd Soviet is set up; the Duma president sends a telegram to Nicholas II warning him of the riots.

Events of the October/November Revolution: Red Guards 'storm' the Winter Palace; members of the Provisional Government are arrested; the Second Congress of Soviets agrees to Lenin's Decree on Land; Sovnarkom is set up to run the government; Kerensky's opposition forces are defeated; Kamenev and others leave the Bolshevik Party.

Assess the Validity of This View

a **Lenin:** convinced the Bolshevik Central Committee to agree to an armed uprising; provided inspiration and direction; proposed a Decree on Peace and a Decree on Land to the Second Congress of Soviets, which had widespread appeal.

Trotsky and the MRC: Trotsky organised the takeover of power; Kerensky's attempt to reduce the power of the MRC triggered the revolution; the MRC meant the Bolsheviks had the backing of the majority of Petrograd garrisons during the revolution.

Bolshevik Central Committee: agreed to the armed uprising, giving full Party support to Lenin.

Red Guard soldiers and sailors: captured key positions in Petrograd; took the control of the Winter Palace.

The Second Congress of Soviets: the revolution transferred power to the All-Russian Congress of Soviets; the Congress voted to approve Lenin's Decree on Peace and Decree on Land.

b Your answer should consider the contribution of Lenin compared with other individuals or groups. Consider the aims of the revolution so you can be clear about what 'success' constituted.

Plan Your Essay

a Failures of the Provisional Government could include: Kerensky's failure to control Kornilov; Kerensky's failure to stop the Bolsheviks before it was too late; failure to get full control over the army because of the influence of the Petrograd Soviet; failure to become the real government of Russia, instead of a 'dual authority'; failure to deliver the Constituent Assembly elections; failure to end the war/improve Russia's military performance; failure to give land to the peasants.

b **Provisional Government weaknesses** that contributed to the revolution could include (among others):
- Failure to control Kornilov, as this convinced many ordinary Russians that the old authorities were trying to regain their power, and led to the arming of the Red Guard.
- Kerensky's attempts to reduce the Bolsheviks' power in October 1917, which gave the Bolsheviks an excuse for starting the revolution.
- Failure to improve the economy, which meant that people were still suffering from the food shortages that had caused the February/March Revolution.

Other factors contributing to the October/November Revolution could include (among others): the role of Lenin; the role of Trotsky; the war; Bolshevik fears about the results of the Constituent Assembly elections, which the Provisional Government had set for November.

c Your plan should aim to make a number of points on either side of the question (Provisional Government failures versus other factors), and bring in evidence to support your arguments. Plan a conclusion in which you make and support a judgement (i.e. state whether you agree or disagree with the view).

Key Concept

a The Bolsheviks' political authority rested on their seizure of power.

b The Bolsheviks' political authority by the end of 1917 was limited: Bolshevik control of the Congress of Soviets meant they could pass decrees (e.g. the Decree on Land) but had limited power to enforce these decrees outside of Petrograd and Moscow.

c Key points that you could include in your paragraph are:
- In October the Bolsheviks took power in the name of the All-Russian Congress of Soviets, sharing power with Mensheviks and SRs; the State Bank and civil servants were reluctant to cooperate.

- The walk-out of Mensheviks and right-wing SRs left the Bolsheviks only sharing power with left-wing SRs, who had limited influence; armed intervention was needed to ensure cooperation of state civil servants.
- The establishment of Sovnarkom helped to consolidate the Bolsheviks' political authority. It sidelined the Petrograd Soviet.
- In December, Vesenkha started to establish Bolshevik control over the economy, including the State Bank.
- Shutting down anti-Bolshevik newspapers, imprisoning members of the opposition, and establishing the Cheka all gave the Bolsheviks greater political authority by the end of 1917, although large areas of countryside were still not under their control.

Chapter 5

🔍 Source Analysis

a **The soviets:** Kropotkin thinks they are good in principle but the Bolsheviks are not allowing them to have any real significance.

The election process: Kropotkin describes the elections as not being free, but instead carried out under pressure by the Bolshevik Party's dictatorship.

The Bolsheviks' 'dictatorship of the proletariat': Kropotkin sees this as a 'party dictatorship', so there is complete control of the state by the Bolshevik Party and no control by the workers. The source is critical of the lack of press freedom and the lack of free elections.

b **Author:** anarchists are opposed to any kind of control by a central state, so the author would automatically be critical of the Bolsheviks' approach. While the author's political views might make him more critical of Bolshevik action, his testimony provides valuable evidence of the sort of criticism the Bolsheviks faced.

Date: 1919 makes the source valuable because it is still from the early stages of consolidation, less than two years since the October/November Revolution.

Audience and purpose: written for readers in Western Europe, presumably to inform them about the political situation in Russia. This suggests it would not have been possible to publish the article inside Russia, which could increase its value to the historian as contemporary criticism of the process of consolidation.

c You will need to assess the provenance and content of the source to answer this question, as well as use your own contextual knowledge. The source has limitations but you should recognise that it represents concerns among the radical left, both inside and outside Russia, that the Bolsheviks were acting to create a state controlled by the Party and run for its benefit. Such concerns wouldn't necessarily make this true, but it is valuable in helping us to understand what the concerns were about.

⚙ Apply Your Knowledge

a Other details you could add to the map include: 63 million people lost, one sixth of Russia's population; 2 million square kilometres of land lost – responsible for one third of Russia's agricultural production; a quarter of Russia's railway lines lost; three quarters of Russia's iron and coal lost.

b This answer will depend on your own views. Make sure you explain your answer, for example: the loss of Russia's western territories would have been the most significant loss for Russian people because they were proud of the Russian empire and would not have wanted to see it made so much smaller.

✏ AS Plan Your Essay

a **How the Constitution granted power to the people:** the Constitution stated that the Congress of Soviets, which was made up of deputies from elected local soviets, had supreme power.

How the Constitution granted power to the Party: in practice, Russia was run by Sovnarkom, not the Congress of Soviets, and the members of Sovnarkom were selected by the Party, not elected; full citizenship rights were limited to workers and peasants; many of those who had been members of 'exploiting classes' (e.g. landlords, merchants, priests) were excluded from having a vote or taking part in government.

b This answer will depend on your own decisions about the question. One possible paragraph could be:

The Constitution of 1918 did not grant power to the people, because although the Constitution looked on paper as though it guaranteed that Russia's government would be democratically elected, in practice anyone with an interest in getting rid of the Bolshevik Party was excluded from having a vote. The Congress of Soviets was made up of elected deputies but it only met twice a year at most. In practice, Russia was run by Sovnarkom, and the members of Sovnarkom were selected by the Party. This means that the 'power' given to the people by the Constitution was limited and superficial. Instead, the power of the Bolshevik Party was strengthened as the Constitution made it harder for anyone to oppose their decisions and actions.

⚖ A To What Extent?

a German troops were advancing into Russia and the Bolsheviks faced almost certain defeat; the Bolsheviks had promised peace; the Bolsheviks needed peace to consolidate their rule; Marxist theory predicted that Germany and other industrial countries in Europe were on the brink of their own socialist revolution, so any peace treaty the Bolsheviks agreed with Germany would only be temporary – when Germany joined Russia as a socialist state, the treaty would be torn up; the Bolsheviks saw the First World War as a capitalist and imperialist struggle that oppressed the workers, so ending Russia's part in the war was ideologically important to them.

b See the highlighted answers above.

c There is no single correct answer to this question. However, you should balance the importance of Bolshevik ideology against other factors. Showing how different reasons link together should enable you to display judgement about which were the most important.

Chapter 6

⚙ Apply Your Knowledge

a Other reasons could include: Reds were able to conscript from large peasant populations in central Russia; Reds had effective propaganda targeted at ordinary Russians; Whites had far fewer soldiers than the Reds; Whites did not have control over industrial areas or areas with large populations; Whites were not united with the same aims and ideology; Trotsky took an active role in leading the Red Army, constantly visiting the fronts; Trotsky ensured the Red Army had sufficient supplies; Trotsky's train improved Red Army morale; Trotsky made the Red Army a professional and disciplined fighting force.

b See the highlighted answers above.

⬆ A Improve an Answer

Your introduction should make similar points to the following example answer:

Although many of the features of Soviet government continued from the structures set up by Lenin immediately after the Bolsheviks' seizure of power in 1917, the experiences of the Civil War influenced many aspects of how the USSR was governed. On the one hand, the centralised control of the Bolshevik government under Sovnarkom continued through to the dominance of the Politburo after the Civil War, while a one-party state was already almost achieved before the Civil War. On the other hand, the Civil War was very influential in, for example, creating the central controls of the economy of war communism, the use of terror to eliminate possible opponents, and the massive increase in the bureaucracy, which were all central features of the Soviet government.

✏ AS Plan Your Essay

a One cause of discontent would be more significant than another if its consequences were more important or wide-ranging than the other, or if the discontent would not have occured at all without it.

b Main reasons could include: the Treaty of Brest-Litovsk; the closing of the Constituent Assembly; the confiscation of private property (with the exception of peasant land) from Russians who had land or money or owned businesses; continuing food shortages; moves for independence by some national minorities.

c This answer will depend on your own view.

d A possible conclusion could be:

The Treaty of Brest-Litovsk was the most significant cause of discontent with Bolshevik rule in 1918. The treaty involved such huge losses to Russia and its empire that it became a cause of great resentment against the Bolsheviks, to the point where it brought different opponents together and therefore helped to trigger the Civil War.

⚖ A Assess the Validity of This View

a Political authority is not secure; it is under multiple threats. Examples might include not having the authority to get laws passed, or not having the authority to enforce those laws.

b **Political opposition in 1921:** political opposition had been minimised as the Bolsheviks had banned all other political parties (and arrested thousands of Mensheviks and SRs); defeated the separate White armies; murdered the Tsar and his family.

International opposition in 1918: Germany (until the Brest-Litovsk Treaty, 3 March 1918); the Czech Legion; Russia's former allies against Germany: Britain, France and the USA; Japan. **In 1921:** Poland; Russia remained excluded from the League of Nations.

Social challenges in 1918: widespread dissatisfaction over the losses from the Treaty of Brest-Litovsk; strong divisions between those social classes favoured by the Bolsheviks and those who were not; concerns about Bolshevik promises to grant self-determination. **In 1921:** nationalist conflict with Poland resulting in independence for Poland and Baltic states; peasant revolt in Tambov; the Kronstadt rising of 1921.

Economic challenges in 1918: ongoing food shortages and severe rationing of essentials; distribution problems; the heavy losses of agricultural and industrial resources in the Treaty of Brest-Litovsk. **In 1921:** the harvest of 1921 only produced 48 per cent of 1913's harvest, resulting in famine; workers left the factories to return to their old villages to find food: industrial output was only 20 per cent of pre-war levels.

Internal divisions in 1918: divisions over peace talks with Germany. **In 1921:** the Workers' Opposition group; objections to the introduction of the NEP; Lenin's ban on factions.

c Your answers to **b** will provide you with the basis for a well-balanced thematic essay. While the statement 'By March 1921, the Bolsheviks still only had a fragile grip on power' is likely to be one that you will wish to challenge, you should take care to carefully consider areas where Bolshevik control remained relatively weak, for example regarding the post-Civil War economic challenges.

Chapter 7

(AS) Source Analysis

a **Source A:**

- *Author:* Lenin. Valuable as he was the leader of the Bolshevik Party.
- *Context:* the NEP had been formally introduced at the Tenth Party Congress a month earlier. Lenin had anticipated opposition to the NEP from Party members.
- *Purpose/audience:* Lenin wants to explain to a wider audience the reasons why the NEP is necessary, and to shut down opposition. The source was published in a pamphlet, which suggests it was intended to go out to a big audience (as a pamphlet is easily distributed and short to read).

Source B:

- *Author:* N.V. Valentinov. Valuable as he had helped to plan the NEP but was also critical of Lenin's theories.
- *Context:* the source was written a long time after the period it describes. It refers to a conversation that was probably held shortly after the NEP was introduced.
- *Purpose/audience:* the purpose of political memoirs is for the writer to look back on their life in politics and government, and give their personal memories of significant events and people. The audience is probably people in the USSR interested in politics and political history.

b **Source A**'s key message is that it was absolutely necessary to step away from war communism because otherwise the economy would collapse. Lenin accepts that this is a step back ('a revival of the petty bourgeoisie and of capitalism') but argues that it is so obviously necessary that it would be 'simple minded' to question it.

Source B's key message is that Lenin's decision to introduce the NEP was difficult for many Bolsheviks to accept because it seemed to go against 'whole chapters of Marxism'. In fact, the source reports that 'virtually nobody agreed with Lenin' in the Party. Lenin himself, according to the source, did not accept anyone's right to tell him what was or was not Marxist.

c You should make sure that both the provenance and content of each source is analysed in relation to your own knowledge, and that there is some judgement between the value of the sources. You should recognise that the sources both have some value as both show arguments for and against the introduction of the NEP.

Apply Your Knowledge

a **Private trade:** trade carried out by individuals for their own profit.

Requisitioning: demanding the supply of something on the basis of an official order (e.g. from the government).

Nomenklatura system: a system where government posts are filled from a list of loyal Party members.

Nepmen: private traders who bought up produce from the peasants to sell in towns and consumer goods in towns to sell to peasants.

b
- **Private trade** was banned under war communism but permitted again under the NEP.
- **Requisitioning** of grain was a key feature of war communism, while the NEP ended grain requisitioning.

- The Bolsheviks introduced the **nomenklatura system** in 1923, making Party loyalty more important in government employment.
- **Nepmen** were seen by opponents of the NEP as evidence of the dangers of reintroducing capitalist elements.

How Successful?

a **To revive the economy:** private businesses reopened and grew quickly; private traders became a feature; agricultural production recovered quickly; but by 1927 the NEP had failed to produce the growth many leading communists expected; the USSR was still relying too much on foreign imports.

To appease workers in the towns: cities regained services such as shops and restaurants; rationing ended; workers could be paid according to how much work they had done.

To appease peasants in the countryside: grain requisitioning ended; peasants were able to earn money from private trade; but there were few incentives for peasants to sell their grain; this led to the grain procurement crisis in 1927–28.

b One possible introduction could be:

How successful the NEP was is best assessed by considering the original aims of the NEP in 1921 and the extent to which they were achieved by 1928. Lenin recognised in 1921 that the Russian economy and society were facing collapse. There was famine across much of the country, caused by the forced grain requisitioning of war communism. One key aim of the NEP was to improve agricultural production as rapidly as possible to improve food supplies. Russian industrial production had also collapsed, but the Bolshevik state was too weak to provide the investment needed for industry to recover. The NEP aimed to give incentives to smaller companies to boost production, so the state could focus on the 'commanding heights' of heavy industry. The Bolsheviks faced serious opposition in the countryside (Tambov) and cities (Kronstadt/Petrograd) in 1921, and the NEP had to address this threat to their political control. The NEP was successful in all three of these aims.

Plan Your Essay

a **Nationalisation:**

- *Solved a problem:* ensured that industrial production was focused on meeting the needs of the Red Army.
- *Created a problem:* depended on state investment. After the Civil War ended, industries ground to a halt because the state couldn't provide the resources they needed.

Grain requisitioning:

- *Solved a problem:* ensured the Red Army always had the food it needed to feed its soldiers.
- *Created a problem:* meant peasants were not left with enough grain to plant the next harvest. This led to declining harvests and widespread famine. Grain requisitioning also caused resentment against the Bolsheviks and led to peasant revolts.

Labour discipline:

- *Solved a problem:* ensured the factories supplying the Red Army ran efficiently.
- *Created a problem:* caused social problems because workers resented the strict discipline.

Rationing:

- *Solved a problem:* ensured the Red Army always had the food it needed to feed its soldiers.
- *Created a problem:* caused social problems by contributing to malnourishment and starvation.

b You should use your table to help you plan a balanced essay. Whether you agree or disagree with the view should depend on which side of the argument you have more convincing evidence for.

Chapter 8

Apply Your Knowledge

a **October/November 1917:** the October/November Revolution.

3 March 1918: the Treaty of Brest-Litovsk.

April 1922: the Treaty of Rapallo.

b The **October/November Revolution** damaged foreign relations with Russia because it overthrew the government in an armed, communist uprising. For Russia's allies in the First World War it threatened Russia's commitment to the war.

The **Treaty of Brest-Litovsk** improved relations with Germany but damaged other foreign relations because it allowed Germany to transfer troops from the eastern front to the western front of the war.

The **end of fighting in the First World War** meant that foreign powers such as Britain still intervened in the Civil War against the Bolsheviks, but with less commitment because they no longer needed Russia to help them win the war.

The **Treaty of Rapallo** improved relations with Germany and also opened the way to improved relations with other countries.

Plan Your Essay

a **Ending Russia's involvement in the First World War:**

- *Evidence of success:* the Treaty of Brest-Litovsk succeeded in getting Russia out of the war without Germany defeating the Russian army and toppling the Bolshevik regime.
- *Evidence of limited success:* this was achieved at great cost to Russia and was an important trigger for the Civil War.

Promoting socialist revolutions in other countries:

- *Evidence of success:* although the Bolshevik revolution was not followed by other socialist revolutions as Lenin had predicted, the Bolsheviks did encourage a socialist revolution in Hungary.
- *Evidence of limited success:* the Hungarian revolution did not survive for very long. Germany seemed on the brink of a socialist revolution in 1919, but the Spartacist uprising was crushed by right-wing forces.

Gaining international recognition for Bolshevik Russia/the Soviet Union as a country:

- *Evidence of success:* the Treaty of Rapallo was signed in April 1922; trade deals with Britain were based on the beginnings of a recognition of Bolshevik Russia as a legitimate country.
- *Evidence of success:* Bolshevik Russia was excluded from the League of Nations and the Paris Peace Conference.

b A possible conclusion could be:

The Bolshevik regime was largely unsuccessful in its dealings with foreign powers in the years 1918 to 1924. This was because the aims of its foreign policy through most of this period were based on the expected spread of socialist revolutions across the industrialised nations, following the lead set by Russia in 1917. When revolutions failed to materialise, the Bolsheviks' aims became more practical: gaining international recognition from and securing trade deals with foreign powers, in order to aid the rebuilding of the country after the Civil War. Here the Bolsheviks had a little more success, especially in regards to Weimar Germany, as the two countries signed the Rapallo Treaty in 1922.

Assess the Validity of This View

a **Russia's involvement in the First World War:**

- *Lenin's actions:* Lenin ordered Trotsky to reach a peace deal with the Germans, resulting in the Treaty of Brest-Litovsk.

- *How successful?*: this succeeded in Russia ending its involvement in the First World War, but it also triggered a civil war.

  Political opposition to the Bolshevik seizure of power:
  - *Lenin's actions*: Lenin's response was to close down the Constituent Assembly, shut opposition newspapers, outlaw opposition parties, and use terror against possible class enemies.
  - *How successful?*: this succeeded in preventing opposition but came at the cost of a secret police force that replicated the methods of tsarist oppression.

  Food shortages in the towns and cities:
  - *Lenin's actions*: the NEP allowed peasants to sell surplus produce (after meeting government quotas) on the private market.
  - *How successful?*: peasants responded quickly to the opportunity to sell directly to towns and cities, reducing food shortages.

  Division within the Bolshevik Party:
  - *Lenin's actions*: the 1921 ban on factions meant that once the Central Committee had made a decision, every Party member had to follow it.
  - *How successful?*: alongside increasing terror and introducing the nomenklatura system, this reduced Party division.

b You should make sure that your answer identifies the major problems facing the Bolsheviks in 1917. You should explain how Lenin acted to solve these problems, and assess the success of his actions. As part of this, you should make it clear how 'success' will be measured.

🔘 Key Concept

a The Treaty of Brest-Litovsk reflected the expectation of a worldwide communist revolution: Lenin was able to accept such huge losses because he was confident they would not matter once Germany had its communist revolution. Lenin's 21 Conditions at the Second Comintern Congress also reflected his confidence in the coming revolution.

b • The Russo-Polish War was a reflection of changing expectations because Lenin had expected a communist revolution in Poland, but when this didn't happen and Poland and the Ukraine allied against the Bolsheviks, the Red Army was ordered to counter-attack.
  - The Rapallo Treaty was a response to the failure of worldwide revolution: part of a search for better diplomatic relations with other countries.
  - The Third Comintern Congress in 1921 reflected a recognition of the failure of worldwide revolution to occur as expected.

Chapter 9

🔘 Apply Your Knowledge

Stalin had a bad temper and was prepared to use violent methods: a weakness because it was why he fell out with Lenin (rudeness to Lenin's wife, ruthlessness in dealing with Georgian independence). Even though Lenin's Testament was not made public, senior Party members knew Stalin had done something wrong. Potentially a strength if other Party members feared or respected him because of it.

Stalin became General Secretary of the Party in April 1922: a significant strength as this position allowed Stalin to control Party appointments and build up an extensive power base of Party members who were loyal to him.

Stalin was able to conceal his long-term aims and ambitions: a strength in that Stalin was able to manipulate his rivals into forming alliances with him by portraying himself as the moderate voice; by presenting himself as less as a threat than he was, his rivals did not seriously try to block him until it was too late.

Stalin was not seen as one of the Party's intellectuals: a strength as it meant intellectuals like Trotsky and Bukharin underestimated him. A weakness as it meant some Party members did not take him seriously.

🔘 🅰 Assess the Validity of This View

a **Evidence that Trotsky himself was responsible for failing to become leader:**
  - His arrogance meant he did not build a base of followers in the Party, and was so self-assured that he attacked the Party bureaucracy instead of trying to get the Party on his side.
  - He was inconsistent and indecisive – e.g. having opposed Zinoviev and Kamenev, he joined with them against Stalin.
  - He was a former Menshevik rather than an 'old Bolshevik', which would have been held against him by some.
  - His formation of the Left Opposition against Stalin, Kamenev and Zinoviev was a mistake because it allowed his enemies to accuse him of factionalism, which the Central Committee censured him for in 1924.

Evidence that other factors prevented Trotsky from becoming leader:
  - Trotsky's great successes made other leading members of the Central Committee loathe and resent him (e.g. Tomsky detested Trotsky).
  - Trotsky's position with the Red Army meant some Party members feared him. As a result, other leadership contenders allied with each other to oppose him, even before Lenin's death.
  - Stalin became leader in the end because he was more skilful at political manoeuvring, and also because his position as General Secretary allowed him to put his supporters in key positions in the Central Committee.
  - Trotsky might have benefited most from Lenin's Testament being read out in the Party Congress of 1924, but Stalin, Kamenev and Zinoviev conspired to prevent this from happening.

b This will be your personal choice. There are no right or wrong answers as long as you can substantiate your decision.

c A possible conclusion could be:

It was Trotsky's successes and Stalin's response to these that prevented Trotsky from becoming leader, rather than Trotsky's own failings. Trotsky's successes and abilities, including the respect he gained from the Red Army, made him the leading figure in the Central Committee after Lenin became ill, and it was these factors that made it essential for the other leadership contenders to reduce his influence in the Party. It was relatively easy for Stalin, in his triumvirate with Zinoviev and Kamenev, to use his influence over the Central Committee (many of whom owed their positions to Stalin) to censure Trotsky for factionalism. Trotsky fared no better than the other leadership contenders against Stalin – even when Zinoviev and Kamenev joined with Trotsky, Stalin was easily able to outmanoeuvre them.

Chapter 10

🔍 Source Analysis

a After a long period of alliance with Kamenev and Zinoviev, Stalin broke away from this 'triumvirate' and was in the process of allying with Bukharin. This was happening during a phase in which the majority of Party members broadly agreed with Bukharin that the NEP should continue.

b Kamenev's purpose was to damage Stalin's chances of becoming Party leader. Instead of being able to unite a collective leadership, Kamenev accused Stalin of wanting to be the 'Chief', 'more important than others'.

c A possible paragraph could be:

Source A is valuable in understanding the opposition to Stalin because it was made by one of the rivals to Stalin's leadership, and dates from the period concerned. It contains some criticisms of Stalin that partly help to show why there was opposition to him, and confirms that support for or opposition to Stalin divided the Party during these years. However, the source does not really help to explain why there was opposition to Stalin or give a sense of the shifting alliances and ideological positions in the Party during the second half of the 1920s.

🔘 🅰 Assess the Validity of This View

a Relates to Stalin's opposition to the NEP; relates to Stalin's support for the NEP; events not related to the NEP

Jan 1924	Lenin's funeral: Stalin makes the most of Trotsky's absence
May 1924	Lenin's Testament blocked from being read at the Thirteenth Party Congress
May 1924	Trotsky criticised the Party bureaucracy at the Party Congress
Oct 1924	Trotsky criticised Kamenev and Zinoviev for not backing Lenin in 1917
Dec 1925	Kamenev and Zinoviev criticise Stalin for his move to the Right and support for the NEP; Stalin's supporters vote them down
1926	Kamenev, Zinoviev and Trotsky form the United Opposition, calling for an end to the NEP (which Stalin supports)
Nov 1927	Kamenev, Zinoviev and Trotsky are expelled from the Party for factionalism
Early 1928	A serious food shortage; Stalin moves against the NEP; harsh grain requisitioning
April 1928	Bukharin criticises 'excesses' of officials following Stalin's methods
Dec 1929	Bukharin and supporters removed from the Politburo following their defence of the NEP at the Fifteenth Party Congress, which Stalin opposes

b This answer will depend on your own view. Remember to explain your reasoning.

c Your consideration of the events contributing to Stalin's victory will provide you with a range of themes to consider in evaluating the reasons for his victory, with your answers to **a** and **b** providing a framework for your assessment of the significance of Stalin's opposition to the NEP. Even if you are certain from the outset that it was not Stalin's opposition to the NEP that was most important to his success in the leadership struggle, make sure you give it a full evaluation rather than dismissing it out of hand.

🔘 Key Concept

a **Communist beliefs about how the economy of a state should operate:** communists believe that the state owns and controls the wealth of the country, and that citizens should be rewarded according to their needs, in proportions equal to the amount of labour they give to create that wealth.

The Leninist approach to the working of the economy: Lenin was pragmatic and, from 1921, Leninism involved state control of banks, transport and major industries combined with some capitalism, in the form of private trade.

Stalin's approach to the working of the economy: Stalinism brought central state control, with the total abolition of private trade and the collectivisation of agriculture, but wage differentials were introduced to incentivise workers.

b Differences between the three approaches are likely to be more significant than the similarities.
  - While Stalin's approach to the economy had superficial similarities with communist beliefs – particularly in the state control of industry

and agriculture – there was something of a gap between the brutal reality of life in Stalin's USSR and the vision of the communist society.

- Lenin's pragmatic approach recognised that the Bolsheviks had to win control over Russia before they could even begin to build towards socialism. It shared the communist vision, but accepted that conditions in Russia were very far from achieving it, and argued that private trade was required in order to keep the economy running.

🔶 Apply Your Knowledge

In 1924, much evidence suggested that Trotsky would succeed Lenin as Party leader: Lenin's Testament said he was 'the most capable man in the Central Committee'; Trotsky was a hero of the Revolution and Civil War; he had the support of the Red Army; he was an inspirational speechmaker; Trotsky did not think he needed to undermine Stalin in 1924, as his own position was so strong.

One of the reasons for Stalin's success in the power struggle was the position he held and the influence he wielded in the Party: Stalin's role as General Secretary meant he could appoint his supporters to key Party positions; it meant his supporters voted down Trotsky's criticisms of Stalin at the Thirteenth Congress, voted down Kamenev and Zinoviev's criticisms of Stalin at the Fourteenth Congress, and confirmed the expulsion of the Left Opposition at the Fifteenth Congress.

Stalin used his theory of 'Socialism in One Country' to damage Trotsky: Stalin used his own theory to accuse Trotsky of a) contradicting Lenin and b) dismissing the USSR's potential. Stalin's theory suggested a faith in the Soviet Union and its people that Trotsky appeared to deny.

Stalin used debates over industrialisation and the NEP to damage his rivals: the Left Opposition called for an end to the NEP and promoted rapid industrialisation. Stalin allied with Bukharin to oppose them. When the Left Opposition was eliminated, Stalin used the grain crisis of 1927 to argue against Bukharin – using the same arguments as the Left Opposition about rapid industrialisation.

Lenin's ban on factionalism in 1921 was significant in Stalin's rise to power: Stalin used the ban on factions to get the Left Opposition expelled from the Party after they organised demonstrations.

Chapter 11

⚖️ 🅰️ Assess the Validity of This View

a Other reasons could include: the leadership struggle; the war scare; Stalin's 'Socialism in One Country'; ideological concerns about the NEP.

b Your paragraph should mention that the 'Great Turn' involved Stalin changing his position on industrialisation, from opposing the Left on rapid industrialisation/supporting Bukharin on gradual industrialisation, to arguing for rapid industrialisation/going against Bukharin by supporting harsh grain requisitioning.

c Your answer needs to consider whether Stalin's 'Great Turn' was motivated by his desire to reinforce his leadership, by targeting Bukharin after the Left Opposition had been neutralised; or whether he did so to stay in step with majority Party opinion as it cooled towards the NEP; or whether Stalin was really convinced by the war scare and the threat posed by the kulaks to socialism.

🔶 Apply Your Knowledge

a Historians could learn that the aims were very ambitious, with even the lowest target still calling for a huge increase in production; and that the most stretching target was for the production of electricity.

b Answers could include:
- Through propaganda-led work campaigns in which workers were encouraged to achieve or exceed targets.
- Through fear of punishment for workers and managers who failed to meet targets.
- Through the use of technical experts.
- Through state planning.
- Through the provision of new infrastructure (e.g. railways and canals to improve the transport of resources to factories).
- Through the development of new industrial facilities on a large scale (e.g. Magnitogorsk).
- Through switching investment from agriculture to industry.

📝 🄰🅂 Plan Your Essay

a **Evidence that Stalin's main motivation was the elimination of the kulaks:**
- The decision to accelerate collectivisation was triggered by the grain procurement crisis. Stalin blamed the crisis on kulaks hoarding grain in order to drive up grain prices.
- The drive for collectivisation followed Stalin's endorsement of the Urals-Siberian method, in which requisition brigades seized grain quotas from peasants – especially the kulaks.
- Collectivisation was accompanied by mass deportations of kulaks.
- In his speech of December 1929, Stalin announced the 'liquidation of the kulaks as a class.'
- The 25,000 urban Party members who were sent to promote collectivisation were tasked with identifying and removing kulaks.

Alternative motives for accelerating collectivisation:
- Stalin had economic motivations – peasant farming was too small-scale and inefficient to produce enough food to feed the urban workers; collectivisation would increase production.
- Collectivisation was part of the Party's rejection of the NEP.
- Socialist theory saw collectivisation as the right way for agriculture to be organised, and many Bolsheviks were glad to accelerate the collectivisation process as it put the USSR back on a 'true' socialist route.

b Your plan should show balance in order to come to a substantiated conclusion. You should consider how far you think the elimination of the kulaks was carried out as a way of removing an obstacle to achieving the main aims of collectivisation (e.g. providing the food security needed for industrialisation), or whether you agree that eliminating class enemies was Stalin's central aim (e.g. in order to ensure that the state was in control of the countryside).

🔶 Apply Your Knowledge

a **1928, January:** Stalin's demand for 'extraordinary measures' in tackling the grain crisis

1928, April: Bukharin outvoted in the Politburo on agricultural policy

1928, November: Bukharin attacked by Stalin for 'Right deviation'

1929, November: Bukharin removed from the Politburo

b The timeline shows that Stalin was hesitant at first (despite the grain procurement crisis happening in 1927, only 5 per cent of farms had been collectivised by 1929); that he became bolder towards the end of 1929, but still wanted the action to come 'from the Party'; that he eventually took action against the kulaks regardless of the consequences.

Chapter 12

🔍 Source Analysis

What does the attribution tell us about the author of the source, and how might this affect what he says? George Kennan was a former US diplomat who had lived in the USSR. This gives his views credibility as he has 'inside' experience of politics in the USSR, but his nationality means he is likely to be biased against Stalin.

What is the purpose of the source and how might this affect its value? The purpose is to communicate Kennan's view of Stalin's intentions and motivations to an informed audience. Kennan ideally would have given a lecture that was objective/unbiased, but his own opinions/biases are likely to have shown through, and he might have wanted to persuade others of these. This means the source needs to be treated carefully.

What view is put forward in the source about Stalin's foreign policy? That his primary motivation was Soviet control over foreign communist parties, even if this reduced their chances of coming into power.

In what ways could you support or challenge the view of the source from your own knowledge? Stalin exerted tight control over communist parties in other countries, e.g. by making sure they all followed Party policy. But it is not clear whether his main motivation for doing so was to prevent these parties from becoming too powerful.

What are the strengths of the source to an historian studying the change in Stalin's foreign policy in 1929? It supports the view that there was a 'Stalin revolution' in foreign policy, with a more aggressive approach that focused on ensuring central control, party discipline and ideological conformity in foreign communist parties.

What are the limitations of the source to an historian studying the change in Stalin's foreign policy in 1929? It does not provide evidence to back up its assertions. It is not contemporary to the events it describes, and it is likely to be affected by bias against Stalin, coming from the viewpoint of an American during the height of the Cold War.

⚖️ 🅰️ To What Extent?

a **The power struggle:**
- *Examples of the use of forceful methods*: not a factor.
- *Examples of other methods*: the power struggle relied on political manoeuvring. A key to Stalin's rise to power was his control over Party appointments. Stalin also expertly manipulated his position as a moderate within the Party to remove his rivals, occupying a moderate central position while first portraying the Left of the Party as factionalists, then turning on the Right of the Party with accusations of a Right deviation.

The implementation of forced collectivisation:
- *Examples of the use of forceful methods*: collectivisation was imposed by special brigades, accompanied by local police, OGPU officers and soldiers, who identified and removed kulaks by force.
- *Examples of other methods*: the brigades also used propaganda/positive messages about the benefits of collectivisation to encourage peasants to collectivise. The implementation of collectivisation was supported by the increasing mechanisation of agriculture.

The implementation of the first Five Year Plan:
- *Examples of the use of forceful methods*: the use of forced labour was central to the achievements of the first Five Year Plan. The rapid increase in the industrial workforce was achieved by forcing peasants out of the countryside through enforced collectivisation. Managers of key industries faced harsh punishments for missing targets.

- *Examples of other methods*: the first Five Year Plan was implemented through central planning (Gosplan). It also relied on massive increases in industrial investment. Propaganda was key as well.

b This answer will depend on your own reasons; remember to give your reason why. For example, 'Force was clearly less important in Stalin's rise to power than his ability to split his rivals and form alliances with some to destroy others. This was what enabled him to outmanoeuvre and isolate first Trotsky, then Zinoviev and Kamenev, then Bukharin.'

c In your answer you should balance the importance of forceful measures against other factors. Showing how different causes link together (for example, the relationship between propaganda and force) should enable you to show judgement about which was the most important. Remember to use information from the table to support your evaluation.

Plan Your Essay

a **Evidence that Stalin was cautious in his foreign policy:** this could include Stalin's attitude towards China. There was an opportunity for the USSR to back another communist party (the CCP) in a neighbouring country, with potentially huge strategic benefits. However, Stalin chose to put the security of the USSR first and backed the GMD on the grounds that GMD rule would be more likely to avoid destabilising China. The Rapallo Treaty and the Treaty of Berlin were both examples of the USSR portraying itself as moderate and reasonable rather than seeking to provoke communist revolution across the world, which could also be described as cautious – further evidence of Stalin wanting stability and security for the USSR first and foremost.

Evidence that Stalin was bold in his foreign policy: not supporting the CCP in China was a bold move in terms of the USSR's internal policies (Stalin was criticised in 1927 by the Party Congress at a time when his hold on power was far from secure). Stalin's changes after 1929 to Comintern could also be seen as bold, since they risked foreign communist parties rejecting control by Moscow, which could be destabilising for the USSR and might undermine Stalin's leadership.

b Plan how you will evaluate the evidence for and against the statement, then consider the points you will include to substantiate your judgement in the conclusion.

Chapter 13

Apply Your Knowledge

Extract 1: b) because Stalin is saying the USSR could not have survived on what the collective and state farms were producing in 1927.

Extract 2: c) because Bukharin was arguing against all-out war on the kulaks (who had been the foundation of the improvements in farming and grain production under the NEP).

Extract 3: c) because Stalin is criticising the 'opposition' of Bukharin, who was still arguing for the NEP approach of controlling capitalist tendencies in the countryside. a) because Stalin is directly targeting the kulaks as a class that needs to be eliminated.

Plan Your Essay

a **Economic effects:** during the period of peasant opposition, agricultural production fell dramatically (sometimes even to 1913 levels). Grain output did not exceed pre-collectivisation levels until after 1935. Grain exports increased (despite declining harvests); since the state bought grain at a low price, these profits funded Stalin's Five Year Plans.

Social effects: in the famine of 1932–34, approximately 6–8 million died. The money from grain exports funded industrialisation, while the poor conditions on collective farms fuelled

migration to the cities. In 1939, 50 per cent of Soviet citizens were working class; in 1929 it had been only 18 per cent. Living standards fell both in the countryside and the cities.

Political effects: grain exports increased, justifying Stalin's 'Great Turn' to rapid industrialisation and the rejection of the NEP. The Party agreed with Stalin that the kulaks needed to be destroyed, weakening Bukharin's opposition. There was great enthusiasm for Stalin's model of building socialism.

b A possible conclusion could be:

'Collectivisation was a political success but brought economic and social disaster' is a valid view. If the social costs only included the famine of 1932–34, that would be enough to be classed as a disaster, but collectivisation also alienated peasants from the state due to the extortionate way in which the state set quotas and made payments to the collective farms, while also failing to meet its commitments to the workers, who faced lower living standards and wages. Economically, collectivisation sent production into reverse as it removed the most successful farmers from the countryside, stripped out any incentive among kolkhozniks to increase production, and failed to supply enough tractors to replace the horsepower lost in opposition to collectivisation. Politically, though, Stalin was entirely victorious: his strategy of switching back to the arguments of the Left enabled him to isolate Bukharin and end any further challenge to his leadership, as the Party enthusiastically embraced dekulakisation and collectivisation as part of Stalin's 'revolution from above.'

Source Analysis

a **Source A:**
- *Strengths*: an article by Stalin, giving an insight into his views; an article written at the end of the first phase of collectivisation.
- *Weaknesses*: the article could be considered to be propaganda.

Source B:
- *Strengths*: by an outsider with more freedom to report objectively; provides eyewitness evidence about Ukraine during the height of the famine.
- *Weaknesses*: published anonymously, which limits an analysis of its origin; published in a left-wing British newspaper that might have been sympathetic to the aims of the Soviet government; the reporter may have been sent especially to find out more about the famine, which could have influenced who the reporter talked to and the information they chose to include in their report.

Source C:
- *Strengths*: written by a government official and released as a top secret document, meaning that it could include information the government would not want to be made public knowledge; written during the famine in a famine-struck area; the purpose suggests a relatively objective, fact-based report.
- *Weaknesses*: we have little information about who the regional health inspector was (e.g. their political affiliations). The purpose of the report could have been to get more funding for the region by selecting the most extreme cases. The language used in the report suggests a level of disgust at the conditions experienced, which could suggest bias.

b **Source A** has value as it gives insight into Stalin's decisions about how he wanted collectivisation to be presented, following the chaos and suffering that its implementation caused. However, it is not objective and could be considered a piece of propaganda.

Source B has value as a view from outside the USSR, which gives an eye-witness report of the famine, although from a left-wing British newspaper that

might have been sympathetic to the aims of the world's first 'socialist' state.

Source C has value as secret official document, which can be expected to have a level of scientific objectivity about what it reports, and to be less affected than Source A of having to present something suitable for public viewing.

Chapter 14

Apply Your Knowledge

a False (steel production exceeded its target in the second Five Year Plan).

b Electricity.

c This answer will depend on your own view as to whether the achievements of the first Five Year Plans were significant enough to justify the broad objective of achieving the rapid industrialisation of the USSR (even though individual targets were not met), or whether you think that the fact that some targets were so far from being met is evidence that the target setters had no real idea what the challenges were going to be in rapidly increasing production.

d • *Strength*: the first two Five Year Plans achieved very impressive growth rates in heavy industry.
- *Limitation*: with the exception of steel in the second Five Year Plan, no economic area made its target. Although this was not revealed to the public, it does suggest the Five Year Plans were not successful on their own terms.

Apply Your Knowledge

a **Created opportunities:** training programmes were made available for workers to develop new skills. The purges created opportunities by removing white-collar workers, experts and intellectuals. The provision of childcare facilities meant that mothers could work.

Made life harder: more people migrated into the towns from the countryside, leading to further overcrowding in the cities. Industrialisation focused on heavy industry so there were few consumer products available. Harsh discipline was used for workers.

b An example paragraph could read:

Although living and working conditions did not rise significantly under the first Five Year Plans, it is likely that this was a side effect of the way the Five Year Plans were carried out, rather than the reason for why industrialisation was achieved. It is certainly true that workers' living conditions declined still further as millions more peasants migrated to industrial centres to escape life under collectivisation, causing a housing crisis. However, this was an effect of collectivisation, which helped provide the workforce for industrialisation. Living conditions were badly affected by a shortage of consumer products, but this resulted from the focus on heavy industry at the expense of light industry in the Five Year Planning process. Strict labour discipline did help to achieve industrialisation, and this made working conditions very tough for many, which could be an exception to this argument.

Apply Your Knowledge

Other factors could include: a six-day working week and longer working hours; poor working conditions; poor living conditions; corruption and bribery; Stalin's purges removed many experts; many workers struggled to feed themselves even after rationing ended.

To What Extent?

a **Rapid industrialisation:**
- *Limitations to its success*: Stalin's targets were set too high and few were achieved. Fear of missing targets meant false data, corruption, bribery and poor-quality products.

A focus on heavy industry:

- *Example of its success*: steel production exceeded its target in the second Five Year Plan; other heavy industries significantly increased their production.
- *Limitations to its success*: Stalin's targets were too high to be met, and the focus on heavy industry starved light industry of investment, causing shortages for Soviet people.

The development of new industrial centres:

- *Example of its success*: large industrial centres such as Magnitogorsk and Komsomolsk were built in central and eastern USSR.

Collectivisation to feed the urban workforce and fund industrialisation:

- *Example of its success*: grain exports increased and the urban population was fed (rationing ended in 1935).
- *Limitations to its success*: collectivisation lowered agricultural production for many years. It was a factor in the death of 6–8 million in the famine of 1932–34.

b Part **a** of this activity will help you to establish the aims for industrial development that you will be considering in your answer, and provides you with some evidence for and against their being met. You will need to link this evidence more firmly to the Five Year Plans in order to answer the question directly.

Chapter 15

🌞 Apply Your Knowledge

Extract 1: the focus of socialist realist art should be labour – the work done by working people. A real socialist hero is someone who works hard and finds ways to achieve more than expected (like Stakhanov).

Extract 2: socialist realism should explore the (positive) impact that socialism has on people's lives, both emotionally and intellectually, and consider how it transforms them as people.

Extract 3: all the art produced by the USSR should be fully dedicated to guiding and encouraging the proletariat of all countries to rise up against capitalism and overthrow it. Anyone not doing this should be excluded from making art.

Extract 4: Soviet artists should work as a collective rather than as individuals, and this collective should be organised so that all its members are working to promote an official view of Soviet culture.

⬆️ Ⓐ How Important?

a **Evidence to support the idea that propaganda was important:** propaganda dominated all media; propaganda was particularly strong for young people; propaganda helped with the implementation of the Five Year Plans; propaganda encouraged Stakhanovites.

Evidence to support the idea that propaganda had limited importance: complaints from workers about conditions and corruption suggests that propaganda was not convincing workers completely; resistance to collectivisation suggests propaganda was not effective in convincing peasants of the benefits of collective farms; other factors (such as fear and aggression) were required to keep Stalin's regime functioning.

b There is no single right answer to this question, but your table might lead you to judge the importance of propaganda in the USSR to be very considerable, but not total. You might consider that propaganda had a stronger influence on young people, when it could be at its most aspirational, but for older people it may have been most important when it supported what they wanted, and least important when it went against their material interests or when reality seemed a long way from the promised communist future.

💡 Key Concept

a Examples could include: youth propaganda moulded the way young people thought and behaved (e.g. through the example of Pavlik Morozov); propaganda in cities emphasised the importance of working hard to contribute to the Five Year Plans; radio broadcasts idealised Soviet achievements and warned audiences about enemy threats.

b Socialist realism was used to exert ideological control in the USSR during the 1930s both over Soviet artists themselves, who had to produce propaganda for the state if they wanted to earn money from their work; and over the Soviet people who were the audience for socialist realist art. This art was purged of any criticism of the Soviet system or any view opposing the Party's doctrine.

Chapter 16

🌞 Apply Your Knowledge

Industrialisation:

- Strengthened the USSR because it helped the USSR to outproduce the Germans. Victory in the Great Patriotic War was in many ways due to the success of Soviet industrialisation.
- Weakened the USSR because the centrally planned nature of industry ignored consumers, making the Soviet population dissatisfied with the continuing gap between what they had been promised and what their reality was.

Urbanisation:

- Strengthened the USSR by contributing to its industrialisation/modernisation.
- Weakened the USSR by creating overcrowding and poor living conditions in the cities. These led to dissatisfaction that made it harder to keep the Soviet people in line.

Collectivisation:

- Strengthened the USSR by extending state control over the countryside. Helped the USSR to increase grain exports, which helped to fund industrialisation.
- Weakened the USSR by reducing grain levels, and by contributing to the deaths of 6–8 million in the famine of 1932–34.

State ownership of the means of production:

- Strengthened the USSR because it allowed the state to quickly turn the USSR over to military production, including the enormous task of moving factory production away from the west of the USSR to safety in the Ural mountains and further east.
- Weakened the USSR because the state, through Gosplan, had become responsible for managing an ever-more complex production system. This complexity led to inefficiencies and delays, especially in the production of consumer goods.

Centralisation:

- Strengthened the USSR because it enabled military decision-making during the war to become highly effective and efficient, and this certainly contributed to victory in the war. Centralisation also meant a coherent political, economic and cultural system for all the very different nations and ethnic groups making up the vast Soviet Union.
- Weakened the USSR as it led to bureaucratisation of the USSR. This contributed to inefficiency and corruption. It also created elitism in the Soviet system (as the bureaucrats made sure they had access to the best things), which was resented by ordinary people.

📝 Ⓐ Plan Your Essay

a Central planning in the Soviet Union was the process of planning targets for each sector of the economy

and then monitoring the extent to which these targets were achieved. Gosplan was responsible for central planning.

The relationship between central planning and economic development was a direct one: the aim was that central planning would direct investment into the areas that would deliver economic development.

The Soviet Union's economic development in the years 1929 to 1941 was impressive: Western analysis of Soviet era records suggest at least a 5 per cent growth rate per year in the 1930s (the USSR claimed 10 per cent).

Central planning was very important to this economic development because state central planning almost completely replaced private markets in the USSR.

b **Propaganda:** propaganda campaigns enthused workers to meet or exceed their targets.

Prison camp labour: many of the mega projects (e.g. Komsomolsk) could not have been completed without free prison camp labour.

Collective farm private plots: accounted for a significant part of the food production of the USSR, without which economic development might have slowed significantly.

Foreign expertise: essential to achieving the rapid industrialisation of the USSR, e.g. the Dnieprostroi Dam relied on expertise from Canada.

Fear: central to the USSR's economic development, e.g. managers were punished for failing to meet targets, workers faced severe disciplinary measures for absences or lateness.

c You can use the points you've made above to help structure your plan. An introduction should explain central planning and its relationship to economic development, and outline the direction of your argument.

You will need to develop your argument by considering ways in which central planning was significant, probably through a consideration of the aims and achievements of the Five Year Plans.

Counter these with any relevant points about other factors. You should make your judgement clear in the introduction and repeat it in your conclusion.

⚖️ Ⓐ Assess the Validity of This View

a **Row 1:**

- *Present in the USSR?*: by 1941 the USSR was far more proletarian than in 1917 and the peasants had been forced into a socialist form of production: the collective and state farms.

Row 2:

- *Meaning*: individuals will no longer be allowed to own things just for themselves. All property will be shared.
- *Present in the USSR?*: the state did own everything: industry, land, housing, control over the economy. The Soviet people all technically shared in this ownership.

Row 4:

- *Meaning*: once capitalist control of industry and agriculture was overthrown, the communist economy would be much more productive.
- *Present in the USSR?*: by 1941 the USSR had succeeded in achieving rapid industrialisation of heavy industry.

b A communist state should have a centrally controlled economy with no private ownership. It will be largely a proletarian society in which the workers, who will share the same values as workers everywhere, will devote themselves to increasing the country's wealth.

c You should discuss the features of communism in your answer, and consider whether these had been achieved or not by 1941 in the USSR.

⬆ A Improve an Answer

a **Strengths:** the paragraph has some relevance to the question (the lives of Soviet citizens), it makes a relevant point (living conditions on collective farms were often very poor), and it makes a judgement about 'to what extent' ('the Five Year Plans didn't improve living conditions for peasants in the countryside'). Consideration of living conditions in the countryside and in the gulags shows balance as most answers are likely to focus on living conditions in cities and factories.

Weaknesses: the paragraph does not address the question's focus on 'by 1941'. There needs to be relevant detail about living conditions on collective farms – saying they 'were often very poor' is inadequate. The same is true for 'harsh conditions' in Siberian prison camps. The link between the Five Year Plans and poor conditions on collective farms and in prison camps needs to be made explicit. The judgement made lacks the balance required for a good A level answer.

b Your improved version should address the weaknesses identified in part **a**.

Chapter 17

⚙ Apply Your Knowledge

Article 17: Stalin would not allow republics to secede (leave) the USSR. His attitude to the republics is shown in his ruthless suppression of republic leaderships during the purges, replacing them with people loyal to his regime.

Article 122: although employment opportunities did become more equal, women received less pay, had fewer opportunities, and were generally expected to do all housework.

Article 125: people were arrested for anti-Soviet conversations, so there was no freedom of speech in practice. Writers had to be members of the Union of Soviet Writers and were often censored, showing there was no freedom of the press.

Article 127: the arbitrary arrests and sentences without trial during the Yezhovshchina show how little the machinery of Soviet state terror was affected by this article.

⬆ A How Significant?

a **Examples of Stalin's use of terror between 1929 and December 1934:** the Shakhty trial (an early show trial) in 1928; the 'Industrial Party' trial in 1930; purges of Ryutin, Zinoviev and Kamenev in 1932.

Examples of Stalin's use of terror after December 1934 until 1939: Zinoviev and Kamenev's arrest (January 1935); the extension of the death penalty to those engaging in subversive activity or guilty of not reporting subversive activity (June 1935); the Trial of 16 (1936); the Trial of 17 (1937); the military purge (1937); the Trial of 21 (1938).

b Depending on your view, your conclusion could consider Stalin's use of terror to have changed after Kirov's murder, with Stalin using the murder as an excuse to launch purges that had no parallel in the USSR before 1934. Your conclusion in this case would need to review in what ways the use of terror was different (e.g. in its focus, scale, and methods of operation) in order to justify this view. Alternatively, your conclusion could argue that there was continuity in the use of terror before and after 1934.

🔍 A Source Analysis

a **Source A** is an account of a show trial published in Britain. This may mean that the author, Denis Pritt, is able to give his true feelings about the trial without offending the Soviet authorities. If that is the case then Pritt's purpose is to defend the verdicts of the show trials and the actions of Stalin's regime for a British audience. If Pritt's purpose was to justify the

show trials because of his strong support for Stalin, then this would make the source highly biased.

Source B is a private note. This means the author, Stalin, was more likely to be honest with his thoughts and views. The source is valuable because it indicates Stalin's personal views about the show trials, including how they should be undertaken and with what aims.

Source C is an extract from a trial. The record of Kamenev and Zinoviev's confessions was important to the show trial because it was intended to be read widely so that many Soviet people could understand the reasons why they had been sentenced to death, and to understand the threats that the Soviet Union was facing.

b **Source A:** the author is Denis Pritt, an eyewitness at the Zinoviev and Kamenev trial and a Labour MP. As a Labour MP in the 1930s it is possible that he was a supporter of the Stalin regime, which might affect the value of this source because he might not have wanted to accept the criticism of the show trials as being based on lies and forced confessions. As an eyewitness to the trial, his account is more valuable than if he was merely commenting on something he had seen reported in a newspaper.

Source B: the author is Stalin. This makes it a valuable source as Stalin ordered the show trials, the public reason for which was his concerns about a dangerous conspiracy threatening his leadership in particular and the USSR in general. An alternative view is that Stalin ordered the trials in order to get rid of old rivals. A source written by Stalin that indicates his reasons for the show trials would therefore be valuable.

Source C: gives written accounts of statements by Zinoviev and Kamenev. These are valuable as a record of the confessions made by both men. However, while people at the time may have viewed them as genuine statements, there are strong reasons to suspect that these are confessions the men were forced to make. As such they are valuable as records of what the state wanted them to say.

c Your answer should include the points made above but also recognise how the sources can still be valuable to/have limitations for an historian studying the show trials of the 1930s.

Source A: the value of Source A is limited by the author's insistence that just because Zinoviev and Kamenev were hardened revolutionaries with long experience of how prisons and interrogations worked, this made them in some way immune to forced confessions. In fact, the author is naïve enough to say he thinks forced confessions are 'intrinsically impossible'. However, the source is valuable in another way: indicating that some foreign observers of the show trials were prepared to believe that the Soviet authorities had not extracted confessions from the defendants by force.

Source B: valuable especially because of the way Stalin says that getting the accused to confess to their crimes ('admitting their mistakes'), while at the same time admitting how powerless they are to overthrow the Soviet state, would 'not be bad'. Since this is what happened in subsequent show trials, this source is valuable in supporting the view of Stalin as the architect of the show trials and their main beneficiary. Source B's limitations could include its being about a relatively minor and early show trial, so e.g. it is not providing evidence about Stalin's views on Kamenev and Zinoviev's show trial, which may have been different.

Source C: has many limitations – contextual knowledge strongly suggests that both men were coerced to make these confessions, which makes them unreliable. However, the value of Source C is that it tells us what the regime wanted these two senior Bolsheviks to confess to: the assassination of Kirov (which legitimised Stalin's purges), the continuing threat from Trotsky, the attempts to

wreck Stalin's great achievements, and the attempts to split the Party.

Chapter 18

⚙ Apply Your Knowledge

Your timeline is likely to add some or all of the following events:

1930	The Industrial Party Trial
1932	Stalin's wife commits suicide; Ryutin imprisoned for his attack on Stalin; Kamenev and Zinoviev expelled from the Party
1933	The Metro-Vickers Trial; Party purge with over 570,000 'Ryutinites' expelled
1934	Kirov's murder
1935	Secret trial and imprisonment of Kamenev and Zinoviev
1936	Kamenev and Zinoviev show trial
1937	The Trial of 17; the military purge and Great Purge
1938	The Trial of 21; end of the Yezhovshchina
1940	Yezhov executed

⚓ A To What Extent?

a **Stalin:** started the Yezhovshchina by approving NKVD Order 00447. Had the power to end the purges, but chose not to. The highest profile targets of the show trials were Stalin's rivals for power.

Bolshevik leaders: Lenin had left a legacy of terror – perhaps 100,000 people were killed in the Red Terror (1918), which gave the Cheka extra-judicial powers of arrest and sentencing. Bolshevik leaders considered terror to be an acceptable method of control. Yezhov ruthlessly implemented NKVD Order 00447.

Local Party officials and activists: NKVD quotas were often pushed up by zealous local officials who wanted their commitment to be obvious. 850,000 people were purged from the Party between 1936 and 1938, so there were lots of opportunities for ambitious people to further their careers by showing their commitment to the Party.

Ordinary individuals: as terror escalated out of control, individuals denounced others in the hope of saving themselves or their families, as well as to settle scores or remove rivals.

b There is no correct answer to this (though you are not likely to absolve Stalin from any responsibility for the Yezhovshchina). Your judgement will need to be supported.

c Your answer should develop the points made in part **a**. You should identify the links between these different points, e.g. Stalin's concerns about opposition to his policies was not only reserved to the senior leadership of the Communist Party; he was worried about opposition at local levels too, which helps explain why NKVD Order 00447, with its focus on former kulaks, criminals and anti-Soviet elements, served Stalin's purposes. Your conclusion should clearly state the extent to which you think Stalin was responsible and substantiate this with reference to your assessment in the main part of your answer.

⚙ Apply Your Knowledge

1. Prison camps/forced labour camps.
2. Heads of the NKVD: Yagoda was replaced by Yezhov in 1936 (and executed in 1938), Yezhov was replaced by Beria in 1938 (and executed in 1940).
3. Leonid Nikolayev.
4. Kamenev and Zinoviev.
5. Former kulaks, criminals and other anti-Soviet elements.
6. Tomsky, because he committed suicide.

🔆 Key Concept

Elements could include: the secret police, state terror, censorship, one-party rule, central control over regions and over the economy and society. Remember to add supporting detail to each, e.g. the cult of personality represented Stalin as infallible, the 'Great Helmsman'.

🗹 🅐 Plan Your Essay

a **Stalin's 'Great Turn':** Stalin took control of the ideological debates within the Party over the NEP and proceeded to set the social and economic agenda of the USSR in the 1930s.

The growing threat of war from Germany and Japan: the USSR/the Politburo was more inclined to look for a single leader to lead the country against the military threat.

Collectivisation and the Five Year Plans: Stalin championed these transformative social and economic movements, although they also created opposition.

Stalin's cult of personality: this created an image of Stalin as an infallible leader whose political dominance should be impossible to challenge.

Mass terror and repression: real or imagined opposition to Stalin's political dominance was ruthlessly repressed.

b This answer will depend on your own view. Make sure you explain your reasoning.

c The table provides five themes that could be evaluated for significance in this essay. The introduction to your essay could mention each of the five themes and give a view on their relative importance in terms of their contribution to Stalin's political dominance. The conclusion should give your judgement on the significance of mass terror and repression, with a brief summary of the supporting evidence that has led you to form this view.

Chapter 19

🔆 Apply Your Knowledge

Other qualities could include:

Party-minded: dedicated to the Party and its needs, putting the Party above family and friends.

How this was expressed or encouraged: people were encouraged to denounce family and friends during the Yezhovshchina (e.g. following the example of Pavlik Morozov); rapid industrialisation and collectivisation prioritised building a socialist future over improving living conditions for ordinary people.

Urban and modern: *How this was expressed or encouraged:* the urban workforce grew considerably in the 1930s; religion was repressed; socialist realism glorified the worker.

Not private or independent: *How this was expressed or encouraged:* overcrowded living conditions in the cities meant very little privacy; Soviet propaganda, socialist realism and mass terror all encouraged people to conform/not show independence or individualism.

🎏 🅐 Assess the Validity of This View

a **Evidence to support the statement:**

- Article 122 of the Stalin Constitution gave women 'equal rights with men in all spheres of economic, state, cultural, social and political life.'
- By 1940, around 43 per cent of the workforce was female.
- 60 per cent of collective farm workers were women.
- The Party ordered managers to employ more women in heavy industry for the second Five Year Plan. From 1936, the Party responded by making it easier for women to enter management training programmes.

- State provision of nurseries, crèches and child clinics meant that women were free of childcare responsibilities during their working hours.

Evidence to counter the statement:

- By 1940, women still only received 60–65 per cent of the pay of men for doing the same job.
- Most women were employed in medicine, education and domestic service: all areas with low pay and lower status.
- Managers continued to give the best paid, highest skilled jobs to men and were reluctant to allow women to get training to improve their skills.
- In 1923, working women did three times as much housework as men; by 1936 it was five times as much.

b A possible conclusion could be:

Stalin's USSR did not achieve equality for women and men during the 1930s. Article 122 of the Stalin Constitution was more about ideology than reality. The USSR in the 1930s advocated equality for women, but the gains women made in getting equal access to jobs were limited in important ways. Career opportunities were restricted and the top jobs in most industries went to men, while managers often kept skilled jobs for male workers. Equality was not present in everyday life either; women were still expected to do housework and childcare after their working day was over.

🗹 🅐 Plan Your Essay

a Benefits could include: improved opportunities from training and education; wage differentials (from 1931) meant skilled workers were paid more; the Stakhanovite movement (from 1935) gave some workers some power over managers; a skills shortage in the 1930s meant good workers were in high demand.

Ways this group suffered could include: long working hours; harsh work discipline; poor living conditions; the purges often targeted 'experts'.

b **Women:** had better access to management training programmes after 1936; benefited from tax breaks if they had six or more children; but were still expected to look after their children and homes on top of full-time work.

Young people: benefited from membership of Komsomol as this provided free summer and winter holiday camps; young people who joined Komsomol had access to better jobs and opportunities; young people benefited from free education; but education was limited and restrictive; young people were encouraged to report their parents to the authorities; Western culture and fashion were banned.

Party members: benefited the most under Stalinism, with high-achieving Party bureaucrats getting access to more living space and a higher quality of life; but Party members were also heavily purged in the terror of the 1930s and never fully secure.

c A possible introduction could be:

Skilled workers certainly did better under Stalinism than unskilled workers. Factory managers were usually keen to keep hold of skilled workers, so working conditions for them were not so harsh. Skilled workers were paid more and had better opportunities for training and job progression, while the Stakhanovite movement provided a way in which they could put pressure on managers to improve their working conditions further. However, conditions even for skilled workers were not easy. Nor were skilled workers the only social group to benefit from Stalinist policies. There were some gains for women and some benefits for young people. However, the social group that both benefited the most (while also being at high risk of Stalin's purges) were the Party bureaucrats who became the elite of Soviet society.

Chapter 20

🔆 Apply Your Knowledge

a **The Treaty of Berlin:** reaffirmed the 'trustful cooperation' between Germany and the USSR which the Treaty of Rapallo had established. Good relations (including substantial loans for the USSR's industrialisation from German banks) continued between the USSR and Germany until Stresemann's death in 1929 and the beginning of the global economic crisis.

Hitler becomes Chancellor of Germany, 1933: the USSR's relationship with Germany had been with the Weimar Republic; Hitler's open hatred of communism and explicit plans to expand Germany to the east forced a change away from the USSR's previous policy of cooperation with Germany.

Japan and Germany sign the first Anti-Comintern Pact, 1936: the signatories committed to resisting the spread of communism sponsored by the Comintern. This alliance between the two countries that posed the most threat to the USSR confirmed the Soviet leadership's view that an attack on the USSR was probably imminent.

The USSR is excluded from the Munich Conference, September 1938: the conference aimed to find a peaceful solution to Germany's claims on part of Czechoslovakia, but Czechoslovakia and the USSR were both excluded from the conference. The exclusion confirmed Stalin's suspicions that he could not expect to be included in any alliance against Germany, and pushed him towards a Nazi-Soviet alliance.

The German invasion of Czechoslovakia, March 1939: this showed Stalin and the world that Britain's appeasement policy had failed, and that Hitler was intent on gaining territory for Germany in the east. In choosing between an agreement with Britain and France or one with Germany, Stalin could see that Britain and France had little to offer. War in Europe seemed certain. This made the Nazi-Soviet Pact a logical solution to the USSR's situation.

🎏 🅐 Assess the Validity of This View

a The correct order (from top to bottom) is:

1. From 1934, the Comintern encouraged communist parties to cooperate with democratic socialists.
2. The Franco-Soviet Pact of Mutual Assistance (May 1935).
3. Soviet intervention in the Spanish Civil War (1936–39).
4. The Nazi-Soviet Pact (August 1939).

b 1. It was a complete reversal of the 1928 policy.
2. Making this treaty with France (Germany's enemy) undermined the Berlin Treaty.
3. The League of Nations aimed to resolve conflicts peacefully; it called for non-intervention.
4. The Nazi-Soviet Pact enabled Germany to invade Poland without any threat of Soviet intervention.

c Arguments could include: Stalin believed the USSR to be encircled by capitalist enemies, all waiting for the opportunity to attack it. From Stalin's point of view, Britain and France wearing themselves out in a war against Germany with a neutral USSR looking on would have been a win for the USSR, whether he was allied to Germany or to Britain and France.

Stalin's foreign policy was consistently pragmatic rather than principled: survival by any means possible. The Nazi-Soviet Pact was the best option available at the time since it bought Stalin time to prepare the USSR for war. If Britain and France had taken a resolute stand against Germany, Stalin might well have continued with a policy of collective security. In the same way, reversing the policy on the Comintern was pragmatic: it made sense to work together with other enemies of fascism rather than help the fascists take the Left apart.

d A possible conclusion could be:

The evidence clearly shows that Stalin's international policy changed direction in the 1930s, and specific policies certainly contradicted others, particularly in the case of policies aiming at collective security against the threat of aggression from Germany. This could be seen in the Soviet entry into the League of Nations in September 1934 and the reversal in Comintern policy from 1934, as well as policies that increased cooperation between the USSR and Germany. The most striking of these was the Nazi-Soviet Pact of 23 August 1939, but there was also the renewal of the Berlin Treaty in 1931. Even if Stalin's underlying aim was to seize every opportunity to defend the USSR, a contradiction remains and helps to explain why the USSR was so vulnerable during the first six months of the Nazi invasion in 1941.

⬆ 🄰 Improve an Answer

A possible introduction could be:

The Western countries' ineffective policy of appeasement and the exclusion of the USSR from the Munich Conference were the main reason why Stalin chose to make a pact with Germany rather than relying on collective security. There were practical reasons for Stalin's decision to sign the pact, such as avoiding a war on two fronts against both Japan and Germany, but fundamentally the lack of any resolute stand against Hitler by the West after the invasion of Czechoslovakia convinced Stalin that the West was going to sacrifice the East to Hitler to keep themselves from having to fight Germany – and that included letting Germany invade the USSR.

Chapter 21

⚖ 🄰 Assess the Validity of This View

a **Military reasons:** the command economy was linked to wartime production being focused on the needs of the Red Army; the command economy was closely linked to rapid mobilisation for total war; the command economy was linked to Soviet military design strengths (e.g. the T-34 tank), because that design process was centrally organised and then disseminated so that it was possible for one factory to stop making aircraft and start making tanks, for example.

Other reasons: the command economy permitted the efficient organisation of labour and resources. Centralised planning ensured that factories were rapidly adapted to the demands of war and sufficient workers were provided for key industries.

b **Military reasons:** Stalin's war leadership; Germany having to fight a war on two fronts (from December 1941); Hitler's strategic mistakes; mass Allied bombing campaigns; Allied secret intelligence.

Other reasons: the Soviet people's determination to defend their communities (e.g. 4 million people volunteered for citizens' defence in 1941); the state's religious concessions (30,000 churches were re-opened); Lend-Lease aid ($1.3 billion-worth by end of the war).

c This answer will depend on your own views. Make sure you can justify your choices.

d Completing the table is likely to have given you a variety of ideas about how the command economy directly or indirectly contributed to victory in the war. It also should have prompted you to consider counter-arguments and then helped you to decide the validity of the statement in the question. Make sure your answer presents your judgement on the statement in the question, and considers a variety of different viewpoints.

🔍 🄰 Source Analysis

a **Source A:**

- *What does the source tell us about the reaction to Operation Barbarossa?* Stalin's reaction was a call for total war, with everything and everyone totally focused on the defence of the USSR.

- *Why might this source be valuable for an historian studying Operation Barbarossa?* Its content shows how Stalin responded to the invasion (e.g. his call for a total focus on the needs of the Red Army, and for an escalation of coercion and control over the Soviet people). Since the author is Stalin, this shows how he viewed the situation – his expectation of 'disorganisers on the home front' points to his continued suspicion of enemies within.

- *What are the limitations of the source to an historian studying Operation Barbarossa?* The speech is propaganda so it presents only the official side of the Soviet people's reaction to Operation Barbarossa. The source does not tell us anything about people's reaction to Stalin's speech (either its content or timing).

Source B:

- *What does the source tell us about the reaction to Operation Barbarossa?* Stalin announced that the most severe measures possible would be taken against deserters from the Red Army, suggesting that Stalin saw mass desertion from the Red Army as a danger.

- *Why might this source be valuable for an historian studying Operation Barbarossa?* This source suggests that Stalin was concerned about Red Army desertions, which would undermine his message of Soviet people dedicating everything to the Red Army against the hated Germans.

- *What are the limitations of the source to an historian studying Operation Barbarossa?* We do not know from this source what the levels of desertion had been prior to Order Number 270 or what happened as a result of Order Number 270 being given.

Source C:

- *What does the source tell us about the reaction to Operation Barbarossa?* The source suggests that some people were critical of Stalin's reaction to the invasion, because his Nazi-Soviet Pact had made the Germans stronger while not preparing the USSR for the invasion. The critics compare the lack of enthusiasm for war with the inspiration felt among partisans during the Civil War.

- *Why might this source be valuable for an historian studying Operation Barbarossa?* The source provides insight into possible opposition to/criticism of the regime and the reasons for that criticism.

- *What are the limitations of the source to an historian studying Operation Barbarossa?* We do not know from the source how reliable the reports are, how general or exceptional the criticisms were in Archangel'sk, or how far these criticisms were shared by people in other regions of the USSR. We do not know from the source whether the reports were shared with the Party leadership in Moscow and, if they were, what happened as a result.

b **Source A:** Stalin's reaction to the invasion is widely thought to be a sign of shock and panic, since Stalin had signed the Nazi-Soviet Pact in the expectation that the German invasion would not come before 1942.

Source B: desertion was punishable by death in the Great Patriotic War, and this covered both soldiers surrendering to the Germans and soldiers running away. Stalin's Order 270 gave military councils the right to execute any soldier guilty of desertion, which led to a rapid increase in the number of executions.

Source C: when Source C talks about 'our government's being feeding the Germans for two years', this refers to trade deals following the Nazi-Soviet Pact that saw large amounts of food and raw materials being exported to Germany on good terms from the USSR.

c You should include all the points you considered in part **a**, evaluated where appropriate with context from part **b**, as this will give your answer range and balance. Make sure each of your paragraphs

explicitly explains the source's value to *the reaction to Operation Barbarossa*.

Chapter 22

🄰 Apply Your Knowledge

a **Geographical reasons:** the USSR's vast size (the regime could move industrial production out of reach of the Germans; the German army's supplies became overstretched); the USSR's vast natural resources; Germany's lack of self-sufficiency in raw materials; the USSR's large population (three times bigger than Germany's).

Military reasons: effective Soviet military leadership (once interference by the Party was reduced); Stalin's war leadership (ability to learn from early mistakes; decisiveness); Germany having to fight a war on two fronts (from December 1941); Hitler's strategic mistakes (e.g. insisting on the defence of Stalingrad); mass Allied bombing campaigns (which weakened Germany's war production); Allied secret intelligence.

Political reasons: the creation of the Stavka (enabled effective decision-making); central control (e.g. the GKO (State Defence Committee) as the highest level of command); the command economy enabled rapid mobilisation for total war (e.g. engineers and other skilled workers could be ordered to move from one factory to another); effective propaganda.

Contributions by the Allies: Lend-Lease aid ($1.3 billion-worth by end of the war); mass Allied bombing campaigns; Allied secret intelligence; agreement from General Eisenhower that the Red Army should take Berlin.

Other factors: the Soviet people's determination to defend their communities (e.g. 4 million people volunteered for citizens' defence in 1941); Soviet industrial production (e.g. Soviet weapons production increased by 450% through the war).

b Use the reasons you listed in part **a** and follow the approach modelled on page 116. Another possible set of links could be: the USSR's huge size and vast natural resources (geographical reasons) meant the regime could move industrial/military production out of reach of German attack (military and strategic reasons). As a result, Soviet industrial production increased through the war (economic reasons) in a way that Germany could not match.

✅ 🄰 Plan Your Essay

a Your sentence should consider both what constituted success for the regime (e.g. meeting the targets of the fourth Five Year Plan) and broader social criteria such as whether people had enough to eat, whether housing had been reconstructed to pre-war levels, or whether production from consumer industries had been reconstructed to pre-war levels.

b **Industrial reconstruction:**

- *Evidence for success*: many of the fourth Five Year Plan's targets were met, especially for heavy industry (e.g. coal and oil); some successes also in consumer industries (e.g. cotton and wool fabrics); recovery of average Soviet incomes; by 1950, Ukraine's industrial output was higher than before the war.

- *Evidence for limited success*: some consumer products (e.g. shoes, clothes and furniture) were still in short supply.

Agricultural reconstruction:

- *Evidence for success*: agriculture's recovery was slow and patchy but some targets were met (e.g. potato production was higher in 1950 than in 1940).

- *Evidence for limited success*: grain, cotton and cattle production in 1950 was lower than in 1940; famine in some parts of the USSR in 1946–47.

c A possible introduction could be:

The post-war economic reconstruction of the USSR was certainly a remarkable success when viewed in terms of what success meant to the Soviet leadership. The fourth Five Year Plan aimed to exceed pre-war production figures and investment was targeted on heavy industry and the reconstruction of Ukraine, where destruction had been especially severe. Soviet statistics for 1950 show remarkable successes in achieving these aims (although these statistics are not necessarily to be trusted). There were also successes in some consumer industries, but these were not complete, and agriculture was one area where successful reconstruction was not achieved.

Chapter 23

⊙ Apply Your Knowledge

a Socialist realism: all creative writing and art should celebrate the achievements of socialism and show the people of the USSR what their glorious socialist future was going to look like. It was important for all writers to follow socialist realist principles in their work because the regime demanded it; artists were responsible for being the 'engineers of people's souls', showing people what the socialist future would be like and how they should think and act as Soviet men and women. From the artists' point of view, if they wanted to earn money for their art, they needed to follow socialist realist principles.

b Instead of a retired soldier being depicted as a Red Army hero, he is an old man on his way to the bathhouse, already a bit drunk and dressed like a scarecrow (i.e. shabbily). Instead of the retired soldier behaving honourably, he aims to catch the monkey and sell it to buy more beer.

c Being called an individualist meant being accused of not thinking and acting for the good of the state but only thinking and acting for yourself. By thinking of himself as an individual, Zoshchenko was not helping society to improve. In a socialist state, individualism was against what the state was trying to achieve.

☑ Revision Skills

Your timeline could include the following (blue = political, yellow = economic, purple = military, grey = social/cultural):

1946	beginning of Zhdanovism; fourth Five Year Plan launched; Marshall Zhukov demoted to a regional posting in Odessa
1947	post-war famine; law passed outlawing marriage to foreigners
1948	Berlin blockade; average Soviet incomes reach 1938 levels again
1949	Leningrad affair; Soviet atomic bomb developed; huge celebrations for Stalin's seventieth birthday
1951	Mingrelian Case (Georgian purge)
1952	Doctors' plot and new political purges; military spending at 25% of total expenditure; first Party congress since 1939
1953	death of Stalin

💡 Key Concept

Your spider diagram could include: Stalin's dictatorship was unchallenged; a one-man dictatorship (no Party Congresses between 1939–52); propaganda reinforced Stalin's dictatorship (Stalin seen as an infallible leader); Stalin built his dictatorship on a fear of enemies both within and outside the USSR; Stalin had absolute power of life and death over anyone.

⬆ Ⓐ Improve an Answer

a A totalitarian state is when ordinary people have no power and every aspect of their lives is completely controlled by the state. A one-man dictatorship is when the rule of one person is not restricted by a constitution, but (despite his theoretical power) a dictator may not be able to control every aspect of his subjects' lives.

b Ways in which the USSR was a totalitarian state:

- The USSR was a police state in which ordinary people could be arrested, tried and punished without even knowing what it was they were accused of.
- Ordinary people had no power to change the party of government. Although they voted in elections, candidates were selected by the Party, making the process superficial.
- A system of internal passports meant that people were not free to move to new places or new opportunities without approval by a bureaucratic system that was corrupt and controlled by the state. Foreign travel was almost impossible, and foreign influences such as radio or newspapers were blocked.
- Education, work and leisure were all controlled by the Party apparatus. Citizens were subject to propaganda and censorship; the media was controlled.
- Scientists and artists had to follow Party dictates; religion was directly attacked; it was forbidden to provide religious education or instruction.

Ways in which the USSR was not a totalitarian state:

- There was a constitution (1936) which made the USSR, in theory, one of the world's most democratic states; it recognised a wide range of rights for its citizens (although largely ignored in practice).
- Ordinary people could complain about their treatment by the state; democratic centralism allowed them to put forward their views at a local level.
- Some state attempts to control people's personal lives failed (e.g. state attempts to increase the birth rate).

c A better conclusion might be:

In a totalitarian state, ordinary people have no power and every aspect of their lives is completely controlled by the state, whereas in a one-man dictatorship, although the leader has complete political power his control over people's lives may be incomplete. Under Stalin, the USSR had many features of a totalitarian state. For example, the USSR was a police state in which ordinary people could be arrested, tried and punished without even knowing what it was they were accused of, and were utterly powerless to save themselves or their families. In the economy, in politics and in culture, the Soviet state controlled what people did, what they were allowed to say, and how they were supposed to think. However, even during the period of 'High Stalinism' after 1945, when Stalin's dictatorship was at its most extreme, the state did not have complete control over every aspect of citizen's lives, which suggests that it might more appropriately be called a one-man dictatorship (even though Stalin ruled in the name of the Communist Party). Ordinary people did complain about their treatment by the state, and state attempts to control people's personal lives were largely a failure. Therefore, while the USSR under Stalin may have come close to controlling every aspect of its citizens, total control was never achieved.

⊙ Apply Your Knowledge

a Dictatorship:

- *Evidence for a change after 1945*: after leading the USSR to victory in the Great Patriotic War, Stalin's sole leadership was unchallenged. The Politburo and Central Committee approved whatever Stalin

decided. There were no Party Congresses between 1939–52.
- *Evidence for continuity after 1945*: Stalin became frail in the last years of his life. His insistence on people following his orders was based on fear and paranoia of men like Beria, Malenkov and Zhdanov growing more powerful. His power as dictator did not increase after 1945.

Personality cult:

- *Evidence for a change after 1945*: the USSR's victory in the Great Patriotic War was seen as due to Stalin's leadership. This intensified the god-like aspect of Stalin's personality cult.
- *Evidence for continuity after 1945*: Stalin's cult had portrayed him as having god-like powers before the war (e.g. in the 1930s he was also called 'all-knowing', 'universal genius', 'shining sun of humanity').

Command economy:

- *Evidence for a change after 1945*: the Great Patriotic War transformed the USSR into a superpower because the command economy was used to open up many more of the USSR's vast natural resources.
- *Evidence for continuity after 1945*: the command economy that had developed through the 1930s helped achieve rapid reconstruction after the war, but the way it worked (e.g. Gosplan) was not new.

Industrialisation as a priority:

- *Evidence for a change after 1945*: industrialisation benefited from war reparations from Germany, which brought new technologies to the USSR. However, rather than industrialisation being the top priority, military spending escalated.
- *Evidence for continuity after 1945*: the fourth Five Year Plan for the reconstruction of the USSR had most of the same aims as the first Five Year Plan: heavy industry prioritised, consumer industries largely side-lined, minimal agricultural investment.

Cultural control (socialist realism):

- *Evidence for a change after 1945*: Zhdanov's crackdown on literature and the arts began in 1946. In 1948, Lysenko was granted total dominance of the Academy of Science, burdening Soviet science with false ideas based on 'Marxist principles'.
- *Evidence for continuity after 1945*: socialist realism had been imposed on the artists and writers of the USSR since 1932. Zhdanov's criticisms and the expelling of writers such as Zoshchenko and Akhmatova from the Union of Soviet Writers was a renewal of 1930s repression.

Chapter 24

🔺 Ⓐ Assess the Validity of This View

a & b

- February 1945: the 'Big Three' meet at Yalta, with discussions focusing on post-war plans for Germany and Poland. Stalin's aim was to get agreement for a Soviet 'sphere of influence' in Europe after the war and to make sure reparations from Germany would contribute as much as possible to rebuilding the USSR.
- July 1945: the 'Big Three' meet at Potsdam. Stalin's aim was to ensure post-war Germany was no longer a threat to the USSR.
- 1945: the USSR takes control over the Baltic States and eastern Poland; the Red Army remains in control in liberated Eastern European states and occupies East Germany. Fear of the West was a factor in this, as Stalin wanted a buffer zone of countries sympathetic to the USSR between it and the capitalist countries of the West.
- 1946–48: pro-Soviet governments take power in East Germany, Hungary and Czechoslovakia.

- 1947: the Molotov Plan launched as the USSR rejects the Marshall Plan and prohibits its satellite states in Europe from joining the Marshall Plan. Stalin and his foreign minister Molotov feared that the Marshall Plan was designed to pull countries in Eastern Europe out of the Soviet sphere of influence and into the Western sphere.
- 1948–49: the Berlin Blockade – a response by Stalin to the introduction of a separate currency in the Western zones of Berlin. Stalin saw the new currency as another step in the creation of a separate West Germany that would potentially threaten Soviet interests.
- 1949: Comecon founded: an organisation for economic cooperation between the USSR and its satellite states in Europe. Comecon was another response to the threat to the Soviet sphere of influence of the Marshall Plan.
- 1949: the USSR successfully tests its first atomic bomb. Until this point, the USA was the world's only military superpower, but a Soviet nuclear capability gave the USSR an equivalent superpower status and made the use of force against the USSR far less likely.
- 1949: Stalin meets Mao Zedong in Moscow to agree a treaty of alliance between the USSR and the People's Republic of China. The agreement was shaped by the growing Cold War hostility in the West to the USSR and to communist ideology: it committed the USSR and China to a military alliance in which each would help the other if either were attacked by another country.

c   Use your answers to **a** and **b** to write your answer and ensure it has balance. While Stalin's foreign policy motives are not fully known, it is reasonable to assume that his long-standing conviction that the USSR had to be defended from Western attack was a significant factor, although how this balances against other motivations, such as a commitment to spreading communist ideology, is up to you to determine.

Revision Skills

1924   Stalin convinces Trotsky to support him in arguing that Lenin's Testament should not be read out at the Party Congress. This was vital since Lenin's criticisms of Stalin could have ended Stalin's hopes to lead the Party.

1927   Stalin's alliance with Bukharin sees the United Opposition (headed by Trotsky, Kamenev and Zinoviev) defeated and these rivals for power removed from the Central Committee.

1928   Stalin argues for the extension of 'extraordinary' measures to ensure enough grain is collected: this ran counter to the policies of the NEP but proved popular with the Party.

1928   Stalin attacks Bukharin for 'right deviation': Stalin makes his move to remove his last real rival for power.

1929   First Five Year Plan launched: the realisation of Stalin's 'Great Turn' to rapid industrialisation and collectivisation.

1929   Bukharin removed from the Politburo and Trotsky expelled from the USSR, making Stalin's position stronger by removing potential rivals.

1932   Stalin's wife commits suicide, reportedly intensifying his ruthlessness and suspicious, paranoid nature; possibly influencing the nature of his leadership and desire for absolute control.

1932   Ryutin calls for Stalin's removal; Stalin gets him imprisoned. Zinoviev and Kamenev expelled from the Party for not reporting Ryutin's 'platform'.

1934   Kirov's murder: Stalin defeated a serious rival and used the murder as justification for increased repression and purges of potential opposition from the Party, including Ryutinites.

1934   The whole system of policing and state repression is put under the control of the NKVD, which in turn is controlled by Stalin, consolidating his power over coercion.

1936   The Stalin constitution declares that socialism had been achieved: a great triumph for Stalin's ideological approach.

1937–38 Purges of the Party, of leadership rivals and the military mean that survivors are terrified of Stalin and do nothing to displease him.

1945   Soviet victory in the Great Patriotic War. Stalin's leadership a significant factor in the victory, making his leadership position unchallengeable and his dictatorship complete.

⬆️ Ⓐ Improve an Answer

A better introduction might be:

A superpower is a state with a powerful military and economy, and with an international political influence that far exceeds that of other powers. In many respects, the USSR deserved the title in 1953 because it had an enormous and powerful military which had just won a global conflict, and it had developed its own nuclear weapons, making it the equal in military technology with the USA. In terms of global influence, the USSR also had superpower status: it controlled satellite states in Eastern Europe and was the leading partner of the world's socialist countries. Consequently, it was also a superpower insofar as its views and possible reactions had to be considered in conflicts around the world, especially in Asia. Economically, however, the USSR was weaker. Its command economy was inefficient, its consumer industries weak and its agricultural sector struggling. Nevertheless, despite its economic weaknesses, the military might and global ideological influence of the USSR certainly made it a superpower.

⚙️ Apply Your Knowledge

a   **Extract 1:** Soviet leaders portray the West/other countries as being unfriendly to the USSR/enemies of the USSR.

   Extract 2: the Soviet leaders' portrayal of the USSR as being surrounded by enemies was the justification for making the USSR a police state.

   Extract 3: the USSR believes it is very important to have a strong global position, and all steps must be taken to achieve this.

b   The 'Long Telegram' led the West to view the USSR in the same way as the Soviets themselves viewed the outside world – 'evil, hostile and menacing'. The West grew more fearful of Soviet aggression, seeing the vast Soviet police and military forces as instruments to advance Soviet strength.

Glossary

A

autocracy: rule by one person who has no limits to their power

C

Cold War: the state of hostility that existed between the communist Soviet Union and its satellite states, and the liberal/democratic/capitalist Western powers between 1945 and 1990

command economy: the top-down approach based on Marxist theory that the state should control the 'commanding heights of the economy' to enforce socialism on business and eliminate capitalism

containment: the Truman Doctrine of 1947 asserted the need to contain the spread of Soviet communist influence

D

dictatorship: a form of government in which absolute power is exercised by a single person or small clique

F

Five Year Plan: a five-year programme covering all aspects of development and transformation including industry, wealth and communication, with the aim of improving the supplies of power, capital goods and agriculture

G

Gosplan: the State General Planning Commission, which from 1921 helped coordinate economic development and from 1925 drafted economic plans

K

Komosomol: the all-Leninist Union Young Communist League was the youth division of the Communist Party

kulaks: Russian peasants who were wealthy enough to own a farm and hire labour

L

Leninism: Lenin's version of Marxism, which embraced policies like the NEP and the ban on factions, which contradicted his socialist goals

M

Marxism: Marx used the term 'communism' to describe his theories, but Lenin preferred 'Marxism' to refer to the distinct economic, social and political philosophy of Marx

N

Nepmen: speculative traders who bought up produce from the peasants to sell in the towns and consumer articles in the towns to sell in the peasant markets

nomenklatura: Party members who were appointed to influential posts in government and industry

O

Old Bolsheviks: the Old Party Guard – those who had been members of the Bolshevik Party before 1917

P

permanent revolution: the concept that continuing revolutionary progress within the USSR was dependent on a continuing process of revolution in other countries

R

Red Guards: loyal, young and old volunteer soldiers mostly recruited from factory workers and given basic training

S

satellite states: countries that retained their national identity but had pro-Soviet governments

social fascism: the view that social democratic parties in Western Europe were helping fascism as they compromised with capitalism and prevented progress towards class revolution

Socialism in One Country: the concept that efforts should be concentrated on building the socialist state in the USSR irrespective of what went on elsewhere in the world

socialist man: a person who was publicly engaged and committed to the community

socialist: supporting a political and economic theory of social organisation which believes that the means of production, distribution and exchange should be controlled by the whole community

Stalinism: a term used by Stalin's critics to describe his dictatorial rule, which contradicted Marxist philosophy and placed the national interests of the USSR above the struggle for world revolution

state capitalism: a 'compromise' economy, which embraced some elements of socialism by imposing a degree of state control but retained elements of capitalism such as private markets

state terror: a means to control the population and remove opposition through control and fear

T

totalitarianism: a political system that demands absolute obedience to the state and where every citizen is subject to central state authority

W

war communism: the political and economic system adopted by the Bolsheviks during the Civil War in order to keep the towns and Red Army provided with food and weapons

wrecking: acts perceived as economic or industrial sabotage, such as failing to meet economic targets, lowering morale in the workplace or incompetence

Y

Yezhovshchina: the period 1936–40 when Nikolai Yezhov led the NKVD and there was a large number of purges

Z

zemstva: elected councils responsible for the local administration of provincial districts

Revolution and Dictatorship

The History revision tips on this page are based on research reports on History revision and on the latest AQA examiners' reports.

General advice

☐ Make a realistic revision timetable for the months leading up to your exams and plan regular, short sessions for your History revision. Research shows that students who break down their revision into 30- to 60-minute sessions (and take short breaks in between subjects) are more likely to succeed in exams.

☐ Use the **progress checklists** (pages 3–4) to help you track your revision. It will help you stick to your revision plan.

☐ Eat healthily and make sure you have regular amounts of sleep in the lead-up to your exams. This is obvious, but research shows this can help students perform better in exams.

☐ Make sure your phone and laptop are put away at least an hour before you go to bed. You will experience better quality sleep if you have had time away from the screen before sleeping.

Revising your History knowledge and understanding

☐ Using a variety of revision techniques can help to embed knowledge successfully, so don't just stick to one style. Try different revision methods, such as: flashcards, making charts, diagrams and mind-maps, highlighting your notebooks, colour-coding, re-reading your textbook or summarising your notes, group study, revision podcasts, and working through the activities in this Revision Guide.

☐ Create a timeline with colour-coded sticky notes to make sure you remember important dates (use the **timeline** on page 9 as a starting point).

☐ Make sure you understand key concepts for this topic, such as communism, Stalinism and Marxism. If you're unsure, attend your school revision sessions and ask your teacher to go through important concepts again.

☐ Identify your weaknesses. Which topics are easy and which are more challenging for you? Give yourself more time to revise the challenging topics.

☐ Answer past paper questions and check the answers (using the AQA mark schemes) to practise applying your knowledge correctly and accurately to exam questions.

Revising your History exam technique

☐ Review the **AQA mark scheme** (page 8) for each exam question, and make sure you understand how you will be marked.

☐ Make sure you revise your skills as well as your knowledge. In particular, ensure you know how to approach the sources question. Practise identifying the overall interpretation in sources.

☐ Find a memorable way to recall the **How to master your exam skills** steps (pages 6–7) – it will help you plan your answers effectively and quickly.

☐ Ask your teacher for the examiners' reports – you can find out from the reports what the examiners want to see in the papers, and their advice on what not to do.

☐ Time yourself and practise answering past paper questions.

☐ Take mock exams seriously. You can learn from them how to manage your time better under strict exam conditions.

Topics available from *Oxford AQA History for A Level*

Tsarist and Communist Russia 1855–1964
978 019 835467 3

Challenge and Transformation: Britain c1851–1964
978 019 835466 6

The Tudors: England 1485–1603
978 019 835460 4

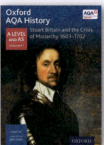

Stuart Britain and the Crisis of Monarchy 1603–1702
978 019 835462 8

The Making of a Superpower: USA 1865–1975
978 019 835469 7

The Quest for Political Stability: Germany 1871–1991
978 019 835468 0

The British Empire c1857–1967
978 019 835463 5

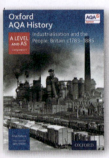

Industrialisation and the People: Britain c1783–1885
978 019 835453 6

Wars and Welfare: Britain in Transition 1906–1957
978 019 835459 8

The Cold War c1945–1991
978 019 835461 1

Democracy and Nazism: Germany 1918–1945
978 019 835457 4

Revolution and Dictatorship: Russia 1917–1953
978 019 835458 1

Religious Conflict and the Church in England c1529–c1570
978 019 835471 0

International Relations and Global Conflict c1890–1
978 019 835454 3

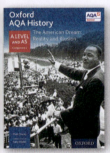

The American Dream: Reality and Illusion 1945–1980
978 019 835455 0

The Making of Modern Britain 1951–2007
978 019 835464 2

The Crisis of Communism: the USSR and the Soviet Empire 1953–2000
978 019 835465 9

The English Revolution 1625–1660
978 019 835472 7

France in Revolution 1774–1815
978 019 835473 4

The Transformation of China 1936–1997
978 019 835456 7

eBook Available

Student Books and Revision Guides also available in eBook format

Revision Guides

 RECAP    **APPLY**   **REVIEW**    **SUCCEED**

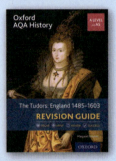

The Tudors: England 1485–1603 Revision Guide
978 019 842140 5

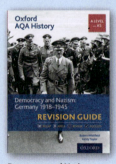

Democracy and Nazism: Germany 1918–1945 Revision Guide
978 019 842142 9

Tsarist and Communist: Russia 1855–1964 Revision Guide
978 019 842144 3

The Making of Modern Britain 1951–2007 Revision Guide
978 019 842146 7

The Cold War 1945–1991 Revision Guide
978 019 843253 1

Revolution and Dictatorship: Russia 1917–1953 Revision Guide
978 019 843252 4

Oxford AQA History for A Level Revision Guides offer step-by-step strategies and the structured revision approach of Recap, Apply and Review to help students achieve exam success.

Order online at **www.oxfordsecondary.co.uk/aqahistory**   OXFORD